THE BOOK
FAERY
MAGIC

Lucy Cavendish and Serene Conneeley

THE BOOK OF FAERY MAGIC

National Library of Australia Cataloguing-in-Publication Data:

Cavendish, Lucy and Conneeley, Serene
The Book of Faery Magic
1st edition
ISBN: 978-0-9805487-2-3
        398.45

1. Faeries.
2. Nature – religious aspects.
3. Spirituality.
4. Folklore.

Published by Blessed Bee
PO Box 449, Newtown, NSW 2042 Australia
Website: www.SereneConneeley.com
Email: SevenSacredSites@yahoo.com.au

Cover image: Jessica Galbreth (www.enchanted-art.com)
Cover design and faery illustrations: Daniella Spinetti
Wheel of the Year illustrations: Justin Sayers
Layout: Serene Conneeley

"Know you what it is to be a child?
It is to believe in love, to believe in loveliness, to believe in belief.
It is to be so little that the elves can reach to whisper in your ear.
It is to turn pumpkins into coaches, and mice into horses,
Lowness into loftiness, and nothing into everything.
For each child has its fairy godmother in its soul."
Francis Thompson, English poet

With love and gratitude...

To my sweet husband and precious beloved Justin, for making me endless cups of tea as I worked, motivating me when I was too tired to keep going, inspiring and encouraging me to follow my heart, supporting me in the battles that always seem to come when you manifest your dreams into reality, and seeing my potential and my light even when I couldn't.

To my gorgeous friends and my wonderful family – my parents Di and Rob, who always believed in me, my sister Amber, her husband Stevie and their sweet little faeries Lily and Grace, and Margie and Pete, my "other mum and dad", for love, laughter, dinners and debates.

Thank you to the inspiring faery folk I interviewed for this book – writer Juliet Marillier, who creates magical worlds that lift the spirits and open the heart, artist Jessica Galbreth, who captures our dreams and whimsy so beautifully, environmentalist Cara Walker, who is so dedicated to helping the planet, Lady Amaranth, who brings beauty into the world with her work, author Doreen Virtue, whose passion for healing people and the earth is so moving, and Cassandra Eason, a wise woman who gives so much to so many. And much gratitude to my Fairyland friends, who are kind and sweet and lovely, and embody all the traits of the fae (including their cheekiness, sometimes!).

Love and blessings to Daniella Spinetti, for the beautiful faery illustrations and the gorgeous cover design, and for patience, sweetness and generosity of spirit. And to Jessica Galbreth, for the pretty and oh-so-magical cover image, and for being such a dream (and so professional!) to work with. You really are the Guns 'N' Roses of the art world ☺

Immense love and thanks to my dear faery friend Lucy, for making this project so delightfully, deliciously magical, and so much fun to create, and for being so wise, so kind, and so honourable. Weaving this magic (and sharing the struggles) with you has filled me with joy.

And to all those taking on the role of the faeries and working to preserve the earth, from wisdom keepers and environmental groups to the individuals who protest about logging, plant trees, write about global warming, sail pirate ships on the high seas to save the whales or do any of the million other little things that make such a difference... thank you for making the world a better place.

With love,

Serene Conneeley

Thank you...

To my family and friends, for their love, laughter and support – thank you to Mum, and her faery reports from Mount Warning, or Fern Gully. To my daughter, Thomasina Clementine, for her faery incarnate self, her sweetness, generosity and kind good heart, and to Mister Love, for his research into plant auras, merfaery investigations, building me a faery healing herb garden, willingness to learn to "see", and inspiring me so much with his fun, laughter, music and positive energy.

To my publisher at Blue Angel, Toni Carmine Salerno, for his support and blessings with this Blessed Bee project, and to all the beautiful faery people I have encountered all over this beautiful blue and green planet.

I am also very grateful to all the people I interviewed for this book, including Wendy Rule, Selina Fenech, Izzy Ivy, Karen Kay and *FAE* magazine, Amelia Sayers, Tom Byrom, Maggie Sinton, Billie Dean, Donna Morgan, Brendan Hancock, Petal, Belinda, Chris and many many more, and to Jessica Galbreth for creating our beauteous cover faery, and Daniella Spinetti for her wonderful design and pretty illustrations (and for being so easy to work with!). What an amazing international community of faery people there are! Thank you, so very much, for your wise insights and fascinating personal stories, and I look forward to meeting many more of you in the coming years...

Thank you mostly and muchly to Serene for being so strong and inspiring, and for being so clever and brave. She is a blessed bee, sweet and good as honey, kind and considerate, gentle and powerful, oh-so talented and lots of fun too! Joy to you and Cutes!

And most of all, I wish to offer my gratitude to the faeries, for all that they do for this green and blue planet. They are the ultimate conservationists and eco warriors, the creative source behind every blade of grass and shimmering rainbow... and they create all this with such joy and pleasure. Thank you, my faery friends. I love you, and love being part of your world.

With love,

Lucy Cavendish

Contents

"I do believe in faeries... I do, I do!"

They say in the old tales that if we do not believe in faeries, they die. But I do not believe this. If we do not believe in faeries, it is not that they perish, but that a part of our soul dies, and fades away, and the magic of life stays just out of reach, when it would often help us most...

You see, faeries are real, and we can learn how to see them, feel their power, heal with them and create a wonderful life by learning the secrets of working with the beautiful energy of these nature spirits and guardians! These powerful natural beings have been on the planet since the earth was born, and have been working with we humans for a very long time. Now we are at a turning point in our relationship – and the closer we get to fae-reality, the more in touch we shall be with our own true nature, and this beautiful planet!

For thousands of years, humans and faeries have lived alongside each other, sometimes harmoniously, sometimes in great fear and mistrust. In these times of magical change and energetic evolution, it is more important than ever before to connect with our faery kith and kin! For from them we can discover the secrets to laughter, love, and living long, healthy lives overflowing with purpose and joy.

From the faeries we can rediscover who we really are – beings of vitality, strength, deep natural wisdom and courage. Through faery interactions, we change our vibration to one which naturally attracts positive experiences and people, wonderful friendships, caring lovers, beauty and prosperity into our lives!

The faeries can share with us the secrets of our ancestry, reveal whether we have the wise faery blood, and teach us how to create health, prosperity and personal happiness. Most of all, rediscovering our natural and long-lived relationship with the elemental realms reconnects us to our own power – nature – the very source of life itself. When we work with the faeries, we awaken our own natural abilities to create wonderful, enchanted lives full of meaning and purpose – and fun and delight!

This book contains many blessings direct from the realm of the fae, offerings which I hope bring you enjoyment, enrichment and inspiration. When you open its magical pages, you too may begin to wonder at those times in your life when you thought you saw something – but dismissed it. A flash of bright light, a sparkle on water, a sweet perfume floating on the breeze, a bevy of butterflies gathered in a glade. All are faery sightings, to me. The wonder they invoke and the curiosity they ignite will result in more and more faery sightings, interactions and, ultimately, gifts of great imagination, beauty and whimsy.

I feel that we are so wired to our left-brain and the consciousness of logic and rational thinking that we have forgotten how to connect and tune in to faery. But we all have that capacity to let go of the thoughts that keep us separate and suspicious, and tune in to connection and expanded consciousness.

For we all dream, and day-dream, and can enter into trance and go within. Most of us now trance and connect when we are watching television, which is why communing with nature and connecting with the faeries is so essential to our physical and imaginative health and wellbeing. I do see and feel and hear the fae, but mostly, I just know. I know because this world which they have helped create is so full of beauty, and I thank them every day for their gifts, and for the love they share with us.

We have filled this book with whimsical first-person accounts of interaction with the fae, clear instruction and grounded guidance to working with the elementals, and inspiring ideas for faery re-connection. *The Book of Faery Magic* is truly for anyone

Photo © Thomasina George.

wanting to grow closer to nature and to their own wild selves. And it is a deep, creative and magical path that will help us move through this challenging stage of earth history in ease, grace, delight and gratitude.

Thank you, faeries, for your trust and your belief in us. I believe in you.

Lucy Cavendish

Mabon/Ostara, 2010

"*We are the beings of light and beauty...*"

I've always loved faeries. When I was little I adored the magical stories my parents read to me. I loved going to ballet class and wearing faery tutus on stage. I spent hours outside in the bush, peering at wildflowers and trying to see the tiny faeries I imagined were dancing within them.

Now that I'm all grown up I still love reading magical tales of enchanted realms. I love dressing as a faery for parties, festivals or just for fun. I walk through the city and its parks, inhaling the sweet scent of flowers and delighting in butterflies and bees dancing and swooping from blossom to blossom. I have paintings of the fae on my walls, which inspire me when I write. And I've made beautiful faery friends from around the world in a virtual faery garden, where people embody the kindness and consideration we attribute to the fae. I love the imagery, the legends and the sense of beauty and magic that faeries symbolise, but I don't believe they really exist.

Yet the essence of the faery archetype is powerful and healing. When we read stories about them we are reminded that we can achieve all that we dream of. When we write about them, paint them or embody them through dance or design, we bring beauty into the world, inspiring and uplifting those touched by our creativity. When we connect deeply with the spirit of nature through environmental consciousness, we re-establish a link to our own faery self, and see our own life as more enchanted and more beautiful. We reawaken our inner heart, and our innate sense of spirituality and joy.

I think we can all create a faery glamour on ourselves and our life with the power of our thoughts and actions, and by allowing the essence of Faeryland, real or imagined, to wash over us. I have the most magical life imaginable because I live like a faery, finding happiness in nature and the natural world, attuning myself to the seasons of the earth, connecting to the phases of the moon. I spend time outdoors, breathing in the sunshine, dancing in the rain, marvelling at rainbows and thunder, inhaling the scent of jasmine and frangipanis in my city street, feeding the ducklings in a nearby park.

I find the sacred not just in the ancient monuments of faraway lands, but in my own home and my own life, in the work I do and the everyday existence I lead. I create my own "luck" through hard work, dedication and passion, see beauty in the so-called mundane, and experience magic and potential in every moment of every day.

Of course it would be lovely if faeries existed. If they gifted people with special talents, sprinkled pixie dust to calm the atmosphere during an argument, cleaned the house while we slept, healed illness and soothed hurt. But this world is so beautiful and magical already that faeries don't have to exist. We can do all this – and more – ourselves. We have our own immense and extraordinary inner power and will. We can bless our own lives, solve our own problems, and bring magic to ourselves and each other. We can protect the environment, create the change we desire, and be the muse and inspiration to ourselves and others by letting our own light shine.

We can still love faeries. The imagination is a powerful, wonderful, beautiful thing, and I think a little part of us dies if we shut it off and deny the wonder of what we can dream up. It makes me smile that Mum has created a faery garden for my nieces, and leaves little gifts and messages for them from their magical friends.

And we can learn a lot about ourselves from the way each generation and culture portrays their faeries, for they are a reflection of our own longings, and our fears. Fears of industrialisation, in the time of the flower faeries, of the uncertainty of nuclear war, seen in the darker faeries of last century, and of today's environmental destruction, resulting in the healing faeries more common now.

I think we should all embrace our inner faery, and enjoy the wonder of this incredible existence. Step up and realise that we are

Photo © Justin Sayers.

the creatures of magic, potential, inspiration and wisdom. We are the beings with the power to transform our lives. Einstein said: "The imagination points to all we might yet discover and create." Infinite worlds and possibilities, infinite love, light and joy. These are the things we can gift ourselves, not from an external source, but from within.

Serene Conneeley

Samhain/Beltane, 2010

Frequently Asked Questions About the Fae

1. What are faeries?

Serene: Faeries have been present in the folklore and legends of all cultures, and in myriad forms, for countless centuries. They've been credited with helping humans, saving lives, causing plants to grow and bringing good fortune – and they have also been blamed for natural disasters, failed crops, animal deaths and human illness, abduction and even murder. They are variously described as tiny and delicate, or tall and imposing. Made of light, or created from darkness. Loving or cruel. Cheeky or serious. Beautiful or ugly. Helpful to those they meet, or likely to lead them astray...

Faeries are different things to different people, which is part of what makes them so magical and mysterious. Some believe they are supernatural beings we can see and interact with, here to help us to evolve and grow, while to others they are the spirits of departed loved ones or ancestors, which fits with the old Celtic view of Faeryland as the realm of the dead. Some see them as a race of ancient deities diminished in stature and power – the goddess Maeve becoming Queen Mab, the horned god becoming King Oberon, Loki the trickster god portrayed as Puck – and there are those who believe they are lower level angels or celestial beings who fell to earth and are destined to remain here, helping humans so they can work their way back up into heaven.

There are also those who see faeries as the anthropomorphisation of nature, our way of humanising flowers, trees and butterflies, like Cicely Mary Barker's flower faeries and May Gibbs's bush babies

Snugglepot and Cuddlepie – beautiful creations of our imagination – or as symbols that our subconscious sends to remind us to be playful and joyous, to lighten up, have fun, dance, sing and celebrate life. Faeries are whatever we want them to be, and their beauty touches our soul, no matter how we perceive them.

Lucy: Faeries are nature spirits, and so they are present wherever there is a touch of nature. They are beings who interact with the process of growth, change, nurturing and nourishment, and death and decay too. They are associated with each element, and they take on the qualities of that element, working with it in myriad ways. For example, some fire fae work with candlelight, and thus are present whenever we work candle magic. Water fae may be present in wells, rivers and dams, cleansing our drinking water and clearing and filtering the oceans and waterways.

Many faery scholars agree that the fae are negatively affected by pesticides and other chemicals, and are helped, nurtured and supported by eco-friendly activities. Faeries appear in different ways to different people, animals and places, as they intermingle the energy they are composed of with the energy of either the being they are communicating with or the place they are working with.

Faeries have social lives and are festive. They have hierarchies and structures in some realms, and are more tribal and primal in others. They are a deep force of nature, and are beloved of many people, even though others fear them or mistrust them.

2. Where are the faeries?

Lucy: They are within the blades of grass and the sap of trees. They are the clouds shifting their shape in the sky, and the negative ions at the seashore. They are large, and small. The large faeries, like the elvish ones, dwell between the worlds in other dimensions, known as Faeryland or the Hollow Hills, which are the realms of beings such as the faery king Gwyn ap Nudd. However there are many dimensional portals, or doorways, which open into the "real world", so there are crossover points, and some people have found themselves walking in Faeryland without having had that intent.

When I was a child, I would go to a secret place I treasured. It was a waterfall in a forest, a short bicycle ride from my home.

I knew exactly how to get there, and this was my own secret special place. Things were different there. Food tasted sweeter, the water was delicious, the air was brighter and I felt so alive, so well and so connected with all-that-is. I saw faeries there, and I would go alone and simply be with them, and nature, the waterfall and the rocks in the sun, and find such peace and beauty. When I reached the age of about 13, and began to devote myself to a final attempt to "fit in", I turned away from my secret place. Years later, when I tried to find my way back to it, it was as if it did not exist at all.

Faeries also inhabit homes and special places – like the guardians of the groves, who work with the goddess Nemetona, or brownies, who can assist around the home – although many are also taking up residence in work environments now, as humans spend less time in their homes and so much more time at their workplace. Faeries, in short, are everywhere...

3. Why do we need them?

Lucy: Because without them, a part of our own soul dies, the part that is wild and free, imaginative and spontaneous, happy and light-hearted, and not so earnest and worried. While the fae do have concerns, their approach is not the heavy, fretful and sometimes very dense and fearful approach some humans have. Faeries inspire us to take part in joyous activities that are fun, and practical, and which benefit the environment and our own natural selves. I think they teach us how to be more fully our true selves, and without them we would have a very ponderous, earnest and dull world.

Without faeries there would be less music and laughter, fewer imaginative worlds where we can play and learn and be nourished, and we'd have no elderberry cordial! The fruits of the earth would not have the love and tenderness the fae pour into them, food would taste less delicious, and we might forget that pesticides and chemicals do not belong in nature, and start pouring them in, willy-nilly, for short term "gain". Oh wait! That has already happened! And that could be linked to a decline in faery faith in the early parts of the 20th century. But this sad state of affairs is on the mend. As people are now more open to faeries, we are slowly evolving into less harmful creatures. Faery belief is returning, so they are more hopeful – and thus, so am I – about the planet and her life force and future!

Serene: The very idea of faeries brings great joy and inspiration to people, touching them on a very deep level, opening their heart and adding so much beauty to the world. These enchanting Otherworld beings encourage us to dream, to believe that anything is possible, and to feel the magic that is everywhere in this world. They embody the essence of lightheartedness and joy, which is so very important in order to counteract the seriousness so many of us feel as we work so hard. And they bring out the child in us, that sense of innocence and wonder that helps us see the world with new eyes. I think they're also a beautiful way of reminding us of our connection to nature, and our need to protect the earth and conserve our precious resources.

Jessica Galbreth: I find that as times get darker, we all reach out to something that makes us feel good. Something that reminds us that there is more than meets the eye in this world. And I think faeries are that to many people.

Cassandra Eason: We need faeries more than they need us, to prove that the world is wonderful, and magical, and that we are creatures of spirit within our physical bodies.

Selina Fenech: Faeries remind us that the world is a living thing that needs our care. They bring us tales of morality. They bring smiles to little girls who are believing for the first time, and smiles to women, who are reminded of the happiness they felt as a child.

Doreen Virtue: We need faeries today because they are the guardians of the environment and the animals, and they are ensuring the health of Mother Earth and her inhabitants. They protect our air, water and earth – the elements necessary to physical life.

Karen Kay: We need faeries as they are the guardians of the land, and the faeries need humans to help them on a practical level, picking up litter, planting seeds... The beauty of working with the faeries is that magic really does come into your life if you let it!

4. Why do you spell it faery?

Lucy: The spelling of faery is very personal. Some people only see "fairies", and that spelling reflects the Victorian view of them as tiny nature beings. Some newly birthed faeries are also "fairy" rather than "faery". The word "faery" implies that the being has been present on the planet for a long, long time, and "faerie" is the even more archaic spelling that has its roots in times when faeries were utterly believed in, and enchantment was everywhere. For me, personally, "fairy" does not resonate quite so much, and so the word "faery" is the one I most often choose to use. I have used "fairy" on occasion though, as it can also denote more modern, newborn fae energies. Yes, it is a conundrum, but a happy one!

Serene: As a sub editor for magazines I use "fairy", as that is the dictionary spelling. It comes from the Middle English "fairie", a borrowing from the 14th century French "faerie", which referred to both the land of the fae and the act of enchantment, and which had itself come from the Latin "fata", meaning the Fates, and "fatum", meaning destiny. The modern French is "féerie" for their realm, and "fée" for a magical being – when I was in France, visiting the enchanted Broceliande Forest, there were many references to the fée.

As a writer though I prefer "faery", for it seems so much more magical and mysterious – referring to myth and legend and ancient times. It's also how it's spelled in the wonderful *Chronicles of Faerie* series by OR Melling, which, despite its title, uses "faery" within the text for a being from Faeryland. The dictionary also includes "faery" and "faerie" as 16th century literary alternatives to "fairy", with a broader meaning including the land or world of the fae. Other sources also acknowledge that the archaic spellings "faery" and "faerie" are often used to refer to the land where they dwell. In the end though, it seems to simply come down to personal preference... And so I, and my faery Tizia, asked some of our Fairyland friends which way they spell fairy/faery/faerie, and why, and got some sensible, some funny and some very sweet answers...

Anita and Fizzy the Busy Aussie Fairy: I use "fairy" for commercial purposes – eg the tizzy dresses and wands for little girls – but "faery" for a heart-connection with fae energy.

Susan and Z'Belle: What a delightful question! I prefer "faerie" because it seems/feels lighter, more mysterious, more ancient, more Otherworldly... It always puts a smile on my face and a sense of ease in my heart.

Tina and Magpie: I love faeries, and I'm in the camp of spelling it "faery". Partly as it does seem so very ancient and more elegant, but also because to me the fae are not just about light – there is always a dark and a light to everything, and "faery" to me embodies both of those elements within it.

Sheridan and Miss Myrabelle: I read a lot of books on mythology, and "faerie" seems to be the most dominant spelling. I also love the *Meredith Gentry* book series by Laurel K Hamilton, and she spells it "faerie" also. Most fantasy and folklore books that I've read spell it this way, but I mostly just have a personal preference for it.

Sharne and Crystal: To me, "fairy" is the most common way I see it spelled, and is more in line with faerytales and Disney-type movies. Whereas "faery" or "faerie" invokes in me the more traditional, sacred and magical workings of the fae.

Naza and Fairy Luna: I spell it "fairy" or "faery". There's no particular reason why, although I do think "faery" looks cuter! ☺

Viv and Nayna: I spell it "fairy" because that is how we were taught it at school, but I think "faerie" is the original spelling from the "old" language (and it looks better! LOL). Love'n'hugs and *faerie* blessings to you! xx

Deidre and Bell: I spell it "fairy" because that's the correct standard spelling. Although it's not listed, "fairie" is Middle English from the Old French "faerie" (a variant of which is "faery"). Did I ever mention I'm an editor? ☺

Nancy and Katrina: LOL at Deidre's answer, because for me "fairy" is the way it is spelled too, although I don't know why. I'm not a history buff or a language buff, just a nurse and a mother and a wife who loves Fairyland.

Cherie and Salena: According to *A Faerie Treasury* by Jacky Newcomb and Alicen Geddes-Ward, it's "faerie", and they base their work on actual contact with the faerie realm.

Melissa and Chrystabella: I use "fairy" when it's for children and "faery" when it's for adults. I always spelled it "fairy" until I saw Brian Froud's artwork, and his influence and knowledge of the faery realms has enticed me to spell it "faery".

Annette and Tossling: I spell it "fairy" because I think that's the usual way. But my spelling control has no worries about "faery" or "faerie". Maybe they are actually better then – deriving from the word fae? Oh, the control doesn't like "fae". Perhaps the control isn't in control here…

Ilene and Peony: I spell it "fairy". I don't know why though, it must be how I saw it spelled growing up.

Claire and Freya: "Fairy" for me, or "fae", just because I'm Old English. I think it just depends on where you live. I say "fairy" as a whole, "fae" meaning just one.

Michelle and Mistletoe: Mistletoe is also wondering how you spell fairy/faery/faerie, and why… But when your human is a Kiwi [New Zealander], it usually sounds like ferry!

Annalie and Charlotte: LOL Mistletoe! Good comment… I spell it "fairy" (ie ferry), as it's just the way we were taught to spell it in New Zealand, but you've given us food for thought now, thank you!

Sandee and Twylight: I spell it "fairy". I'm not really sure why, I think just because that is usually how you see it spelled in the US, so it's familiar to me. I think the other spellings look much older and more European though. And I actually like them better!

Carolyn and Thistledown: "Faery" or "faerie" – it's the Irish way ☺

Sylvia and Harmony: It's "fairy"! Always has been and always will be. The others just look wrong, LOL.

Stephanie and Morwenna: I spell it "faerie". Not entirely sure why except that it's how my parents spelled it when I was a wee one!

Lisa and Isabeau: I usually spell it "fairy", but lately it's been "faery". I don't know why, I just do!

Vivian and Kyra: My response is "fairy", as I don't think I'd actually seen it spelled any other way until I became a Fairyland player ☺

Jenny: I was brought up spelling it "fairy", and to spell it any other way just seems weird and awkward. I've tried "faery", but when I do, I feel like I'm spelling it wrong.

Allyson: I spell it "faerie". It's Middle Englishy (although it originated from French), and I like that form of our English language m'lady. You can also shorten it to "fae". "Fairy" doesn't shorten to "fai"!

Sharlene: Hmmm... I think it should be "fairy" to muggles, and "faerie" to us non-muggle folk, hee hee.

5. Why so many stories about changelings and abductions?

Serene: The faeries have been blamed for many things, particularly the awful charge that they take healthy babies and leave a sick fae child, or an enchanted bunch of twigs, in its place. But we must consider the context of the era in which the charges are made. When infant mortality was high and medical knowledge was scant, it was easier for parents to say their baby had been abducted by the faeries than that it had died too young, so it gave comfort to the grieving. And if a young child had a medical problem or deformity, the parents could say it was a changeling, and that their own healthy babe had been stolen by the faeries and replaced with one of their sickly children. Likewise if a child was too smart or well developed for its age, it was often accused of being a faery changeling.

All kinds of illnesses were blamed on the faeries too, such as tuberculosis, then known as consumption, which caused a person to waste away – people believed it was because the faeries had forced them to dance each night at their revels, causing them to die of exhaustion, as they didn't understand sickness and disease, or the causes of them, or have any idea how to cure them.

There are also documented cases where husbands murdered their wives, and tried to avoid prosecution by declaring that she had been taken away, and a fae woman left in her place, and that it was this evil faery that he had punished by drowning. Like witchcraft later, accusing your wife of being a faery was a simple way to get rid of her. Many diseases were also blamed on faeries (and witches), and it was claimed that faeries shot people with flint arrowheads, known as elf shot, to cause pain and sickness.

The fae were reputed to kidnap the musically gifted too, as well as young mothers to nurse the faery babies. They also – apparently – seduced people, sent them mad, bewitched cattle and destroyed crops. There were even stories that they stole healthy humans to pay the devil his tribute, especially once the Church demonised the nature spirits that had once been honoured. Such accusations became a way to discredit the idea of the fae, and also to explain those who ran away or were killed in accidents or by legitimate illnesses that were not understood at the time.

Lucy: A few centuries ago the faeries were seen as cruel and troublesome, and worthy of fear, because the Church – and not just the Christian church, but many religions with strict dogmas and mistrust of the natural world – were threatened by the power of the fae, and the devotion of their followers. It is easy to forget just how strong the faery faith was in so many parts of the world. The faeries, being so very much a part of nature, had special healing powers, and could – and still can – shapeshift, bring energy to a situation, and promote growth and vitality.

In a time when you were meant to feel ashamed of having a body, and to work hard at being "good" to pay off your sins, the faeries – and their belief in us, and nature, as pure and perfect, and whole and complete – were a definite threat. The faeries also enjoy dancing, which was banned in many countries, such as Ireland and Puritan New England, they like rhythm and drumming, and they love making love. All highly suspect activities, according to the Church! Faeries generally challenge institutions that go against natural laws – and of course the best way to undermine the faeries was to promote an image of them as nasty, baby-stealing tricksters. It is a great injustice, and an image that is still promoted today, woven through popular books such as the Sookie Stackhouse vampire novels. Which faeries quite like reading, due to the sex scenes, but are slightly sad about some of the misrepresentations of their nature. But they know it's "only a book"...

6. Can I work with faeries if I am a Christian?

Lucy: Yes. There are many branches of Christianity which are very beautiful, and which have a deep reverence for nature. In the early Celtic branches it was a faith that embraced the natural world, and acknowledged (to a degree) the wisdom of the druids. So yes, any Christians who are tolerant and loving can develop their relationship with the faeries as they develop their relationship with nature.

Some Christians, however, might disapprove, and can be quite fearful of faery energy. But it would be wonderful to see more and more Christian people opening up to the green world and its loving energy. In Victorian times, the god Pan was known to many as the "Green Christ". There is definitely room for eclectic faiths, and personal blends that make sense to the individual and the path their soul is yearning for.

7. What if I am a pagan?

Pagans, as people who revere nature and her cycles, get along splendidly with faeries, and there are various forms of purely faery paths. One is the Feri Tradition, begun by Victor and Cora Anderson, which has been studied by pagans Starhawk and T Thorn Coyle. Another is faery craft, a blend of witchcraft and faery faith, which is explored in books such as *Druid Power: Celtic Faerie Craft & Elemental Magic* by Amber Wolfe, and *Faeriecraft* by Alicen and Neil Geddes-Ward. Paganism is exceptionally broad, and incorporates so many varieties, traditions and developments, which all acknowledge nature spirits, so there is no conflict for pagans in working with faery energy along with god and goddess forms.

8. Do faeries exist only in the British Isles?

Lucy: No, although it is easy to understand why some people would have that impression. The faery faith is very strong in Ireland and Scotland, as for many years prior to the 1600s there was less interference from the more repressive and strict forms of Christianity. For a thousand years, Catholicism and faery faith, although not always great friends, had lived together in a kind of awkward but mostly peaceful alliance. And it is from these pockets where there was less interference that we get most of the faerytales and stories we know today.

There are faery stories from all over the world however. What is most interesting is when the faery beings, the nature spirits of different locations, migrate with the families they are kin to, such as Irish and English fae going to the New Worlds of America and Australia. Fantasy writers like Charles de Lint and Terri Windling explore these collisions of Native American and Irish faery culture in their beautifully written and very wise novels. Ultimately, as there are faeries wherever there is nature, faeries are therefore everywhere. We simply need to connect, feel their energy, communicate with them and remember the stories.

9. If I eat faery food, will I be trapped in Faeryland?

Lucy: It is not so much that you will never return home if you visit Faeryland and eat the food, because all food is faery food. It is simply that if you partake of faery essence, if you have that true experience, the world will never ever seem quite as it was – you will be forever changed. And this is a wonderful thing, although it can make fitting back into a very mechanistic, unmagical and "logical" world quite challenging!

But the rewards and benefits of eating that faery food absolutely overwhelm the difficulties of having partaken of the faery experience. So eat, be changed, and live a wonderful, healthy, magical life, full of enchantment!

10. What is the faery star?

Serene: The seven-pointed star is known as the faery or elven star, heptagram, septagram and septacle. Physically it is any self-intersecting heptagon (a seven-sided polygon). The number seven corresponds to spirituality, which is why this symbol is associated with elves and faeries and magic. There are also seven colours in the rainbow, seven chakras, seven endocrine glands, seven musical notes, seven sacred planets and seven days in the week.

The seven-pointed star is used in magic to represent the seven elements or seven directions – air, water, fire, earth, upper world, lower world and spirit, or east, west, north, south, above, below and within. In some witchcraft traditions it's regarded as a symbol of authority, as well as of the seven virtues required for magical workings – humility, respect, trust, kindness, truth, honour and dignity. Aleister Crowley and his order used it, referring to it as the Star (or Seal) of Babalon. Rock bands Marilyn Manson and Tool incorporate it into their artwork and imagery. Even the flag of Australia has five seven-pointed stars on it, a large one known as the Commonwealth Star, whose points represent the unity of the six states with a final point for the territories, and the others forming the Southern Cross.

Superstitions

Serene: As times have changed, people's opinions of the faery folk have changed too. Today they are considered harmless and even helpful to humans, yet just a few centuries ago people were terrified of the terrible powers of the Otherworld, and so there were many charms created that people believed would keep them safe from the fae. Now most people would welcome a meeting with a magical creature or a visit to Faeryland, so they would ignore all these superstitions, but they make for interesting reading if nothing else...

☆ Laying the father's trousers over a cradle or hanging an open pair of scissors above it – which sounds a bit dangerous to us! – was believed to prevent a baby being abducted.

☆ A necklace made of peony seeds will protect children from being kidnapped by the fae. Which is odd, as faeries love peony flowers!

☆ According to some, you should never lay a baby in an elder wood cradle or the faeries will spirit it away.

☆ Referring to the faeries as the Good Folk, the Fair Folk, the Shining Ones or another favourable name was also believed to protect you, and your child, from abduction.

☆ Iron saps their strength and repels them, and can even kill them – a charm used to great effect in the Sookie Stackhouse books to battle evil faeries, but more superstition than fact.

☆ In a similar vein, you can guard against faeries with malicious intent by keeping a nail under the bed – which comes in handy in the beautiful OR Melling series *The Chronicles of Faerie*.

☆ Wearing your clothes inside out, sprinkling salt around you, the sound of bells, running water, an untidy house, rowan leaves and primrose flowers are also considered to keep you safe.

☆ The herb Saint John's wort can break faery spells and cure the sickness caused by faery darts. Or the same herb can attract the faeries... Sometimes it depended on which part of the world you lived in as to whether a plant would attract or repel the fae!

☆ Throwing a lady's glove into a faery ring as they dance will stop their revelry. Just why a lady would be out walking in the middle of the night, in the dark, wild countryside, is another matter.

☆ Faeries love to look at their reflections in pools of water, but they hate mirrors, so it is said, so hanging one near the entrance to your home will apparently ward off the fae folk.

☆ Tying up a bundle of oak, ash and thorn twigs guarded against the faeries – although, ironically, finding the twigs for this bundle would require you to walk beneath the three trees, which have long been considered the faery tree trinity, and a place the fae feel safe.

☆ If you visit Faeryland for a night and a day, you will return to your own home and find that 70 years or more have passed.

☆ Leaving offerings for the faeries of food and drink would protect against the mischief and mayhem they caused – and we still leave out snacks for Santa Claus and his reindeers and elves...

☆ On the flipside, faeries will be offended and disappear if you insult them with gifts of money, clothes or worldly goods.

☆ Tossing a hot coal into the butterchurn as you work will prevent the faeries from stealing your butter.

To See the Faeries

Of course, not everyone wanted to avoid the fae, and there were also many folk charms that were believed to help you see them.

☆ According to Reverend Robert Kirk, in his 17th century pamphlet *The Secret Commonwealth of Elves, Fauns and Fairies*, to see a faery you should:
> 1. Take a tether of hair that has bound a corpse to a bier. Wind it around your waist. Stoop down and look backwards through your legs until a funeral procession passes.
> 2. Find an accomplished seer. Have him place his right foot over your left foot and lay his hand on your head. This will confer clairvoyant power to you.

☆ Placing an oak leaf or a four-leaf clover inside your left shoe will apparently help you see the faeries.

☆ Drinking fresh thyme tea will boost your faery sight, as will laying seven grains of wheat on a four-leafed clover.

☆ If you find a small stone or a shell that has a hole worn right through it from the water rushing over it, you will apparently be able to peek through the hole and see into Faeryland.

☆ And perhaps most powerfully, if you look a faery, especially a leprechaun, straight in the eyes and hold their gaze for a long time, you will gain control over them. But don't ever tell a faery your name, or it will have power over you!

Jessica's Faery Magic

American Jessica Galbreth is a magical artist who inspires people with her beautiful paintings of faeries, goddesses, vampires and fantasy and mythological subjects. As well as her amazing paintings and prints, she is the creator of the stunning *Enchanted Oracle* deck, publishes an annual calendar and her own art book, and has a gorgeous line of greeting cards, jewellery, faery figurines, coffee mugs and more. Visit Jessica at www.enchanted-art.com.

As a small child, I always had a vivid imagination. Growing up on the river in northwest Ohio gave me the opportunity to be surrounded by nature. It was a simpler time then, and I was allowed to play for long hours by myself in the woods. It was then that the first glimmer of the fae entered my life. I was enchanted, and instead of fading as I grew up, it only grew stronger. No one else in my family has this interest, but it is something that is very strong within me, and has been there for a very long time.

My communication with the faeries is more that I sense them rather than seeing them. Even now, as I walk alone in the woods, it's as if I can feel them around me – sometimes mischievous, sometimes playful, often times serene and beautiful. And I can say that they are on my mind daily, due to the nature of my business. I'm either painting a faery or related image, filling orders with faery items or doing research on the fae for a project. Not only that, but I'm surrounded by them. My home is literally a shrine to the fae!

I believe in faeries both literally and metaphorically. I wish I could say I've seen them, but sadly I haven't. But I do believe! And while I don't see them with my eyes, I see them with my heart and my mind. I don't think we're meant to see them as physical objects, rather I feel that they're beings of energy that can sometimes manifest in the physical realm, but very rarely.

Being lucky enough to draw them for a living is such a wonderful adventure and brings them even closer to reality for me. Through my work I want to ignite the same passion for the fae in others. I know my visions may differ from others, and that's okay. My message is simply to remind people of the myth and magic that is intricately woven through the history of mankind.

I am inspired by many things... mother nature in all her beauty, the intricate myths and stories of ancient cultures, the shadowy mysteries of the moon, and the innocence and simplicity I see in the eyes of my young children. And the faeries definitely inspire my work too. My favourite part about being a faery artist is the freedom of creativity it allows me. There are no rules, and because they are magical creatures, I'm free to explore different aspects of their nature with my art. I am also a huge mythology buff, and the Celtic myths which are full of faery stories are my favourite. Perhaps it's my Scottish roots – my ancestors are the Galbraith clan that still has a standing castle in Scotland.

I think we need faeries in our lives because as times get darker, we all reach out to something that makes us feel good. Something that reminds us there is more than meets the eye in this world. I think faeries are that to many people. And the wondrous thing about them is that they are not limited to one religion or belief system. I love to see people from all walks of life proudly announce that they believe in faeries.

Jessica is the founder of Fairy Day, an annual holiday for believers, collectors, artists and the young at heart. It's celebrated around the world on June 24 each year by those who love all things fae. For inspiration and ideas for holding your own events, visit www.fairyday.com.

Working With the Faeries

"The wall is silence, the grass is sleep,
Tall trees of peace their vigil keep.
And the Fairy of Dreams with moth-wings furled,
Plays soft on her flute to the drowsy world."
Ida Rentoul Outhwaite, faery artist

Connecting With Your Faery Friends and Allies

Faeries are beautiful energetic nature spirits and beings, most often described as more solid than angels, less so than humans. I feel they are like mist, able to form and reform at will, and that they can utilise the energy sources around them to manifest, if they wish for us to have the gift of seeing them with eyes wide open.

Working with the fae is very healing, energising, healthy and inspiring. They help us to be more than who we often believe ourselves to be, to close the gap between our real and imagined selves. They ignite our potential in so many ways.

The fae folk have many abilities that we seem to have "lost", perhaps through the voluntary switching off of our DNA. Maybe, encoded in the silent DNA that lies slumbering in sequence in our every cell, lie the secrets to shapeshifting, to flying, to manifesting, to long, long life... And perhaps soon they will switch on, with a simple realisation, a vision, a moment in meditation, a shift in energy.

Perhaps it will only take something very small to reawaken us. Perhaps our dormant DNA is already poised and ready to come back to life, like a series of dominoes waiting for a push. Then we may be able to grow our wings, switch on to growing in stature or being small once more, flying, or changing and slowing down time. Perhaps working with the faeries is one mighty way of switching back on!

Being fae does not mean being light-headed, and detached and disconnected, as some people seem to think, based on expressions like "away with the faeries". Many humans who work with the fae experience their energy as extremely powerful and deep.

"They are a primal force, like a storm or a boulder," says Tom Byrom, a natural therapies student and pagan from Sydney, Australia. "A deep feeling of ancient energy seems to surround them. Sometimes I feel they are protecting me. Usually though, they seem to cause a little chaos around me, making life interesting, to say the least."

Some people are frightened of working with faeries and faery energy, because they seem so unpredictable. "I believe the fae care about humanity, but in the same way that nature does," Tom says. "There is a lot of love there, but they live by different rules to us, and certainly have different morals and ethics to us."

Working with the faery realm does require us to examine our morals and our conditioning, to question why we think and feel what we think "right" and "wrong" to be. Working with faeries can create a different sort of consciousness, one which is unbounded by time and place, which is grounded in the natural progression of the cycles of the earth, our solar system, our galaxy and our universe. It's not grounded in the empty ritual of society, economic "reality", politics and other limiting systems we humans have invented. And it can demonstrate to us that we have far to go before we can improve on nature's own clocks and checks and balances. This can all lead to change – people following their true path, taking risks in love, and loving nature and being passionate about the planet.

Faery workings are very enchanted, and can have a very direct purpose. For example, you may approach the fae with a specific request or idea in mind. This may work – but sometimes in the most unexpected of ways. Or you can simply invite them in, and get ready for more whimsy and adventure. There are some basic ways in which to work with the faeries however. It's no good inviting them in willy-nilly, with no preparation or intent, then complaining that your house is topsy-turvy or your life has changed. Faeries thrive best outdoors, and if you invite them in, understand that some of your control over your environment will be abdicated. It is best to work with them firmly, with strength and respect but a gentle heart. It seems paradoxical, but such is the nature of the fae!

People often complain to me about the faeries. "They steal things," they tut. "They are naughty," people love to moan. Faeries do not steal – they take in return for what has been asked of them. They do not simply pick up a ring or a necklace and fly away with it, chuckling the whole time. They may take or move something beautiful to bring it to your attention. They are what some would call naughty – but often, this is because you have welcomed them in. They have a very different value system to many of us over-conditioned and oh-so-domesticated wild creatures, the humans. We have lost our vital spark – and the faeries will bring that back!

Most faery "rumours" are started because of the historic mistrust that developed between humans and the fae after the Church promoted a great deal of fear-based untruths and poisonous propaganda about faeries. The fae are trustworthy and very caring, but they do not have the same rules as us. Yet they are much more likely to share than to take anything.

To ensure that things that are very precious to you do not go missing, you may wish to invoke the dragonfae (part dragon, part fae) being Oroki. Of eastern descent, he is very able to create boundaries and protect what is yours. Many faeries are protective of your belongings, not because of ownership, but because of the energy signature the item carries. Sometimes when a faery carries off an item, it is to cleanse it and return it to the earth, as it may be carrying unhealthful energies. Do not assume to be able to read energy to quite the same degree as the fae, no matter your sensitivity!

Working With the Faeries

"Working" with the fae may seem like a contradiction in terms, as they are so playful and delightful. And when they are earnest, it may be that you've encountered some of the very wise and serious gnomes, whose name comes from the word "gnosis", or knowledge. But faery beings are always at work, in that they're constantly being creative and creating. From the elementals who seed the planet's energetic structures, to the devas cultivating the plants, and the faeries of the meadows and waterways, the fae are continually generating and regenerating life itself.

Working with faeries can, to put it very simply, mean you are willing to live more. To be more conscious of your thoughts and choices, to be aware of what it is you do, to own your own energy, and make adjustments without inflicting your own difficulties on others. While I have seen faeries who are sad – most often at the kind of environmental disregard that leads to trespassing without respect on their territory, and undoing much of their good work, I have never seen a faery feeling self-pity, as so many humans do.

If you approach the fae with pity for yourself, they will most likely avoid you, because your energy will be draggy, heavy and thick, and extremely vampiric. That is not to say that they do not help people – for they do, very much so! But the spirit in which we reach out to them will dictate the exchange, and the quality of our interactions. So, before you work with the fae deliberately, here are some very broad guidelines.

Do clear your energy before approaching them. This does not mean to fake happiness if that is not what you're feeling, or to attempt to seem pure and holy. The faeries will most likely laugh at you if you approach them with great earnestness and with the idea that you are about to give them a great gift.

It does mean to learn to comb through the energy that is yours, genuinely, and that which may belong to others. Clear the cords and attachments as best you can. Even if you feel angry and hurt, and fierce and sad and in pain inside, it is always best to approach the fae honestly, by acknowledging your feelings. This is not the same as directing these feelings at them. Simply say and feel: "Can you assist me with this? What should I do with these feelings? What is the best way for me to use this energy and these feelings?"

Don't approach them with a shield over your feelings, no matter how difficult these feelings are to have and hold within your energy field. You must be genuine to truly connect with them. This doesn't need to be a laborious process, but it does need to be done so you approach them with clarity and self-awareness, and ask for help.

If you do this, they will often help you by clearing the energy which you no longer wish to hold within your light body. They can clear this, and can often make use of it elsewhere – faeries are the great recyclers of nature, and they will not "waste" anything. This energy is the fertiliser of some of the most beautiful aspects of nature, and the earth can transmute most everything...

Where to Find the Faeries

It is best to go to a liminal place – an in-between place. Faeries are neither purely spirit nor purely material, they are both, and they are most likely to appear when you are in a space, both personally and within the world, that is between. In-between places are easy to find. Most of us have been to these spaces without even knowing we were in a sacred faery environment.

Seashores: Where the land meets the sea it is not quite land, yet not quite ocean. The sea fae are known to many as negative ions – an ironic name as it is these tiny fae beings who ionise the atmosphere to make us feel cheerful, happy, uplifted and optimistic.

Shorelines of lakes: Freshwater faeries are very wonderful, refreshing and life-affirming beings. They are also quite busy, so do be sure to let them know you are coming!

Banks: No, not the money-lending institutions where many gnomes work undercover, trying to even things up and spread some of the wealth. No, it's the banks that are on the shores of the rivers and streams. Creek beds and streams are also very much in-between and magical places.

Underground places: Open spaces beneath the ground, otherwise known as caves, are full of faeries, and many dragonfae beings too! Wherever you live, there are some of these enchanted sites nearby.

Doorways and thresholds: The most magical liminal places can exist in what many people see as the most mundane of places. Back doors are especially magical, but all thresholds and doorways are crossing places into the faery realm – just like the wardrobe in CS Lewis's beautiful book *The Lion, the Witch and the Wardrobe*, where Lucy crosses into the realm of Narnia after a mundane game of hide and seek. The right mirror, a screen, even an ordinary piece of glass can become the most magical scrying tool, or an entry point and doorway into the realm of the fae. Don't forget to work with the mundane and the ordinary – by doing so, you make the everyday enchanted!

Gardens: Wherever two or more trees can be found, there are faeries. If you ever see trees leaning towards each other, or forming an arbour, there the faeries will be found.

Hills, mountains or rocks: Special places where there seems to be an "opening" to the world within the world are very powerful – and you will know it when you find one of these places. Mid-mountain, on the hillside, is the most likely entrance point, forming an energetic threshold. Look for an indentation in the earth, a kind of natural seat or an opening. Certain trees have this energy and are entrances to Faeryland too. And wherever there are faery rings, there are fae, even outside your own home!

Rainbows: It is possible to stand within a rainbow and receive an incredible clearing and cleansing from the rainbow sprites, simply by being there. Rainbows can reveal the position of a dimensional halfway point between worlds, so pay attention to the faeries, and if they permit you to enter the rainbow, go ahead and enter. But if they shield you and ask you to leave, do so, as they may have made this request because a clearing is taking place, or some very old, hurt energy is being transformed. It's best not to be caught in this energy, so wait until you have a clear sign to proceed. And if you are asked to enter, well, step bravely forward, and be prepared for healing!

Mist: This creates an in-between landscape where much that is hidden under bright light can be revealed, and what is not pertinent can be obscured to avoid distraction. Faeries are so often seen dancing and twirling and playing catch with the mist!

Rings: Of trees, stones, even homes and plants... Circles create worlds between the worlds, and when they occur in nature they are very sacred. Even the ordinary ring of the sink plughole can create a kind of void, a place where energies can come through and be revealed. That's why so many visions happen in the bathtub, at the kitchen sink or as you wash your face.

Liminal times: The truly great thresholds are those within the cycles of the sun and the moon, and every day we have the opportunity to feel this magic from the faeries. The in-between, liminal times of each day are sunrise, sunset, dawn, twilight, moonrise and moonset.

Visiting Faeryland

If you wish to create a sacred space to connect with the fae, it can be helpful to do so at an entry point that is a liminal place. One of the most amazing ones is the entry to faery king Gwyn ap Nudd's kingdom on the side of Glastonbury Tor in England, but you will find one close to your home if you know how to look. At one of the liminal times, place your offering there as you say:

> *To the faeries, my kith, my kin,*
> *I wish to have an entry in,*
> *To your realm safe and true,*
> *To learn your wisdom, straight from you.*
> *To you I bring this gift of mine,*
> *Some food, some fruit, some milk, some wine.*
> *I ask for you to hear my call,*
> *And bring me home to you once more.*

It is important to ground yourself before leaving for Faeryland. Take within your hand a little dirt, or a leaf, or something very real and tangible that connects you back to the place you are journeying from. A touchstone is perfect.

Draw a seven-pointed star, either physically or by directing your own energy to mark it out etherically, and seat yourself in the centre of this. This is your entry point or portal to Faeryland.

Allow yourself to sink down. It can help, if you are a drummer or like drumming, to simply feel the heartbeat of the earth, slow and steady. You will be taken down... down... down... and be met by a denizen of Faeryland who will guide you through this journey.

The Art of Offerings

It is essential when interacting with the fae, especially when you hope to benefit from their vitality and their wisdom, to exchange something with them. You can make an offering of your energy, your time, your emotions or of an object. Sometimes it can be a beautiful gesture to offer a flower, a seed or a stone that is precious to you, or tie a ribbon to a faery tree – after asking first, of course.

It's important to not add anything to the environment that will be harmful. I've visited many sacred places where you can see the offerings of pilgrims. Some are wonderful, but others choke dreams and cause debris for the faeries to carry away. Do avoid this approach, as it will energetically "choke" the wishes you make.

Leaving food out for the faeries is also a beautiful thing to do. Tiny cakes, cupcakes or small biscuits, especially ones you've baked yourself with wholesome ingredients, will absolutely be appreciated. And it's wonderful to put symbols on your cakes, if you wish – the seven-pointed star, a triskele, the vesica piscis, a moon or sun. This is a great way to put some of your energy into the offering.

Another type of offering could be a simple clay symbol that you create for the faeries. I have a beautiful faery friend who makes altar tiles out of very simple things, like mud and clay that is found, and then paints them using completely biodegradable paints, the idea being that it returns to the earth very naturally after use.

Any ribbons or offerings that you leave on a tree should be made of natural fibres. And of course you can leave fruit and seeds out for the fae too. There is also nothing more beautiful than saying: "Here, I offer you energy, to do with what you will." This is appreciated by the fae, as humans have increasingly earned themselves a very bad reputation with the faeries.

Maggie Sinton is a Romany tarot reader, healer and teacher who lives in Western Australia. Her grandmother taught her a faery rite for the giving of offerings when she was very small. "My grandmother was a remarkable woman and a great healer. She was as blind as a bat, but she'd walk into the woods and somehow find the herbs and objects she needed for healings," Maggie recalls.

"On full moon nights she'd take out her special glass, a stemmed glass, and salute the Wee Folk. It was the only stemmed glass I'd seen until we were on the ship coming here – we drank out of bowls or jars. Which wasn't a drama, it's just the way it was. We were a step below dirt poor, so this rite would have been so important to her."

Maggie's Grandmother's Faery Rite

You will need a special glass for this ritual. Choose one, and use it just for the Wee Folk. You'll also need the cream of the milk – this was the top bit in the days of bottled milk – or some pure cream, and some ground cinnamon or ginger.

☆ Hold your glass up to the moon and allow the moonlight to shine through it.

☆ *Slowly pour in the cream. Salute the moon once more.*
☆ *Take a pinch of the spice. Smell it and feel it, then hold it up*
   to the moon.
☆ *Sprinkle the spice onto the cream and salute the moon again.*
☆ *Place the glass on your back doorstep and call the Wee Folk.*

"My grandmother used the words "Come up" about half a dozen times," Maggie remembers. "But she pronounced it 'cooom ooop'. Then no one left via the back door until dawn. In the morning she would take us out to find and dance in faery rings. I understand how important this must have been to her because the cost of her precious spices must have been like buying gold, and they were only ever used for the Wee Folk."

Maggie's grandmother truly connected with the faeries, sacrificing so much to be able to show them her intent and respect. And the faeries know what is in your heart, so it's no good thinking that you can offer them a little milk and honey then forget about doing something positive and real for the environment.

It's not "this" for "that" – working with the faeries is an energy exchange, and one which is quite intimate. You must offer the fae something of what is in your heart, and ground this by creating the energy in the physical. The very best offerings are the ones which have a real and true impact on nature and her wellbeing. Some very simple offerings include:

☆ Clearing an area of garbage and litter.
☆ Performing an energy healing on the earth. Be open about this. It's not about pouring an energy *you* think the earth needs in, it's about offering open clear energy to the land and the fae for *them* to work with in the way they feel best. Faeries have had plenty of priests "blessing" the earth, and often feel people who do so have ulterior motives, and feel they know best with their human arrogance!
☆ Replenishing the earth. Plant trees, especially ones native to an area, start a worm farm or a compost for your garden, or make a donation to an environmental cause that you connect with.
☆ Being grounded in your appreciation. Picking up other people's litter is a good way of giving back to the faeries. It is not, as some people seem to feel, undignified and too "low" for us to do. The faeries appreciate these acts, and notice where your heart's energy is coming from.

"We have a house spirit living in an old stove in our house that identifies itself as a domovoi," Tom Byrom says. "When I was 19 I lived on the border of Russia and China, and the domovoi was a big part of the culture there. When I first moved to my current home we had many problems – consistently burning or cutting ourselves when we were cooking, power failures, water failures, problems with our phone line. But when we acknowledged the domovoi, and started leaving him offerings, the problems stopped," he explains.

"Sometimes my housemates and I see a small man running through our kitchen. We believe this to be our domovoi friend. I also believe that I have faery blood, brought through from my Irish ancestry. This means that I have a very strong connection to the land and the weather. I am also very skilled in glamour magic and I pick up on other people's emotions very quickly. I believe these gifts also come from my faery lineage," Tom says.

How to Develop Faery Communication

To see the fae more clearly, and develop the Sight, it's often best if you do not see clearly at all. People who are short sighted are often more likely to see faeries, because they have naturally softened the boundaries between all things. There is a different psychology and brain structure that is developed with differently sighted people, and while there are many wonderful things about having perfect vision, sometimes it helps *not* to see.

When we are children we often see faeries, but then well-meaning older people who have already succumbed to the disconnect from their intuition may try to talk us out of it, fearing for us. But fear is not a very wise teacher. If a child is experiencing visions, and you cannot see what they are speaking of, or you think they simply saw a butterfly, ask them about what they saw rather than telling them. Do not rob them of their Sight, or their knowing!

Tom, a vital member of Australia's pagan community, saw faeries a great deal when he was young. "When I was a small child I used to see faeries – mostly small winged sprites that looked like Victorian era faeries – and other nature spirits," he says. "I remember asking my mother about a small man who used to sit on a tree stump outside of our house. She told me I was imagining things, but I knew I wasn't. I never had any more connection with him than just seeing him, but I knew he was real. More recently, the faeries have visited me in meditation and ritual."

Artist and photographer Carolyn Colmore, from New Zealand, also says she sees faeries. "The fae have made themselves known to me through flashes in my peripheral vision, and feeling their energy and mischief," she explains. "They have given me gifts of baby bird feathers and tiny eggshells, perfect pine cones and beautiful coloured leaves. And yes, they've even allowed me to take their photo!"

Sometimes this ability is hereditary. Science student Jean Kerwin, from Victoria, Australia, saw faeries when she was young, and has since learned of her mother's experiences, which mirror her own.

"My mother had two sightings when she was little, both times in her bedroom. One time it was more of a pixie, dressed in ragged brown and green clothes. The other was a pretty faery with blonde hair and a blue dress," Jean says. "Also, when my mother was pregnant with me, living in country New Zealand, both she and my father saw a green ball of light fly through the window and dance around the walls for five minutes, then fly out again. Both were stunned, and asked the other if they had seen it, and both of them had, although they have no idea what it was."

You can also see the faeries without opening your physical eyes – you may simply wish to see them with your spirit eye, and allow them to enter your world through the imagination. As well as methods like meditation, trance and ritual, there are some wonderful traditions we can fall back on when it comes to developing our faery sight.

One way is to rub a herb across your eyelids. Now, please be most careful – no stinging nettles! Take a rose petal (ask the plant first) or a piece of thyme, which is wonderful for faery sight, or even cinnamon basil, which is perfect for meeting sweet plant faeries and helping you remember the quality of the meeting.

Next, soften your gaze. Practise looking around an object, be it a person or a plant or a river. Remember that everything, when you get right down to it, is simply a vibrating energetic field. A shifting, moving mass of molecules bound in relationship to each other, and often far less solid than it appears to be!

This, if we wish to get deep about it, which we will because this information serves a purpose, is achieved quite easily by all of us if we can shift from a left-brain perspective to a right-brain perspective. Human beings, at present, are involved in some big changes in their make-up, energetically speaking, but many of us have a great deal more practise, habit and encouragement at being in the space of the left brain.

The left brain does have a lot going for it of course. It is the logical, detail-oriented, knowledge-based part. It designates between me, we and thee, it divides objects up, compartmentalises many things and is very linear, and very past, present, future. It is helpful and wonderful under many circumstances. In contrast, the right brain is more creative, more philosophical, more big picture, concerned with feelings, emotions and imagination.

Now, go soft... Relaaax, and slow everything down. You are going to begin to change your vibration – by softening, by feeling the pulse of life moving throughout your body and your energy field, and softening your gaze, allowing your eyesight to blur a little, and shift, and go beyond physical borders.

You can move quite easily into the right-brain state. Many ecstatic experiences happen very naturally, and there need never be a sense of *trying*. Techniques include listening to or creating repetitive drum music, staring into a candle flame, slowing the breath, gazing at light refracting off water, or ice, watching shadows move across the landscape, scrying with the clouds in the sky.

Drawing a seven-pointed star, either physically or etherically, for the faeries to enter through, can also assist you with the development of clear and bright faery sight.

Talk to the faeries too. Let them know who you are. Develop a relationship of trust, and in doing so, they may begin to reveal themselves to you. It will take patience, and gentle stillness – think of it as allowing a wild creature to come close to you. Think how shy they can be, and how still, trustworthy, peaceful and in tune you need to be for them to approach you. Adopt and allow that energy to flow through you when you wish to connect, and your results will be wonderful, and very beautiful and inspiring indeed!

Shhh! Faery Secret

Wearing green will let the faeries know you are one of their friends right away, and if you have a good and friendly heart, any colour will do just as well. But if your heart is mean, then they will flee faster than a unicorn!

Clearing and Revitalising Your Energetic Field

For this activity it is best to be outside in nature. Doing this kind of faery working can gift you with what the Celts call nwyfre (pronounced noo-wee-fray), a natural source of pure vitality and energy – sheer, primal life force. Whereas the other great faery gift of awen is creative and divine inspiration, nwyfre affects health, energy supplies and our ability to feel strong and well, and grounded and thriving, growing and connected.

Before working outside, please be aware of your surroundings. So many of us are so cut off from the natural world that you may wish to start gradually. Open a window. Work with natural light. Go for a walk. Get a little familiar with the faeries and the source of this gift called nwyfre before diving in.

For some people there may also be temperature conditions and safety issues with working outside. Please let people know if you are going on a bush walk by yourself, or hiking in a forest. Always have water and some energy bars or food with you.

Once you have ventured into nature, lay down on a rock. The best rocks are those that have soaked up sun and moonlight, which are often at pools – these tend to be places where faeries gather. When I was very young I used to go to a waterfall, a very small, sweet one, which had many deep grey, flat rocks around the water's edge. I would lay on one rock which had a great deal of "sparkle" to it, which was how I knew there was faery energy there. This was not something I had learned, it was just something I felt and knew.

When lying down on the rock, I would often feel a sort of brushing of what I now know is my auric field, with thousands of what felt like tiny brooms sweeping and clearing my energetic field, and tugging and pulling at other parts where energy was stuck and stale. For me, this interaction was blissful, healing and very re-energising.

If a rock by a waterfall is not available (although I would place a bet that one such place is much closer to you than you think!), please just take yourself outside, and hold a piece of crystal. The combination of the rock or the crystal with the sun will call forth the fae, who can sweep through the energetic debris that may be clinging to your auric field and light body.

The faeries often seem to polish your auric egg, or light body, too – quite often I have done this sort of exercise and have glowed afterwards, seeming to shine from within. Faery vitality is so uplifting, surprisingly simple and very easy to access.

For people coping with challenges to their health, this connection and conducting of nwyfre is a wonderful enhancement to their treatment. Always follow your doctor's guidance, but seek out nature's healing too, as it can create miracles in the physical realm.

Working With Faery Glamour

Faery glamour is the art of change, particularly of material appearance. It can be extremely helpful when we need to work within a situation that demands a certain appearance or energy. It is not a disguise, although it can be used as such – it's more a taking on of fae energy within our material form, and accentuating an aspect of our own being that the faeries can sing to, and increase.

It is almost like calling on your own faery blood, and allowing its energy to accentuate an aspect of yourself. Thus, faery glamour can make you appear to be smaller, taller, invisible, more attractive, old, young, male or female. It is an awesome ability, and one which often begins with very subtle effects, which you can grow over time.

Why would we have need of such a thing as this? Glamour has been most helpful to me when I have needed to be in my power but have felt exhausted. When I have needed to feel attractive and beautiful, yet conditioning and old inner voices have risen up again. When I have needed to speak in front of many people, but felt tired or withdrawn. It is not faking it, it is drawing on an aspect of faery energy that exists both within and outside of your own self, and calling on your faery blood, to assist you.

Once when I was walking home late at night, I felt myself being followed. I asked the faeries to lend me their glamour to become invisible... And suddenly the footsteps dropped away, stopped, and turned. I sent a spell of protection for others who might encounter this being's energy, and went on my way.

This does not mean that I became invisible, in truth – but it means that at that point in time I could not be seen. I had not restricted the other person's sight, so much as altered the way in which I could be perceived. This can be of great help when wishing to avoid troublesome folk, or when wanting to hold a surprise party, or simply for moving quickly and gently around the place.

I often drop a faery cloak of invisibility over my shoulders when needed, and what makes the cloak work is this aspect of faery magic called glamour. It can also work very well when you need to be persuasive. It is not a manipulation, I hasten to add. It is a selection and projection of energies most helpful to your own cause or project at the time. And for those of you who wish to truly feel and be more attractive, it is very simple. It can also be helpful as a form of psychic self-defence, for standing in your power, for creating strong boundaries, and for empowering children and other folk who may be frail in body and mind, who could otherwise draw the attention of some predatory energetic or physical types.

Faeries often use glamour themselves to walk amongst us, without us being completely aware they are there. We may sense them, or have a feeling that they are nearby, but their glamour keeps them invisible, and thus they can go about their business more effectively. The faeries may come to you in dreams or visions, and teach you their own methods of glamour. If you are fortunate enough to have a faery guide assisting you in this way, be sure to pay close attention to their instructions!

Glamour can help you to draw energy to you, push your boundaries out, and tell others who are infringing on your energetic, physical, emotional self: "Enough!" and: "Back off!" without needing to say a word. Your energy and the magic of glamour will do it for you. The power of the fae can be very large, very strong and very empowering. This is one of the most under-used aspects of their magic, a kind of self-defence in a world where energy can be stolen too readily, especially from those who are sensitive, giving and kind. Allow the faeries to protect you, and adapt some glamour strategies to ground and develop your own beauty, strength, courage and power.

Messages From the Faery Realm

Interpreting the messages from the realm of the fae accurately can take lifetimes to learn. We know they are with us when a feather drops, or a dragonfly dances around our hands, but what is the message, and what action is best to take when they appear to us so clearly, especially when the sign is repeated over and over?

Remember that the best way to approach faery messages is with an open heart, innocence and pure intent. And while we can never "force" a meaning, we can certainly learn to speak a little of the language of faery messages. Start by being still. Breathe. Let the chatter of your mind grow faint, then quiet, and soft. If you are with others, cease your talk. You do not need to verbalise, or interact that way with the energy. Still all your thoughts. Make room for the faeries to enter. Centre yourself. Breathe. And begin to look about you with the eyes of the fae...

The Rule of Three

Faeries like to send messages in groups of threes, fives, sevens, nines or elevens, and you will definitely know if the fae are speaking with you when there are three or more consistent signs. For example, one day I found a beautiful bird's nest lying outside my back door, whole and perfect. My second sign was a king parrot's feather being sent to me in the mail. The third sign was a beautiful sea eagle circling above me on the seashore. I had asked the faeries to share with me any messages they might have regarding a new love in my life. The bird's nest signified a home, just beyond my door, whole and secure. The second message indicated commitment, which is the meaning of the king parrot, and the third, the eagle, was telling me that freedom could be had in this relationship.

While the messages were delivered by birds, who are friends to the faeries, I knew that the fae had asked them to come to me and help me "see" and receive their message. The way in which the message was delivered took the theme of the birds of the air.

The theme the faeries will send to you, or help you to see, most usually appears over a time frame of three days, three hours or three minutes. If a message does come to you three times, please do not question the faeries any further – act on the message immediately, or simply accept and know it to be true.

Being open to a message means you can receive the message. Many people spend their time intellectualising the messages and wondering what to do, or if it is "really a message", in some ways choking the magic out of the message, harrying and fussing at the detail. Then the faeries can grow weary, and flee!

It is important to be playful, and light-hearted and as honest as possible, when working with the fae. Even if you're feeling very sad, or very angry, there is always a part of you that can ask for help honestly – and sometimes whimsy and humour and delight are easy to find simply by connecting with the possibility of faery energy.

Faeries do not avoid sad or wounded people, in fact they have incredible healing abilities in the physical realm, and have worked with people with depression or cancer, or other serious illnesses, and people who are grieving. They come to us when we are real, and wild. Authenticity is their signal to come on in. So remember to look for these numbers – one, three, five, seven, nine and eleven.

If you are feeling somewhat that being authentic and real are easier said than done, you are right. However, if you can remember, contemplate or just bring gently to mind a time when you did feel free, and when you had let go of self-consciousness, and let that feeling flow through you and extend out from your heart, into the energy field of the world, and ask your question, you will have that sense of authenticity that the faeries regard so highly, and reach out in return for. They may even recognise you as one of their kin!

Faery Numbers

One: This signifies a simple, powerful message. Act now.
Three: This is an issue that has a past and a present impact, and will have an echo into the future.
Five: This number signifies a profound shift, and powerful change.
Seven: This number refers to chakra links, rainbow harmony, and total involvement in your life.
Nine: This means that magical power is yours at present.
Eleven: This indicates mastery, completion and wisdom.
Multiples of these numbers, for example 111, 333 and 555, simply amplify the importance of the message, so pay attention!

Signs of the Nature Faeries

Faeries communicate with we humans very clearly, and with each other all the time. It is simply a matter of tuning in to their world, and beginning to read the signs for ourselves, and sensing their energy about us, within the world, and sometimes within our own blood.

Their signs and their messages are always very clear, and very sweet. However people who have not yet developed their intuition or their sensitivity can seem to be quite blind or immune to the faery signs, and the faery healing magics that are everywhere. Always stay open and aware. Insects like cicadas, ladybirds, Christmas beetles, dragonflies and butterflies all work with the faeries, and have different relationships. Some are faery steeds, and have a close and very bonded relationship with the fae. Bees too are a wonderful sign of faery activity and natural health.

Faeries love to help you by answering your questions, when the question is important! It is true that when you ask them a question they do not understand, for example: "When will I be rich?" they may not answer, or may attempt to divert your attention to the areas of your life in which you are already abundant. By focusing on these, you will develop more and more abundance. It is unlikely that the faeries would give you a series of numbers for a winning lottery ticket, but magically you will begin to attract more prosperity, as this is how magic works. They are also unsure of the source of some of our great unhappinesses, as we say we want certain things, as humans, but we often do not see all the beauty around us, and are very destructive. So when you wish to ask the faeries a question, be sure to consider their world first of all. Faeries value the natural world, gratitude, courage, laughter, sweetness, healing and fun!

Signs From the Stone Kingdom

Hag stone: This is a stone with a hole all the way through it, and it is said to grant the person who possesses it second sight, and the ability to see the citizens of Faeryland in all their forms. They are rare and difficult to find, for some, but for others they appear easily and offer themselves up regularly. I tend to find them on seashores, lakesides and other magical faery places.

Chalice stone: Stones with a small section scooped out of them can gather dew or fresh rainwater. If you've received a faery chalice, put it out at night then gather the dew in the morning, and run it across your eyelids to enhance the Sight.

Small ring of stones: A natural ring of stones in nature (or even in a car park!) means it is time for you to stop for a while and dance with the faeries in the midst of the stones. It is time for a time-out in the world between the worlds, for nourishment and revival of the soul. It's possible you have been going full-tilt in a very straight line, and missing some of the beauty to be found and savoured along the way.

Crystals: These are signs that the faeries are speaking with you. They often drop them onto your path, outside your door, or tuck them into drawers or under your pillow. They do the same with small beads and jewels, but crystals contain such pure, clear energy that they are a direct way for the faeries to help you know what is happening, and how to work with the situation for your highest good.

Signs From the Plant World

Mushrooms: This is a sign that it's time for sheltering your magics, to form a circle of like-minded friends.

Toadstools: It's time to psychically protect yourself, and also a time of lucid dreams and visions. Pay attention to them.

Moss: It's time to become more comfortable, to sleep more and have some time out. To get closer to nature, and to hold on to what matters for you, and to have stronger boundaries.

Clover: Finding a clover, especially a four-leafed clover, is a faery sign that you will soon find new love.

Leaves and foliage from different trees: These do not always appear naturally – sometimes they will appear on a billboard, or strike you as you watch a movie. But trees speak to us, and the fae are always working with the trees, to keep them well, healthy and whole. They appreciate the trees as sacred beings who dwell in a different time dimension to us. Their seasonal cycle is our own natural one, but as we have adopted calendars to arrange and order the procession of the wheel of time, we have separated ourselves further from nature. The faeries are telling you it's time to reconnect.

Gum leaf: It's time for cleansing and renewal.

Oak leaf: It's time to ponder the old ways, to be proud of the challenges you've survived, and incorporate all of your wisdom into strengths. Be compassionate with these strengths, not proud. Oak symbolises strength, endurance and the ability to withstand shock, so if you find an oak leaf, or see an image of one, you're being told by the faeries that you too are very strong, and will go on!

Rowan: Represents protection from persecution.

Holly: This signifies masculine power, potency and seeing.

Mistletoe: This attracts faeries who can assist you in activating your magic and help you invoke the sacred nature of the elements within. Because of this, and mistletoe's connection with the druids, faeries attracted to mistletoe help us reconnect safely with each element, and draw upon the magical tools of the druids and the faeries – the sword, the spear, the cauldron and the stone. (Note how these occur in the suits of the tarot – the swords, the wands, the cups and the coins. If you read tarot, you'll find that simply by recognising the deep meanings to these symbols, you will be able to give stronger readings and experience the magical world far more lucidly, as well as travel between the worlds more safely.) But back to mistletoe! This sacred plant and its faeries can also assist you to heal from past life trauma that's a result of the abusive misuse of the power of these elements, for example if you were persecuted by fire or water during the Burning Times. If you see mistletoe, it's a sign that the druids and their healing energy and bardic ways are calling to you, and telling you that it's time to spend time between the worlds. It is also a powerful fertility symbol.

Willow: The faeries feel that you need to drink more water, detoxify your sources of drinking water, absorb good information and move on emotionally. It also relates to retaining other people's emotions, and empathy leading to headaches and physical pain.

Eucalyptus: This signifies that you will find the correct healing treatment for a medical issue.

Elder: Elder trees protect the faeries, and if they are growing in a circle, they create a strong protective force for many miles around.

Oak, ash and thorn: These trees grown together create an energetic realm through which the faeries can appear more easily to you.

Apple: These trees attract the fae associated with Avalon. You can use the bark in spellworking. Simply use it as fuel for a fire – its smoke sends a message to the faery realm and also smudges you, clearing your energy field to raise your vibration, and thus allowing you to see and work with the faery realm. Particularly wonderful for those who are attracted to the Celtic path, the apple tree is especially sacred due to its fruit, which within holds a secret, the five-pointed star. Cutting open an apple horizontally to reveal the five-pointed star inside is a sacred act – leave an apple cut in this way out on a moonlit night to tell the faeries who you are.

Flowers: If a sweet flower falls in front of you, look to see what kind it is. For example, yesterday, just before I crossed the street, I looked down and saw a beautiful rose on the ground. No stem, just the rose head itself, its petals spread out, lying on the road, absolutely undamaged, utterly perfect and lovely. To me, the fae and the nature beings had left me a sign – that the changes I was about to make (symbolised by crossing the road) were on track, and that there was much love in the approach taken. A wonderful sign!

Rose: These faeries work with deep and abiding love and passion. When a rose appears to you, it indicates that you are following your life purpose. A red rose is one of the earthly passions, and will bring you great happiness, while a white rose symbolises the pure spiritual path, and indicates great insights and intuitive abilities.

Bluebells: Any flowers that are bell shaped are loved by the faeries, who can create homes in their sweet cushiony petals. Bluebell faeries assist too with your own workings within your home – they help to create a home sweet home, and good sleep.

Daisy: Sweetness and innocence, clarity and simple integrity.

Lilac: This pretty flower brings forth the faeries who can assist you with allowing life to have more sweetness and recognising its sacred moments, even in the most everyday situations.

Jasmine: You will soon know a relationship has future potential.

Morning glory: These magical blooms have always fascinated me. As a child, patches of bush near my home played host to these gorgeous blooms. To me, they were a clear sign I was entering a faery realm, where magic happened and time slowed down. Morning glory helps you hold on to your belief in magic, even if all around you the natural world is in peril. They are also a message from the fae to hold on, even when the going seems steep and our aims too high – for we will find a way to reach our dreams!

Thyme: This is perhaps the most magical and powerful of all herbs in terms of attracting and drawing loving faery helpers. Thyme faeries make a safe haven for all other faeries to visit you within, and the aura of the thyme plant itself is cared for and cleansed by the faeries. By growing this herb – thankfully a hardy one that even not-very-green-witches like me are able to grow – you also invite the faeries to work with and cleanse your energetic body, as thyme raises your vibration and assists you in feeling connected to other dimensions, allowing all to flow, and helping you understand and merge with concepts that are outside of logic and linear time – like the faeries themselves!

The position you find your faery message in will also tell you a great deal. For example, a gum nut turned upside down and filled to the brim with sparkling dewdrops is a faery chalice, which may be telling you that you are currently closed from receiving and that it's time to accept some help. So always honour the context in which your magical faery message appears.

Messages From the Small Winged Ones

Please remember that, as with all winged beings, there are hundreds, sometimes even thousands, of varieties, and the more attention you give to the details of your winged messengers, the clearer the message will be to you. When I was little, my message from the black prince cicadas was to work hard at what I wanted to learn, and have friends to help me. The green grocers, as I called the green cicadas, told me to water my plants and eat more green, bright foods, and the yellow cicadas told me to absorb more sunlight.

Dragonfly: A dragonfly is a sign that the strength of the dragonfae is with you – these beings are very strong, and very deep – and that there are some big changes coming your way. When dragonflies come, look closely at their wings, how they are moving, and whether they are still or moving well. You have power and great ability to create what you wish to manifest when a dragonfly comes to visit.

Ladybird: These beautiful spotted creatures are the messengers, the go-betweens, of Faeryland. Whisper a secret desire to a ladybird, and when it flies off, it will share your message with the faery queen!

Butterfly: All butterflies remind us to live in the moment, to look about us immediately and to experience what is beautiful now. Different butterflies have different messages, for example, seeing a monarch butterfly means you have the endurance to change homes, go on long journeys and live in more than one place.

Cicada: Cicadas shed their skins when they emerge from their evolution under the ground, and a cicada appearing to you is an indication that you are shedding your skin and undergoing your own evolution. Another significance of the cicada is that they sing – which indicates it is time for your solar plexus to be bright, and for you to sing out. The cicada's singing is made by a muscle on the abdomen, so while it might seem it is the throat chakra that needs to sing, it is your lower chakras that must be expressed and be sung out. Singing in groups could be wonderful for your power now.

Cicada shell: It is time for you to move on, and leave the past behind. Something no longer "fits".

Bee: Seeing a bee indicates that your health is returning. It also signifies that you should create diversity in your life, and symbolically make honey. Bees are a symbol of love and the intoxicating power of affection and desire, and they are natural life-bringers.

Beetle: All beetles have different messages, but they are wish-bearers, and can carry your wish from you to the faery kingdom. Ladybirds are wonderful at this, and whenever they appear you know the faeries are wishing you well, and supporting your endeavours.

Grasshopper: This is a sign of a great leap forward, strong movement, and that it is time for a change of abode.

Mosquito: Something small you have overlooked will bother you. Take time to clear the karma of your ancestor line.

Wasp: There are many types of wasp. Some are very beautiful and have no sting, and are not aggressive, while others are far swifter to attack, and have painful stings, like the paper wasp. A friend was stung recently by a paper wasp – as she sat down. It seemed right for her to ask who in her life was being a "pain in the butt", because that was what she literally had!

Messages From the Forest Floor

Worm: This little creature indicates that it's time to slow down and to simplify your life. Eat slowly. Go organic. Add more raw food to your diet. It's also time to get more oxygen, and to go deep within, into your own darkness for a while. You should also embrace and work with the element of earth, and the gnomes.

Caterpillar: This signifies that you are becoming... and that can take a long time. Have patience!

Ant: There's a busy time ahead, and it could be most productive to cooperate as part of a group, and be very organised.

Messages From the Sky Beings

Bat: Your clairaudience is waking up. It's time to travel to a safe place, sounding it out before heading to new places and spaces. Find a group of like-minded friends to share a sacred journey with. It's also time to go within, and find the strengths in your darkness.

Owl: They represent wisdom, yes, but for women particularly, seeing owls is a symbol of the wisdom of Blodeuwedd, a faery goddess and Queen of the Celts, who shapeshifted from a form made from flowers during the day to an owl at night. Through the owl, the faeries are suggesting to you that you remember your shadows, honour them, and keep the balance.

Raven: The law of the threefold return of the witches and the faery faith is that whatever we sow we shall reap, to the power of three and far beyond, so be aware of the energy you are choosing to send out into the world. It is powerful, it is your responsibility, it will have an impact in the world, and it will return to you, positively or negatively, depending on what you put out, and many times over.

Robin: Oh, how dear they are! I saw my first robin red-breast at the foot of magical Glastonbury Tor, as I prepared to walk to the top of the mighty faery hill for the very first time. To me, the robin was saying "well done" on my journey, and they are the sign of having done hard work, and now being able to enjoy the rewards. They are the fae's way of saying "congratulations!" to us. They bring us hope, and the knowledge that the future may have its challenges, but it will be bright, and that the faeries are cheering us on. Always make a wish if you see a robin – they will carry the wish to a faery queen of the Seelie Court, who will honour your wishes, should they be in balance.

A feather: It's time to connect with the element of air, and to inspiration and intellect. You may be too grounded and practical at present. It's time to lighten up and be freer in your thinking. All feathers have different energies of course, and when you know the bird that the fae asked to gift you with a feather, you will know an even deeper meaning of this message.

A bird's nest: A bird's nest that is whole and unscathed from its journey from the branch to your hands can be a sign that your home is cared for and protected. It is also a sign to participate in that care and protection yourself. It may be time for a house blessing, or to care for your surroundings and shelter. Birds are meticulous about keeping their nests clean, and the fae help by removing any energetic debris. What is it that you must cleanse from your home?

An egg, whole but opened: This indicates that a new life has sprung forth. Support and nurture the new path in front of you, and honour the learning that must take place as a result.

An egg, shattered: A new project may not come to life in the desired way – but another opportunity will come in its place.

Messages From the Animals

Possum: It's time to find a warm, comfortable shelter, and if one is offered, know that this is a sign that you would do well to go ahead and accept the offer. Alternatively you might want to be careful about who you offer your time, shelter and hospitality to. It is wonderful to extend a welcome, but do not allow someone to "move in" beyond what you are comfortable with. Faery people are notoriously generous, and sometimes have very fluid boundaries, so it may be time to check in with your intuition and see if it is time for some privacy and space again.

Wallaby: This indicates leaving the past behind, and finding a way to move forward. The faeries are saying: "Do not go back!"

Faery hound: This means the Wild Hunt, and a time of cleansing, is approaching! Check to see if the faery hounds have red ears – this is a very powerful sign that change is coming. They're also associated with Artemis, the warrior goddess of the wild hunt.

Rabbit: These creatures represent fertility and are a symbol of Ostara, the goddess of the springtime and fertility. They indicate that it's time for sensual enjoyment, spring energy and lovemaking (something many faery folk traditionally don't need too much encouragement to pursue with great abandon!).

Hare: Related to Andraste, the goddess of battle and victory, these are a strong sign of magic, and indicate that you will win a forthcoming struggle or battle. This is a very powerful omen, and a positive one for faery people who work with white witchcraft.

Faery horse: Some horses have traces of faery horse blood, as some people have traces of faery blood. Seeing any horse when you've asked for a sign is a way of connecting with the steeds ridden by the faeries on their wild hunts. And Rhiannon, the goddess of inspiration and the moon, will be with you.

Stag: This is a sign of Cernunnos, the horned god. If you see a stag, know you are being called to recognise the positive qualities of masculinity – the heroic protective-provider, the good father – and that your own ideas of men may need reworking. The king stag tells also of a time of great change that is approaching.

Deer: These are the consorts of the king stag, but they are also messengers of your own gentle nature. Whatever your true nature may be, when a deer appears, it is a sign to be very aware, to use your senses to be alert to what is taking place, and to be ready to avoid trouble if and when it comes. It can also be a sign that you would benefit from a vegetarian-based diet, as well as from caring for young ones and being with like-minded souls. Deers also show that Elen of the Ways, a great primeval Paleolithic horned goddess who guards leylines and the tracks of the deer herds, is with you.

Moose: This creature represents wisdom, strength, endurance and territory, and can indicate that a loss of your territory may have been taking place over time, pushing you back from what is rightly yours. This is the time to reclaim your purpose and direction, and ground your dreams and inspirations.

Fox: Canny, clever, intuitive and able to survive much, a fox is a beautiful message from the fae to do what must be done, even if it means withholding, staying quiet and being stealthy for a time. Undercover activity may take place with the fox. If you feel this does not connect for you (although it most likely does), think of who may be plotting some kind of attack or takeover – then without becoming worried or fearful, take steps to secure what is precious to you.

Wolf: If you see a wolf, it indicates that it is time to find your pack, search out your people, and discover the like-minded souls who are your true family. Recall your instinctive wisdom, and cease overriding your natural knowledge with logic and learned "advice". You are so strong, and so deeply connected to the lunar cycles.

For a detailed and broad-ranging study of the symbolic language in which animals communicate, please consider Scott Alexander King's wonderful works, Animal Dreaming and Animal Messenger.

Reading the Signs : What's the Story?

How you piece together your own natural-world faery oracle is very unique and individual. It may be a wonderful opportunity to take a faery oracle wander. Give yourself a set time – say, eleven minutes – and set out in a natural area or, if you are in a city, somewhere where there is a park with many trees. Pay attention to what happens, and collect three signs. I did this this very morning, and had a wonderful reading, straight from the heart of the fae!

I went to the beach I love so much, and walked to the headland
on the south side. A sweet-smelling breeze began to lift my hair as
I set out. The first sign was a fallen butterfly wing, golden and
black, that my feet went very close to. There was just one, and it
was tattered in some ways. I collected it carefully and continued,
pondering my question. I went further, and sticking up from the
earth, mingled with sand and beautiful pebbles, was a smooth
stone in the shape of the goddess. Continuing onwards, a feather
stuck straight out in a clearing. The feather was from a parrot,
blue and green streaked, and miraculously, it seemed to me, in
complete integrity. No dampness nor mites had eaten away at the
perfect design of the feather, nor dimmed its beauty.

I carried these back, and lay them in front of me. Silent.

First, the monarch butterfly wing. This indicates that one half
of a long journey has been completed, and that I am feeling
somewhat tattered and windswept, and sometimes exhausted. It
was interesting to note that the wing was a right wing, as I have
problems from time to time with "frozen shoulder" on my left side
– my receptive and feminine side. Were the faeries asking me to treat
this gently, and perhaps have some more of the acupuncture that
had completed this healing journey before? The healing journey
that coincided with a great journey's ending? Perhaps. It felt right
to look at both the physical and metaphysical aspects of this sign.

I looked again. The stone in the shape of the goddess. Time to
ground my goddess energy, and perhaps bring her more into my
home, and honour her in some way. To appreciate my body, and to
know how strong and permanent it is. Strong and everlasting, like
the stone that had been battered and washed up on the shore again
and again by the ocean, and thanks to this, the stone's true and
beautiful shape had been carved out. Ah, the journey, and its
experiences and its losses, had given me some of the grounded
wisdom and compassion of the goddess. Thank you faeries!

And finally, the parrot feather. I gazed at it, its power and beauty,
its hollow centre, its seeming fragility and yet its immense strength.
It indicated that it is time for some changes. For some independence,
and for far-reaching views that will allow me to envision possible
pathways for the future. To get "off the ground" and see my world
from a higher perspective, and to be swift and precise in the changes
to be made. To take off, and fly high!

Working With Faery Oracle Cards

It is not always possible to take the time for a destiny walk to find your faery signs, but you can also connect with the fae through the energies imbued in the many beautiful, energetic oracles available to us in this wonderful and wondrous world.

Faery oracle decks embody the energies of the fae within the cards, and are a tool through which you can easily and beautifully connect with these wise beings, and clearly understand, through the cards you select, the messages they are sending you.

Faery oracles need to have a touch of the earth about them – they need to be balanced. For that reason, I developed *The Wild Wisdom of the Faery Oracle* with beautiful Australian artist Selina Fenech, and *The Oracle of Shadows and Light* with the incredible American artist Jasmine Becket-Griffith, to address the imbalance and misunderstanding of the fae that seems to be out there.

Faeries are not simply sweet little flower creatures – although they are that. They can also be large, wild, essential, deep and above all primal and natural, dignified and very much themselves. There is a great wisdom to the fae that comes from the knowing of this paradox, that they are playful, gentle, fierce and deeply wise. Underestimating them and their power is never a good move, as it sees us mistreating the earth, and treating them as a convenience.

Wonderful faery oracles include the work of Brian Froud and his talented life partner Wendy in their *Heart of Faerie Oracle*, as well as Brian's collaboration with writer Jessica Macbeth on *The Faeries' Oracle*. And artist Jessica Galbreth's beautiful *Enchanted Oracle* deck, created with tarot reader Barbara Moore, has a beautiful balance of light and dark, whimsy and earnestness. To ensure balance, always look for both mirth and reverence in the faery oracle you are drawn to work with.

Please become very "intimate" with your cards. Sleep with them, touch them often, whisper to them, and take them with you on your journeys. Do your readings outside. And ask the faeries for their assistance before starting a reading, as they will help you. While many people like to think that the faeries are not reliable, when the whole story is told, and we look back, we can see how they were clearing our magical path, and pointing us in the best and most blessed direction, every time.

Doreen's Faery Magic

American author Doreen Virtue teaches people around the world to communicate with angels and faeries. A psychic, spiritual healer and environmentalist, she's written many inspirational books, including *Healing With the Fairies* and *Fairies 101*, and created several beautiful oracle card decks, such as *Healing With the Angels* and *Magical Messages From the Fairies*. Visit www.AngelTherapy.com.

Like most children, I was fascinated with faeries. Mum gave me a beautiful book about faeries and I used to stare at the paintings because they made me so happy. Now, the faeries help me to connect with nature, and I credit them with inspiring me to begin each day with a five-mile walk with my little Sheltie dog Valentine. And they regularly remind me to get outside during my work day.

The faeries are the guardian angels of nature, so they're found wherever there are flowers, plants, trees, animals and bodies of water. I also notice there are more faeries in countries which believe in their existence. This is particularly true in Australia and Ireland, two countries which revere nature and the faeries. When I visit these two countries, I always see heaps of faeries everywhere.

Faeries prefer outdoor settings where plants grow naturally. They don't care for pruning, trimming, lawn-mowing or fertiliser, and they avoid pesticides completely. If you want to attract faeries into your garden, let the garden grow free. Plant plenty of flowers, and hang crystals from the trees. Feed the birds regularly, and create little faery circles by putting stones in a round shape on the ground. They also appreciate little wicker doll furniture. And if you put some unwrapped chocolates near your plants, the faeries will be over the moon with happiness!

You can see faeries in your mind's eye and feel their movement as they flit about. Faeries love to dance, sing and play musical instruments.

To connect with the faeries, simply go outside and introduce yourself to them. You can do this silently or aloud, as the faeries can hear your thoughts. You won't hear anything in return for a while, as the faeries scan you to discover whether you're a nature-respecter or not. You don't have to be perfect at recycling etc, but you do need to be conscientious and loving towards nature and animals.

If you "pass" the faeries' scan-test, then they'll give you an assignment that you'll hear as a thought, idea or feeling. Usually the faeries will ask you to pick up any rubbish that is littering your area. If you do so, the faeries will make themselves more known to you. You'll begin to hear their cute, tiny voices in your ear, and see them more clearly in your mind's eye.

We need faeries today because they are the guardians of the environment and the animals, and they are ensuring the health of Mother Earth and her inhabitants. They protect our air, water and earth – the elements necessary to physical life. And the more people who believe in faeries, the more power they have to do their environmental work. The faeries love helping people who join in their mission to clean up the environment and protect animals.

I believe in faeries, and think they are as real as you and me. I can't wait until they are no longer labelled as "mythology", and when folks realise that faeries are sweet, kind and loving. They got their "naughty" reputation because the faeries do have egos, unlike celestial angels, and just like people, faeries will judge those who abuse the environment. And that's who they play tricks upon.

Doreen is the founder of the World Fairy Festival, which was celebrated for the third time on May 1, 2010. For events, visit www.worldfairyfestival.org.

Connecting With the Faeries

"Wherever is love and loyalty,
Great purposes and lofty souls.
Even though in a hovel or a mine,
There is Fairyland."
Charles Kingsley, English poet

Make Your Own Faery Altar

Most people who follow any kind of earth-based spiritual path have an altar in their home, which they use as a focus of their attention, energy and prayers. Witches use theirs for rituals, spellwork and divination, to communicate with their gods and goddesses, and as the physical manifestation and development of their beliefs. For shamans and other medicine people, their altar becomes a powerful healing tool developed over years of apprenticeship and initiations, which grows, changes and becomes more potent as time passes and their wisdom increases. For those who work with the fae, theirs incorporates the light-hearted joy of these Otherworld beings, and the essence of nature.

An altar can be as simple as placing something on a shelf to represent the four elements – such as a candle for fire, incense for air, a crystal for earth and a shell for water – or as large, complex and involved as you like. It can be permanent, or something you create from scratch every time you want to work with it. However you want to set it up, it will become a magical object and a place where you can sit in quiet reflection, perform your spiritual practices and manifest your dreams into reality.

An altar represents a retreat from the outside world, a place where you can be truly yourself, strip away any masks and explore your inner thoughts, beliefs and questions as you send your magic outward. It will probably be fluid and often changing, reflecting your own expanding knowledge and revealing your growth and development. And making one is an ongoing and enchanted creative project that will carve out your own sacred space.

Creating your own faery altar will help you connect with the energy of the fae and more deeply to your own intuition. This sacred space will become a place where you can do readings with your faery oracle cards, prepare faery rituals, herbal blends and other magical creations, channel faery healing, leave offerings to the magical beings you want to communicate with, and reconnect with your own inner faery. It will be a representation of you as well as of your relationship with the fae, reflecting your inner self in addition to your connection with Faeryland and faery energy.

Your faery altar will become your very own portal between dimensions, blurring the lines between the mortal world and the world of the fae. It will be a reminder of your work with them and their energies, even when you're not consciously doing so, a constant physical presence that will maintain the energy, bring beauty to your home and your heart and open a door to the spiritual realms. Having an altar dedicated to the fae also shows them that they are welcome in your home, and will encourage them to become a part of your life.

Setting Up Your Altar

To make your faery altar, first find the place that feels the most magical to you. This might be outside, in a corner of your garden, on a fallen log or a stone slab, under a tree, on your balcony or even in a nearby park or forest. Or you may prefer to work inside, in a corner of your lounge room, on your bedside table so it can fuel your dreams, in your home office, art studio or magical room, or even on a bookshelf or a kitchen bench or windowsill.

It can be set up permanently or assembled only when you want to work with faery energy, and can be your sole altar or one of several different ones that you work with. It's totally up to you – this is your sacred space, symbolising how you perceive the fae and the ways in which you want to work with their joyful, healing energy.

You can create your altar on pretty much anything – on a side table, a special wooden chest, a small shelf, a piece of wood supported by bricks, an upside down milk crate or even a cardboard box with a lid (which you can store your ritual tools, herbs and crystals inside when not in use, and display everything on top of when it is). There are even incredible faery altars available, that have a round table top supported by a carved tree trunk, with a faery door going into the tree, and ivy, toadstools and flowers sculpted around it. But the intent of your altar, and the time and passion you dedicate to creating it and maintaining it, is much more important than how much money you spend. Setting it up on the floor or on the bare earth outside can be just as powerful.

Next, think about your altar cloth or covering. If it's an outdoor altar, you could cover it with moss, a piece of canvas or a faery motif children's party tablecloth. If it's indoors, find a beautiful piece of lush, shimmery fabric that feels good to touch, and choose nature-inspired colours, which can range from earthy red-gold-browns through all the shades of leaf green and water blue, and the vibrant pinky-mauve-yellows of a sunset. Or use a gorgeous shawl that reflects your faery self, or buy (or be gifted) a traditional altar cloth. Or you may want to show off the altar itself, and dispense with a covering, which is fine too. Learning to work with faery energy means letting go of rule books and preconceived notions, and following your heart and your inner knowing.

Now comes the fun part – choosing the objects to place on your altar. This is a totally intuitive process, and will form the basis of your first faery ritual. There are no rules to follow (although we've listed some suggestions), and every single object should have personal meaning for you, whether it be something you found, like an acorn or an autumn leaf, a special gift from a loved one, like a crystal or a faery statue, something you've made yourself as an expression of your love of faeries, like a clay figurine or a picture, or a special item you've bought for your faery workings.

The only limit is your imagination! You can add things or replace things whenever the mood takes you – faery energy is mercurial and light-hearted and very much alive, so keeping your altar from stagnating will keep the energy flowing. And once you start working with the fae, or the faery archetype, you will begin to attract objects too, like feathers, artwork and symbols of magic.

Elements and Elementals

Faeries are aligned with the four magical, natural elements – air, water, fire and earth – so you can use a representation of each one as the basis for your altar set-up. You might have an incense cone or a feather for air, a chalice of water, mini fountain or a shell for water, a cauldron or sun depiction for fire and a stone or crystal, or dish of sand or salt, for earth. You could also use four coloured candles – yellow for air, blue for water, red for fire and green for earth – placing one at each corner of your altar, or small statues of magical beings, such as a winged sylph for air, a mermaid for water, a red-clad faery for fire and a gnome for earth.

Perhaps you feel drawn to work with representations of the four mythical treasures of the Irish fae folk known as the Tuatha de Danaan – the Lia Fail or Stone of Destiny, symbolised by a stone of the earth, the Sword of Light wielded by Nuada, represented by an athame or other air symbol, the Cauldron of the Dagda, symbolised by a chalice for water, and the Spear of Lugh, represented by a wand or other fire object. Like everything about your altar, the things you use to represent the elements can be as elaborate or as simple as you like. A rough sketch of a sword or a sharply pointed crystal will work just as well as a jewel-encrusted athame – as with all magical workings, it is your intent that creates power.

Where you place your elemental objects is also entirely up to you. You may want one in each corner of your altar, or midway along each side. You could place them in a circle in the middle, or in a row along the back. In magical traditions the elements are aligned with a direction, although these too are open to interpretation.

Many people in the southern hemisphere put fire in the north, the direction of the fiery sun at the equator, and earth in the south, although these are usually reversed in the northern hemisphere. Some people put air in the east, as it is the direction of the sunrise and new beginnings, and water in the west, where the sun sets below the ocean at night, although these too can be reversed depending on your geographical location and your particular magical tradition.

If you plan to work a lot with earth elementals such as gnomes, or with the earth archetype and powers, you may want to have your altar in the south of your room or facing south (in the southern hemisphere), or set it up in a darkened room to represent the grounded earthiness and going within aspect of this element. If you're working more with the element of fire or the fire elementals, such as salamanders, genies and other creative, passionate fae, you may want your altar to face north or be placed in that corner of the room, or set it up in a place where sunshine streams through your windows to give your workings some of its fiery energy.

Likewise if you're focusing on water elementals, such as undines and nymphs and mermaids, or the emotional aspects of the element of water, you could face your altar to the west, place it in that section of your room, or set it up outside near a pond, a river or by the sea, or even around you as you bathe – perfect for a ceremony or working that begins with a ritual bath. And if you are wanting to work with the air elementals, with sylphs and delicate winged beings, or the element of air and its energy of new beginnings and initiating powers, you may prefer to face your altar east, place it near an open window, or set it up outside.

Adding and Elaborating

Once the foundation of your altar is in place, you can add and embellish to your heart's content. You can incorporate your favourite faery artwork into your altar with small faery images, or hang a beautiful painting on the wall above it, to provide inspiration in your workings with faery energy and to fire up your imagination.

A vaporiser to burn essential oils and/or a censer to light incense would also be a perfect addition, along with ritual candles that incorporate the energy of the fae, glitter to represent faery dust, colourful ribbons and shiny sparkly objects, tiny faery wings you find or make to represent your love of the faeries, pictures from a faery oracle deck or mini prints, butterfly shaped candles, little pots of flowers or herbs – anything that makes your heart sing and your mind open to the magical realms.

You might want to place a small dish in the centre that you can place offerings in, be it food, tiny crystals, flowers, sparkly glitter or whatever else you feel moved to gift. Don't be offended if it's still there afterwards though – it's said that faeries consume the essence of food rather than its physical aspect. If you're outside, the earth will take your libation of water, juice or mead, and little creatures will consume any food, as a symbiotic partnership with the fae.

Add the things that you find on your nature walks too, such as rocks, feathers, twigs, seashells, leaves, crystals, gum nuts, acorns, sand, driftwood and flowers. You can make a powerful ritual out of these object-finding walks, by asking for signs and messages, allowing the physicality of your body movement to clear your head and put you in a magical state of mind, and having the alone time that helps you hear your inner voice and lets you find the answers to your questions or dilemmas, because being outside in nature is so soothing, and breathing in clear air will wake you up and energise you.

Your faery altar is a reflection of you and your beliefs, the physical manifestation of your spiritual self and your relationship with the fae, so do be open to its changing nature. You might find new things to add fairly often, so it can change whenever you feel the urge. You may prefer to keep just a few things permanently on the altar, then add what is needed when you're performing a ritual, doing a specific faery working, or it's a full moon or faery festival.

It can also be a good idea to have a special faery treasure box to keep your objects safe and dust free. This can be a carved wooden chest, a silver or brass blanket box, a pretty patterned gift box, a drawer in your dresser, a cloth faery bag or even just a plastic container so you can see what you have and where everything is.

You might want to keep a faery journal on your altar or close by, to record all the things that happen during the time you dedicate to the fae, whether that be writing down all your faery oracle readings, any messages they whisper to you, magical recipes you create, be they herbal potions or tasty treats, or realisations you have during your faery time about your self, your life and the magical realms.

Or you can make a faery scrapbook, and collect pictures, poems, pressed flowers, articles, cuttings, your own words, meditations, card readings, herb workings and the messages you receive. This can be a beautiful reminder to you, to lift your spirits if you ever feel down, and will also become a gathering place for all the knowledge you discover, the personal breakthroughs you experience, and the wisdom you gain through looking within and connecting with your inner faery.

Creating a Faery Ring

Another possible way to set up your faery altar is to base it around a faery stone circle or toadstool ring. This would work beautifully for an outdoor altar, but you can also set it up inside, on your altar table. You could buy little ceramic mushrooms from a garden shop to create your faery ring, placing your other objects within or outside this space. You might like to find a collection of pebbles or small rocks on your walks, make little standing stones out of clay or find a mini Stonehenge set to construct your sacred circle.

You may also wish to collect several crystals that are flat at the base and point upwards at the other end with which to create your circle. Rose quartz, amethyst or citrine would be perfect, or choose any other kind of crystal you are drawn to. This ring of power will look beautiful in the centre of your altar, and also be an amazing focal point for your workings. You can charge other crystals within this sacred circle, help plants grow by placing them inside it overnight, create blessed water by leaving a bottle or glass there, or simply keep a beautiful faery statue within it, to represent the manifestation of your faery magic.

A circle of any kind is an immensely powerful symbol. A shape without beginning or end, it captures the essence of unity, eternity and the continuing cycle of life. Magical rituals take place within them because they mark the boundary between the worlds, as well as being able to create a protective barrier that can contain the energy raised and keep out negativity.

Any other magical symbols you feel an affinity with can also be incorporated into your altar, either permanently or for a specific working. You could set your objects up in that shape, include a representation of it as an altar piece or use it in any way that works for you. Here are a few examples, but go within to discover the symbols that have the most meaning to you.

Seven-pointed star. The faery or elven star acts as a portal to bring in faery energy, and represents magic and the harmony of the seven elements. You could sprinkle salt, crystal chips or ground herbs into the shape of this star, then place an object at each point, or embroider it onto your altar cloth, carve it into the wooden tabletop or draw it on paper and place that on your altar.

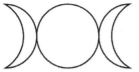 **Triple moon or triple goddess:** This pretty symbol represents the three major phases of the moon – waxing (as it increases towards full, appearing as a crescent), full (where it appears as a perfect round disc) and waning (as it decreases towards dark, represented by the opposite crescent). It is also symbolic of the triple goddess and her aspects of maiden, mother and crone, and the three major stages of the feminine life cycle. In the northern hemisphere this symbol reflects the moon cycle, with the waxing crescent appearing as a backwards C, followed by the circle of the full moon and the C shape of the waning crescent, but in the southern hemisphere this is reversed, appearing as ☾O☽.

Horned god: This symbol represents the horned god of nature and fertility, known variously as Cernunnos, Pan, Caerwiden, Herne and the Green Man. He is the pagan god of the forest, the hunt, wild animals and fertility, and is associated with horned male animals such as stags – and erroneously with the devil. He reflects the seasons of the year and the cycle of life, death and rebirth, and is considered the guardian of the forests and its wisdom, the defender of all animals and the masculine half of the divine.

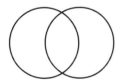 **Vesica piscis:** This is the ancient sacred geometric pattern of two interlocking circles, which symbolises the merging of the conscious and the unconscious, the physical and the spiritual, yin and yang, god and goddess, and the inner and outer worlds. The space where they intersect represents this union, and the Christians adopted it for their own, using it as their symbol, which they called the ichthys. The vesica piscis is also the symbol of Glastonbury's sacred Chalice Well and all the magic it holds.

Triquetra: From the Latin "tri quetrus", meaning three-cornered, this magical symbol represents the eternal cycle of life, death and rebirth, as well as other threefold aspects, such as maiden, mother, crone and physical, mental, spiritual. To the Celts it also symbolised the realms of earth, air and sea that made up their universe – and later the Christians adopted it as a symbol of their holy trinity (father, son and holy spirit). Today, thanks to TV's *Charmed*, it has also come to represent magic and the power of three.

Triskele or triple spiral: From the Greek for three legged, this symbol also represents the triple goddess, and all the triple aspects of life – maiden, mother, crone; life, death, rebirth; body, mind, spirit; waxing, full, waning; sun, moon, earth. It's drawn in one continual line, with no beginning or end, which is how ancient peoples saw life and existence. There is a triple spiral carved in the entrance stone at Newgrange, Ireland's Neolithic burial chamber, which some believe was an initiation chamber and others claim is a faery mound, and the symbol is known to some as the spiral of life.

Yin yang: The yin yang symbol represents the Ancient Chinese understanding of how the universe works, and how everything is interconnected. The outer circle represents all that is, while the black and white spaces within the circle symbolise the interaction of two opposite yet complementary energies that exist within the greater whole. Yin, the black, symbolises feminine, night, passive, cold, introspective energy, while yang, the white, represents masculine, day, aggressive, hot, active, expanding energy. Neither can exist without the other, signified by the dot of the opposite shade within each shape, and we all have elements of both within us.

Faeries As a Symbol of Nature

Your faery altar also represents your connection to nature, so have as many found objects from the natural world as you can. This might be fallen leaves, twigs and seeds you come across outside, feathers, clay figurines or even photos. You can place a vase of fresh flowers in the centre of the altar, even when you're not consciously working with it, or little pots of ivy, violets or marigolds, or specific herbs that suit your workings, as these will attract the fae and also scent the room and help shift your consciousness. Burn incense or herbs to purify and scent the air, and make it easier to slip into a magical trance state, and if you're working at night, illuminate your altar with tealight candles to add to the magical atmosphere.

Your altar can also reflect the shifting seasons, and the environment in which you live. You might like to rework your altar at every sabbat, to incorporate the energy and magic of the seasons into your workings, and make use of the beautiful faery flowers and foliage that bloom at different times as the Wheel of the Year turns.

The Wheel of the Year

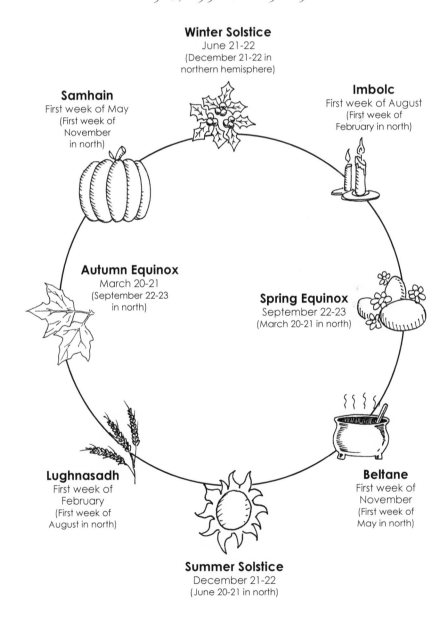

Winter Solstice
June 21-22
(December 21-22 in
northern hemisphere)

Samhain
First week of May
(First week of
November
in north)

Imbolc
First week of August
(First week of
February in north)

Autumn Equinox
March 20-21
(September 22-23
in north)

Spring Equinox
September 22-23
(March 20-21 in north)

Lughnasadh
First week of
February
(First week of
August in north)

Beltane
First week of
November
(First week of
May in north)

Summer Solstice
December 21-22
(June 20-21 in north)

Yule

Yule is celebrated at the winter solstice, the longest night of the year, and marks the middle of winter. When working with the faeries at this time of year you could have a dark blue altar cloth and decorate your sacred space with bunches of mistletoe, holly or pine cones. You could make your faery ring from garnets or blood red rubies, leave an offering of nuts, citrus fruits and spices for the fae, and burn cinnamon or ginger essential oil or incense. If you're in the northern hemisphere you can add a faery to the top of your Christmas tree, or decorate it with faery figures.

Imbolc

Imbolc is the cross-quarter day that falls between the winter solstice and the spring equinox, and marks the first day of spring and the energy of new beginnings. You might choose a light blue altar cloth at this time, and fill a vase with bluebells, snow drops and primroses. Light and powerfully healing crystals such as rose quartz and clear quartz can be used, and herbs such as angelica, myrrh, celandine, basil and bay can be blended together to make your own incense.

Ostara

Ostara is celebrated at the spring equinox, one of the two times of year when night and day are of equal length. It marks the middle of spring, so flowers are blooming, nature is alive and vibrant, and the energy is fertile and bright. You can use a green altar cloth for your faery workings, and incorporate moonstones and aquamarines into your set up. A bunch of daffodils or lilies or sprigs of jasmine will bring the energy of the season inside, and you can present chocolates for the faeries – and for yourself! – because in the northern hemisphere this pagan celebration was transformed into Easter.

Beltane

At Beltane, which marks the first day of summer, you can dress your altar, and yourself, with rich gold material. Pictures or symbols of bees would be perfect, and anything that makes you feel sensuous and joyful, for this is the time where nature is bursting forth, and you can harness the fertility of the season for your own projects. Sunstone, amber, citrine and topaz can be used, and offerings of strawberries, honey, seeds and cinnamon would be most welcome.

Litha

Litha is celebrated at the summer solstice, the shortest night and longest day of the year, which is also known as Midsummer. The faeries are very active at this time, as it's a crossover point where the veil thins a little, so it's a great time to connect with their energy. Light and bright is best – an orange altar cloth and pots of golden herbs such as chamomile, Saint John's wort and lemon verbena are wonderful. Have a vase of honeysuckle, daisies and frangipanis, or stick to roses, the flowers of summer and love. Add their petals to your ritual bath, drink rosebud tea to activate psychic powers, and plant some in your garden to invite the fae to come and play.

Lughnasadh

Lughnasadh is the cross-quarter day that falls between the summer solstice and the autumn equinox, and celebrates the beginning of autumn and the harvest season. Choose a red or gold altar cloth, and use wheat sheaves, corn husks, acorns, oak leaves and juicy ripe berries to represent the day. Make a faery ring of golden topaz or tiger's eye crystals on your altar, and burn sandalwood incense. Leave an offering of honey or oat cakes for the fae, and make a donation to a charity to reinforce the beautiful energy of gratitude.

Mabon

Mabon is celebrated at the autumn equinox, when day and night are of equal length, and is a time of balance and harmony. Choose a rich russetty or golden brown altar cloth to represent the vibrant colours of autumn leaves. Wind ivy around the edge of your altar, place marigolds in the centre, and have a dish of plump berries to share with your faery friends. Magical herbs associated with this day include passionflower, sage, thistle and milkweed.

Samhain

At Samhain, the first day of winter, lay out a black, deep ruby red or orange altar cloth, and perfume the air with the heady, heavy scents of patchouli. This is a time when the veil is at its thinnest, and spirits and beloved ancestors are believed to walk the earth. Divination can be very effective at this time, so bring out your dark obsidian mirror or scrying bowl and use the fae energy to take a peek into your future, then recall your past and let go of any hurts.

How to Connect With Your Inner Faery

"If we opened our minds to enjoyment,
We might find tranquil pleasures around us on every side.
We might live with the angels that visit on every sunbeam,
And sit with the faeries who wait on every flower."
Samuel Smiles, Scottish author

Finding Your Own Magical Self

Faeries have long captured the imagination, inspiring people to weave mystical stories, create beautiful art and protect and hold nature as sacred. The very idea of them lifts the spirits, opens the heart and the mind, reminds us of the secret longings of our soul, and fills us with happiness, spontaneity and child-like wonder.

These magical beings represent a lost part of ourselves, the part that is wild and free, that dives joyously into life, and loves with passion, abandon and fearlessness. And you can regain this essential part of yourself, and bring more joy and magic into your everyday world, by connecting with your inner faery.

The simplest way to acknowledge and celebrate your inner faery is to get back in touch with your child-like self. Not childish as an insult, but as a compliment, as something to aspire to! American author and spiritual teacher Wayne Dyer says: "One of the most responsible things you can do as an adult is to become more of a child." And it's true. It is a gift to be able to see the world through a child's – or a faery's – eyes, to experience life with joy, innocence, truth and beauty. To be filled with awe at the way your life unfolds, and at the wonder that is this magical existence we are all experiencing.

Recapturing this way of seeing the world, and your life, is easier than you might think. Start by giving yourself permission to do any of the things that made your heart sing when you were a kid. Play in the park, sliding down the slippery dip, pushing yourself higher on the swings, feeling the wind in your hair on the spinning top. Feed the ducks, watch squirrels scurrying across the grass and bats soaring from tree to tree, and immerse yourself in their little world within our world for a while.

Get a hula hoop or a skipping rope and reconnect with the joy of movement. Fly a kite. Turn up the music and dance crazily around the room or sing into your hairbrush. Have a costume party or meet your friends for coffee dressed as a faery, a witch or a favourite film character. Spend a day at an amusement park scaring yourself on all the rides or reliving happy memories eating faery floss and playing the clown game. Have cake for breakfast, party pies for lunch or Coco Pops for dinner.

Watch a kids' TV show or movie without feeling you have to justify it to anyone. Learn about the planets and the stars, or do a jewellery-making course. Finger paint. Babysit. Bake a faery cake. Follow your passion, be it salsa dancing, travelling or starting a band. Dance under the full moon, stay up all night, laugh, love. Do something unexpected and fun and playful and wild.

Most importantly, start to tune in to what it is you love to do, rather than the things that are expected of you. This doesn't mean shirking responsibility or running away from any issues you have to deal with, but simply finding time in your life to be light and happy. Connecting to your joyful heart, and allowing that to permeate your senses. Responsibilities will seem lighter and problems less dramatic if you can view them with new eyes, with eyes filled with gratitude and compassion. If you are happy and fulfilled, difficulties will be easier to deal with and challenges will weigh you down far less.

Our inner faery is the part of us that is a free spirit, that knows what it needs to be happy and feels entitled to live in that state. We all deserve happiness, but so many people feel guilt about it, or keep pushing it away because they've become convinced that happiness is dependent on earning more money, having more things, losing 10 kilos, finding a boyfriend, getting a new job or moving to a new town. But your inner self knows that none of these things of themselves bring happiness.

It is we who must find our own happiness, and a happiness that comes not from possessions or status, but from simple – and yet oh so important and powerful and magical – things. From our friendships and our families. From living our life aware of all the wonderful blessings we receive each day. From pursuing our dreams and making a difference in the world. From being proud of who we are and at peace with all the decisions we've made.

The way you handle any challenges will be a reflection of the way you live your life, and the way you see the world. If you believe everyone is conspiring against you, you will no doubt experience life that way. But if you realise that bad things sometimes happen – to everyone – you will be able to put things in perspective, and deal with them in a much easier, calmer manner.

Stepping Outside of Yourself

Another lesson of the faeries is to not take things personally. The faeries don't share our attachment to things and events, and if you can adopt a little of their detachment (without going too far the other way!) it can help you handle situations better.

Most people are just doing the best they can, thinking of themselves and what they want and need to do, and their actions are rarely intended to hurt or upset others. Sometimes this will happen, as an unforeseen consequence, but if you can avoid taking it personally, and simply explain to them how it affects you, the problem can often be solved easily and well for the two parties. But if you take it personally, and feel affronted and defensive, believing that they are out to get you, you're more likely to act badly yourself, and inflame the situation. No one experiences life in exactly the same way as another person, and things are all about perception – which can so easily be misconstrued.

Try to see any issue from a more detached viewpoint. If someone doesn't want to do something, don't automatically assume it's because they don't want to see you. If they say something that upsets you, ask them exactly what they mean, and tell them how it sounds to you, and why it's upsetting. They may have no idea. People rarely do something with the intention of hurting another person, or punishing them in any way, so if something has impacted on you in a hurtful way, gently explain your view, and try to understand theirs.

You can also be more like a faery, and connect with your inner faery, by being truly yourself, and being very honest about what you want, what you need and what you like (and don't like). Some people will do things because they assume you want it done, or they think it will be good for you, even though it is not. So calmly explain what you do want.

They may be surprised, and genuinely believe that they were doing the right thing, so it is important to express how you feel and be clear about what you want. We are perceived differently by everyone based on how we interact with them – you may seem wise and trustworthy to the friend you do yoga or rituals with, but fun-loving and carefree to the one you go out partying with and hide your spirituality from – and they will treat you as such. But you can stop acting the way you think you should, and allow people to see you. The real you. All of you.

Stop apologising too for the things that mean a lot to you. So what if you like a supposedly daggy band, would rather read comics than Dostoevsky (or vice versa), or are considered nerdy because you enjoy studying. Releasing this fear of judgement is so liberating, on the big issues and the small. And really, is anyone going to stop liking you if you say you love Nickelback or Duran Duran? That you'd rather watch a romantic comedy than the latest arthouse offering? That you think faeries are cool?

If they do, then it is their loss. We don't all have to like the same music, read the same books, act the same way or want to do the same things. My dearest friends I love not because we're the same, but because they are kind, and brave, and understanding and true. We have connected deeply, shared intense experiences, laughed a lot, helped each other through low points, celebrated high points, and encouraged each other to shine. We make each other more, not less, when we're together. And we know we can disagree about something and it is not personal, and not catastrophic to the friendship.

We have similarities, but we have differences too, sometimes big ones, and that's okay. There are some fundamental values that should never be compromised, and if that ends a friendship then it's probably for the best, but don't ever apologise or hide who you are or what you believe. A real friend will love you, flaws and darkness and all, and will value you even more if you let your real self shine, and allow them to do the same.

This doesn't mean you should be selfish, far from it! Being true to yourself makes you more alive, more joyful and more understanding, and more willing to be selfless and help others and the planet. Some people confuse being true to themselves with being selfish, and decide that always putting themselves first is the way to be strong and authentic. But when you are truly alive, truly connected to your inner self, there is no competition. No one's needs have to be put before others, because you know there is always a way in which everyone's desires can be met, and that you can discover a solution that is right for everyone.

Spending time helping the planet is another way to connect with your inner faery, for they are the humanisation of nature, and a symbol of it. They remind us of our need to protect the environment, and our desire to connect with the earth. They encourage us to treat the planet and its plants and animals well, consider it sacred, and work with, rather than against, nature.

Many people today have lost this connection, but faeries, and movies like *Avatar* and *The Cove*, remind us to spend time outside in the natural world, to care for the planet and its flora and fauna, and to conserve our resources. We have appointed faeries as the guardians of the earth, and of nature, but it is us who must do the work, and protect the endangered animals, the beautiful forests, the life-giving land, the precious water and the very air itself.

Our need for faeries is a reflection not only of our disconnection from nature, but also of our disconnection from ourselves. Our spontaneous, genuine, real selves, freed of the layers of conditioning that we should be sensible and serious. The part of us that sparkles with enthusiasm, that can't wait to get up in the morning and go exploring. That laughs with happiness at seeing bubbles floating through the air or a butterfly delicately alighting on a flower, and delights in planning beautiful adventures that will nourish the mind and the soul. And it is this wonderfully authentic and precious part of ourselves that we must nurture, protect and celebrate.

Expressing Your Inner Self

Another way to connect with your inner faery is to tap in to your creative, expressive side, embodying the energy of the fae through music, dance, art or writing. The magic and beauty of their archetypal energy stirs something deep within and touches the heart, bringing joy and inspiration. We each have unique talents that not only benefit us, but also the world, when we express them. There are many artists who capture the beauty of the fae through their paintings, and being artistic can be a wonderful way to give voice or vision to your inner faery.

You can paint or draw for yourself or for others, it doesn't matter. Art is incredibly therapeutic, regardless of how good (or not) you think the results are. Paint or draw your own faery image, the manifestation of your inner self. Create your own oracle deck or collect crystals and stones to make a rune set. Write stories, poems or books for yourself or for publication, or keep a private journal to record your faery insights as you get more deeply in touch with the real you.

You can also welcome this energy into your life by surrounding yourself with representations of the fae. Hang pictures of the magical winged beings that live in the mist-shrouded Otherworld. Wear faery clothes or jewellery, slip a faery charm on your keyring or have one embroidered or printed on your bag. Have a faery statue by your bed or a magnet on your fridge, or drink your coffee from a faery mug.

Whether you believe faeries are fact or fiction, you can tap in to their fun, light-hearted and healing energy to fulfil all your dreams, bring magic into your life and improve your relationship with the earth, your self and others. Your inner faery is a source of unlimited creativity and unbridled joy, and connecting with this energy will bring more balance and harmony into your life, and help you more clearly see the blessings around you. It will increase your self-esteem and self-knowledge, and reconnect you to the joys of childhood, and that innocent belief that anything and everything is possible. Because it is, if you work to make it happen…

Cassandra's Faery Magic

Cassandra Eason is a druidess, a solitary white witch and the author of more than 80 books on magic and spirituality. She lives on the rural Isle of Wight, England, with her eldest daughter and baby granddaughter, who is reintroducing Cassandra to the wonders of childhood. Her books include *A Complete Guide to Fairies & Magical Beings* and *Pagan in the City*. Cassandra answers questions about faeries and nature spirituality at www.CassandraEason.com.

I grew up in the centre of an industrial town in the Midlands of England, with a sooty backyard and a solitary nut tree clinging to a patch of earth, from which precariously dangled my swing. Every Christmas my mother took me to a big department store to see Santa Claus in his grotto, where bored shop staff would dress up in tinsel and faery wings. I was totally disillusioned when I saw one having a cigarette behind the toadstool. But what I didn't realise as I creaked to and fro on my swing, clutching the battered faery doll my father had won for me at the fairground, was that the brown creatures scurrying around the nut tree and up and down the roses that grew around the toilet door were *real* faeries.

Hour after hour I watched them flutter their brown, leaf-like wings and hop around the trunk of the tree playing tag. They mainly appeared when it was foggy or grey. My backyard faeries occupied their own world, and I was aware even then that I was of little more interest to them than our old ginger cat, observing them idly as he cleaned his paws.

More than 40 years later I saw similar creatures around an old tree in the forests above the Gold Coast near Brisbane, and realised my childhood fae creatures were more than imagination. And from my ongoing research into nature essences over more than 20 years, it seems that faeries are a manifestation and reflection of nature, wherever and however it appears.

Faeries have been described in mythology and actual experience in almost every culture and age. They are as varied in their forms and attributes as nature itself – gentle and ethereal, magnificent beings of light, hideous black forms with eyes like glowing coals, golden-haired maidens, withered crones, a shadow in the grass, a rustling of leaves when there is no wind, the rippling of sunlight or moonlight on water.

The most famous faery court was that of the Tuatha de Danaan of Ireland. According to myth, they were driven out between 3000 and 1000BCE and became in folk memory the faery people, gods yet not gods. They were credited with building the megaliths of Ireland, which are still seen as gateways to the world of the fae. In earlier times too, benign faeries were regarded as invisible but integral members at the family hearth, working on farms, at looms or in workshops while the human owners slept. And in the 21st century we still need faeries, whether they are sooty brown city fae or golden-haired queens on lush green mounds.

To me faeries exist in a parallel universe, independent of ours yet occupying the same space. Some might be projections of our own fears and feelings, but there may also be whole nations of faeries who have their own path of evolution and are as fascinated by us as we are by them, and who may argue about whether we exist.

We need do nothing and say nothing to see faeries as they go about their own daily life. In the modern 24/7 world, where simulated experiences and theme parks too often take the place for children of playing on a backyard swing or for adults a walk in the woods, we need faeries to prove the world is wonderful, magical, and that we are creatures of spirit within our physical bodies. Sit in the forest, by a river or on your plant-filled balcony, and let the fae world unfold, reassuring you that magic is more than Christmas, Disney or make believe.

History of the Faeries

"The fairies went from the world, dear,
Because men's hearts grew cold.
And only the eyes of children see,
What is hidden from the old..."
Kathleen Foyle, Irish author

The Tangled Tale That is Faery History

Faeries have been here with us – and for us – for a very, very long time. For as long as there have been humans to speak of the fae, we have told tales of seeing them, healing with them, being elf shot by them, stealing away to make love with them in the ancient groves, or entering Faeryland for a day, only to return to our own world years and years later. But how long have the faeries inhabited this earth? They seem, if the old legends have truth, to have always been here, perhaps even before there was rock, or plant, or animal, or sea creature. They are certainly pre-human.

First, perhaps, came the pure elementals, the earth beings (gnomes), air beings (sylphs), fire beings (salamanders) and water being (undines) from the stars themselves. From these elementals the land, the sky, the seas, the rains and the lightning were born and formed. And within that land were seeds, and from those seeds flew the first faeries. And from both the elementals and the fae, these beings of raw material energy, beings of both the physical and the invisible realms, other life forms emerged, nature thrived, the animals came forth in their pairs, the land deepened and changed, and the skies cried their healing waters upon the land, and all things grew, and changed, and were alive together.

For however long it has endured, and it is prehistoric, our relationship with the fae has persisted through the darkest of times. Like the hardiest of plants, our beliefs have taken root wherever they can find fertile ground. Dismissed as make-believe friends, or condemned as soul-stealing devils, the faery faith continues to flow where it can. Thus they find their way to us through our legends, our music, our movies, our homes and our imaginations.

Indigenous people all over this beautiful green and blue planet have worked with the nature spirits, and still do, leaving offerings for them and speaking with them to learn more of the healing arts, the plants and the animals. From the faery faith doctors of Ireland to the people of Ghana in Africa, people leave out food, milk, honey, and even pans of clear water for them to bathe and play in.

And it is said that if you acknowledge them, and if you are fine within your being, pure and true, innocent and wise, if you are a person of good heart and honesty, they will teach you all they can.

The faeries of Ghana squeeze the juice of a sacred plant into people's eyes, for the Sight, into the ears, to hear all, and into the mouth, to sing and speak with them. These are not old tales. Some happened yesterday, as well as ten thousand years ago. It is the same story, the story of a relationship between beings who are alike, who share a planet, and who have a fate that is twined together like ancient vines.

Even their name has a long history. The word "faery" comes from the Latin word "faetae", which loosely translates to mean "the enchanted ones". This evolved into "faery", later "fairy", and was the name given to the nature spirits in France. Elsewhere they had their own localised names, such as sidhe, huldufolk, Tylwyth Teg and aelves. But when the Normans invaded the Celtic and Anglo-Saxon countries in the 1100s, they brought with them their language – French. Their rule spread all over the British Isles, and so did the word faery. And so the many-named Good Folk became the faeries... and so they have stayed.

Today, while they may be called by a French name, they have great power in their traditional realms. In magical countries such as Ireland, the faery faith is resurging once more, even affecting government decisions, such as a multi-million dollar motorway construction. In County Clare an expensive feasibility study was conducted and the decision made to divert the highway around a five-metre-tall faery hawthorn tree that local bards insisted the trooping faeries rested under. It was believed that if the tree came down, the faeries would not be able to rest, the energy would become tired, fretful and unfocused, and there could be accidents.

These would not necessarily be caused by the faeries, but if the tree was taken away, the exhausted fae, having nowhere to rest, would march on – and this, in turn, would create a pool of fatigue. The council decided to save the tree, which has become a sacred site of sorts, albeit one that is ringed by a highway!

This change to a favourable perception began during the Industrial Revolution of the 1800s, when faeries underwent a metamorphosis, being seen less as the fallen angels of uncertain temperament of previous centuries, and more as nature's friends, delightful small beings who bring magical delight to us all, and most especially to children, who are innocent enough to see and believe in them.

Importantly, as the green land began to be sewn over with motorways, traffic, houses and factories belching pollution, as the trees came down to feed this "progress", the faeries were increasingly seen as benevolent beings, bringing love, charms, potions, healing and balm to the troubled souls who were being separated from the land, their true source.

From the Theosophists of the late 1800s to the founders of the Findhorn community in the 1960s and the environmentalists of today, people began to tie the fae not only to the growth of spiritual freedom, but to the protection of the green earth and the beauty of nature. They championed the notion that if you wish for your garden to bloom more lushly, for plants to grow better and forests to be protected, you must interact with these beings – and this belief is as widespread today as it was centuries ago.

The story of the belief in faeries is a heroic tale of survival. Despite fear, persecution, accusations of evil and malignity, faery practices and faiths have evolved, hidden, sprung forth from the shadows, and now walk directly into the light of this new era.

The faeries have indeed shown us how to survive. By shapeshifting and merging with other paths, only to reappear today with more vigour, vitality and verve than ever before, they are wondrous in their strength, vitality and determination to be here, and be seen.

The Fae of Ancient Times

The pantheon of the Ancient Greeks was peopled with the glorious gods of Mount Olympus, but the woods and fields of Greece were alive with dryads, nymphs and fauns. The waterways were brimming with naiads, and the great seas crossed by Odysseus flowed with merfolk, nereids and harpies, those great female shapeshifters loyal to the sorceress Circe. And akin to the elementals in their primal nature were the Titans, those great forces who ruled the world for a time, such as Cronus, and Rhea, the mother of the gods, from whose body life on this planet was said to have sprung.

In the pre-Islamic countries of the Middle East, tales were told of the djinns, pure fire elementals mixed with humanity's blood. Djinns (who had an incarnation as the lead character in the popular television show *I Dream of Jeannie*) have burning eyes of fire, and the power to grant wishes and fly on magic carpets.

In Ancient China the ma-kuh, a fine-boned, tiny faery, lived in a great mother mulberry orchard, and from her realm governed the creation of the fruits and the health of the silkworms, and thus she is the mother faery of the silk, which is why wearing silk has such magical qualities and can create such strong faery energy.

In Ireland, Dana was the great Mother Goddess, from whom all things were created, including the faery people. Her name means "offering", and her children were called the Tuatha de Danaan, the people of Dana. After ruling Ireland for a time they eventually left this world to go into the Hollow Hills, or shapeshifted into many other forms – but not before loving many human women and men to keep their bloodline going.

In the countryside of what is now known as England and Wales, Gwyn ap Nudd, the king of the Fair Folk, was revered across the land, with Glastonbury Tor seen as the entrance to his underworld kingdom. And King Arthur's wife Gwenhyfar's name means "white phantom", which has led faery scholars such as RJ Stewart to propose that she was a faery woman, and that her marriage to Arthur represented the uniting of the faery realm and the human realm for all time. In that view, she is a faery goddess of the land, of justice and of equality, and of love and sovereignty and great earth magic, who brings fertility and enchantment to the realm of Camelot by her presence, and in the form of the Round Table.

There were, and are still, many gods and goddesses who are particularly associated with the fae, including Freya, the Nordic goddess of love, beauty and fertility, after whom the day of the week Friday is named. She is represented by amber, and incorporates the wisdom of the ancient world, plants, love and primal forces. She is honest, transparent and can fly and shapeshift – just as the fae can.

Pan is another ancient god of the fae, and is often portrayed playing music for them to dance and make love to. He was revered only marginally in Ancient Greece, as his home was the province of Arcadia, a place so primitive and wild that the locals were known as acorn-eaters, since at the peak of the Ancient Greek civilisation, circa 500BCE, they had not yet discovered how to make bread.

But in the 18th and 19th centuries CE, there were hundreds of groves devoted to Pan along the riverbanks and in the meadows of Britain. And as the forests were cut down, and factories sprang up to tear the minerals from the earth, Pan worship grew, his popularity creating controversy and frenzy – it was PANdemonium!

Concerned Victorians like the poet Elizabeth Barrett Browning wrote "Pan is Dead" in her poem *The Dead Pan*, to win people back to Christianity and away from this music-loving, goat-footed woodland god. Other Victorians disagreed, and planted living altars to Pan, among them the chamomile lawn of the poet Algernon Charles Swinburne. Lord Byron, Percy Bysshe Shelley and John Keats also wrote of him, and in time his statue appeared in well-to-do London gardens, and even, in 1928, at New York's Metropolitan Museum of Art. Pan had invaded the homeland of the Puritans!

The more the world's population shifted from the wide green spaces to small, smoky towns, and children went to work in the factories, mills and mines, the more the love of Pan grew. With him came the love of the fae, and of all things green and wild. Without Pan worship, would we have had Peter Pan, who then led to the great revival of faery magics in Edwardian times? Perhaps not.

The renowned mystic psychotherapist Carl Jung felt he too worked with Pan, and that he strolled in the garden with him, and listened to him teach about nature and spirits. "There are things in the psyche," the great psychotherapist said of his interactions with Pan, "that I do not produce, but which have their own life."

The Greek warrior goddess Artemis guards her huntresses, these beings of faery who gather in the forests with their faery hounds, who are possessed by no man, and who claim freedom as their right. They come out under the sickle moon, the bow from which she shot her silver arrows. Her domain was for the wild ones, the free ones, the faery ones.

Ceridwen, the great goddess of the sickle moon of Wales, also had long and intense interactions with the fae, who gifted her the secret of the making of the magical potion awen. Awen translates as "flowing inspiration", and is the Muse made in liquid form. It is knowledge and learning, a direct drink of divinity, and its drops grant one the powers of shapeshifting, understanding all the languages of the world, and bright wisdom.

Awen is a core faery gift – it is the power that creates music, poetry, scientific breakthroughs and brilliant performances, and wise ones must have touched awen to their lips to know the source and to have drunk from the fount of inspiration. Ceridwen is one of the goddess keepers of what makes awen, but awen determines where it will go – the faeries have made its power so that no one can control it. It must come unbeckoned and unforced to those who truly have the strength to hold and express awen's creative power.

Cernunnos, also known as Herne and the horned god, is said by some to be another form of the faery king. He is the king of the woodland, the consort of the goddess – and if this is so, then is it not so that the beloved of the goddess would be a faery king? Faery magic is not separate from the magic and influence of the goddess. Brigid works also with the salamanders of flame and the undines of her wells. It is all a great web, and these gods and goddesses are also associated with this in-between realm of magic and mystery.

The Green Man, the god of the fertile world, is represented by a man's face emerging from the trees or foliage of the forests. Often we encounter him while we are out in nature – it is oh so easy to see the Green Man's wild yet wise visage peeping out from the leaves and vines. His image is found carved in Christian churches all over Britain, and so perhaps in the time before the churches were raised, he danced in the old stone circles that were so often torn down to make way for the Church. The Green Man is a fae father figure, and a lord of life, vitality and sheer, pure energy. He is associated with Robin Hood, and all forest-dwelling men.

The Christian Era

There is great beauty to aspects of the Christian path, some of which has been removed by its own followers. The Gnostic gospels, those of Mary Magdalene, the principle of reincarnation and the Book of Enoch are just some examples of the jewels that were burned, banned and declared heretic. There were, however, long periods of tolerance that flourished prior to the seventh century, when the Synod of Whitby decimated the Celtic church, which had been founded as much on druidry as Christianity.

This is evidenced by the way the faery faith thrived alongside the Christian church of the early centuries of the first millennium after Christ. Fae faith and Christianity may have had an uneasy relationship at times, and the former been treated with suspicion by the Church, but for many people, a very eclectic version of their faith was forming, which mingled aspects of the new ways upon a solid and magical foundation of the old ways.

Whether they considered themselves Christian or not (and many did not), our ancestors lived lives that were respectful – and sometimes fearful – of nature. People interacted with nature spirits, and worked with the faeries every day.

Before villages were created, every tribe had its natural beings with whom they whispered and worked, who told them where to hunt, how to find the healing herbs, where the cleanest water ran, and how to stitch deerskin into boots. They showed the symbols of the spiral and of the circle, of the four directions, and of the men and women who mingled with the animals that brought them life.

When the Romans arrived in Britain, they brought with them a religious structure that was already focused on the political and worldly, rather than the natural and the cyclic. For indigenous people, the seasonal cycles were their faith, and the nature spirits were their guardians and primal companions, the energies that danced and worked with those great turns of the wheel.

Christianity, for all its beauties of brotherhood and peace, has not proven itself a friend to pagan faiths throughout Western Europe. One of the great disasters was the destruction by Christian zealots of the Temple of Artemis, located near the ancient city of Ephesus, near the modern town of Selcuk in Turkey. Built around 550BCE, it was one of the Seven Wonders of the World.

Missionaries such as Saint Boniface, who also destroyed many sacred sites of the Jewish peoples, saw themselves as carrying out a divine mission. By destroying the holy groves, such as the Greek grove of Dodoma where an oracular service was offered to the people, these missionaries felt they were saving souls. But these groves were revered greatly by our ancestors, and were the dwelling places of nature spirits, and the loss was keenly felt.

The Angles of Germania worshipped in groves sacred to the earth goddess Nerthus. Roman senator and historian Tacitus wrote, circa 100CE: "After the Langobardi come the Reudigni, Auiones, Angli (Angles), Varni, Eudoses, Suarines and Nuithones, all well guarded by rivers and forests. There is nothing remarkable about any of these tribes unless it be the common worship of Nerthus, that is, Earth Mother. They believe she is interested in men's affairs and drives among them. On an island in the ocean sea there is a sacred grove wherein waits a holy wagon covered by a drape."

There are many modern-day reminders of our ancient nature-loving past. A suburb or place name that ends with the suffix "lea" or "ley", as in Wembley or Waverley, refers to the place of the grove, as they are Old English words that mean "clearing" or "grove". There are thousands of towns with this suffix all over the world, and if we look at the name we can decipher more of its magical meaning. Wesley translates to "grove of the west", Easley is "grove of the east" and Sulley is "grove of the south". Bradley is the "broad grove", Langley is "long grove", Hetherly is "grove of the hawthorn", Oakley is "grove of the oaks" and Hartley is "grove of the deer".

In this way we can trace the history of an area. If it is a new name, my feeling is that the fae have helped us choose this name because it is a place of sacred energy, and we need only translate the name to know what its distinct blueprint is. If there is no grove there now, it is in the invisible world, held there by the faery naming of the place. Such names may also indicate a place where powerful leylines cross, or merge, and thus hold clues to the songlines of the planet, which the faeries, some humans and many animals walk.

Within these groves, called Nemetona by the Celts, faeries gathered along with humans, gods and goddesses, and nature was revered. Truly the touch of the divine was in the breath of the wind, the warmth of the sun, the gentle fall of rain and the fertile earth from which the sacred trees grew, guarded by their fae.

In the changing landscape of the British Isles, the druidic faith and early Christianisation gave way to the Anglo-Saxon invasion and then colonisation of the islands. These newcomers brought their own faery folk with them – elves, trolls, gnomes and dwarves. They also brought their goddesses, such as Freya, who were believed to tend the fae, and to have the same shapeshifting qualities.

The faery faith, the druidic ways and the growing forms of Anglo-Saxon magics with their strong reliance on the fae were dealt a stunning blow by the powerful Roman politician Pope Gregory the Great. Around 600CE he sent a group of missionaries to convert the Celts, Anglo-Saxons and pagans of Britain, Ireland and Western Europe, whose faith in the fae, in nature, in tree worship and the goddess in her many forms, had remained so strong.

He wrote to the head of the group, Abbot Mellitus, who became the first Bishop of London and later the Archbishop of Canterbury, a famous letter known as the Epistola ad Mellitum: "I have come to the conclusion that the temples of the idols in England should not on any account be destroyed. Saint Augustine must smash the idols, but the temples should be sprinkled with holy water... for we ought to take advantage of well-built temples by purifying them from devil worship, and dedicating them to the service of the true God."

The wells, the groves and the stone circles were thus sanctified for the Christian God. Some of the great stone circles, such as the magnificent healing temple of Avebury in England's Wiltshire, had many of their stones pulled down, thrown into pits and burned to "cast the devils out". Other stones were heaved out of their resting place in the earth, split and reworked for constructing churches, houses and farm buildings in the tiny village of Avebury.

While Pope Gregory's instructions gave new and much wider freedom to priests to "drive out devils", the faery exorcisms his words inspired had their precedents. Saint Collen of Wales, who served as abbot in Glastonbury for five years, had earlier made it his mission to purify the Tor, a sacred site watched over by the faery king, whose realm stretched from the mountains of Wales to the mid-levels of England.

The faery king's name, Gwyn ap Nudd, means pure, bright, white and sacred. But that did not stop a faery "exorcism" taking place to drive him out. When Gwyn invited Collen to his faery castle, the abbot went, but instead of eating the food he was offered, which he believed would trap him in Faeryland for countless years, he sprinkled holy water around the hall, causing it, so it is said, to vanish along with its fae inhabitants. After this time, locals did report that their faeries – their protectors and guides, the beings who helped them work the fields and bring forth the fruits – were not so easily seen with the eye, but their songs could be heard across the Tor on moonlit nights.

According to legend, there was a stone circle on the Tor's crown, which some say was the castle of Gwyn ap Nudd himself. Remnants of a stone circle were found atop the Tor during an archaeological dig in 1922, and it is said that the stones, two of which remain as part of the modern pathway up the Tor, were taken down, cracked and split, with many used to build a church on top of the Tor.

The Hollow Hill of the Tor, and its faery king, did not take kindly to this revolution however, and over time the church on the Tor suffered, as it was built on faery ground. It had usurped some of the land of Avalon itself, and trespassed, without respect, permission, innocence or pure heart, into faery realms.

It is not that there was a faery curse, rather that when energy is disturbed, and fear and hatred exist in place of love, mirth and reverence, there are consequences. In 1275 an earthquake destroyed the church. A new, smaller church was rebuilt on the site, which lasted until 1539, when it was destroyed during the Dissolution of the Monasteries, and today only the stone tower remains.

Other stones from the stone circle were used to build Glastonbury Abbey, which was also destroyed in 1539. As the abbey was abandoned and left unprotected, these stones were taken and used to build the houses that line the streets of Glastonbury today. Thus it is possible that the remains of the original stone circle of the Tor could be scattered among the homes and shops themselves. Could this be why there are so many faery sightings on the streets and within the walls of Glastonbury's homes?

Shhh! Faery Secret

Some faery scholars, like Reverend Robert Kirk, believed you must never eat faery food. But others say we'd all be healthier, stronger, wiser and longer-lived if we did eat it. And the faeries say all food is faery food anyway!

The faery persecution of the Dark Ages inspired the literary great Mark Twain. In his beautiful, perhaps channelled, book *Personal Recollections of Joan of Arc*, he wrote passionately about the exorcism in medieval times of known faery sacred sites.

He wrote: "All the children pleaded for the faeries, and said they were their good friends and dear to them, and never did them any harm, but the priest would not listen, and said it was sin and shame to have such friends. The children mourned and could not be comforted; and they made an agreement that they would continue to hang flower wreaths on the tree as a perpetual sign to the faeries that they were still loved and remembered, though lost to sight."

Faery faith always springs back to life, because its roots run so deep. And as it's an ancestral path, it is not possible to obliterate it. The fae, often our own ancestors, are us, our bloodline, and as the fae create the earth and dwell beneath it and tend the plants, we eat faery food at all times. Thus, no matter how we try, we are them, and they are us, and we interact with them, always.

Faery faith did not die when churches were built over their sacred sites. At Glastonbury, faery fairs were a magical part of living near the Tor, and a faery fair was also held with the human fair at nearby Pitminster near Taunton. But by the Middle Ages, superstition and rumour had done their work. Faeries were seen as beings you must never traffic with. Written in the late 1300s, Geoffrey Chaucer's epic work *The Canterbury Tales* speaks of an army of friars sent out to "bless" the woods and streams, the trees and rocks, villages and homes and castles too, to "maketh that ther ben no fairies".

Another method the Church used to deal with the persistence of faery faith was to steal their name and appropriate their powers. The faeries of the Tor, or of the stones and groves, were simply not spoken of, and wells were transformed into the Virgin Mary's well, or a saint's well. Sometimes, as with Brigid, a goddess was turned into a Christian saint (and thereby continued her work!).

Many people continued to commune with the faeries, but their faery faith was polluted with fear, as the belief began to be twisted from trust in pure nature spirits to fear of malevolent ones who must be placated, because they bore humans so much ill will they would harm them. The priests carried out "clearances" of sacred faery areas, in alignment with Pope Gregory's decree, which echoed down through the centuries.

In the Middle Ages, witch burnings, imprisonment and suspicion spread amongst a population driven by fear, guilt and shame. And women, daughters of Eve, were the most conspicuous targets for the persecutors. Faeries became aligned with witches, midwives, wise women, healers and seers, who were suddenly, fiercely persecuted. And yet, because the 11th century monks wrote down much of the older forms of faery faith, albeit through biased eyes, we have them to thank for preserving some of the knowledge.

Every house, humble cottage and castle had their brownies, every field had their meadowfae, every spring had its sprite. But when The Malleus Maleficarum was published in 1486, a kind of guide to witch inquisition, any version of faery was ordained to be derived from "their master, the devil". During these dangerous times, the fae shifted again, and transformed once more.

Cunning Folk, Wizards, Wise Women and Faery Doctors

The faith of our ancestors during this time was very eclectic. Anglo-Saxon spells reveal that it was not uncommon to call upon an angel and a faery to help with healing. Rites and spells from the 10th and 11th centuries were preserved in the Lacnunga, a magical text that contains details on blessing the land and the Nine Herbs and Land Ceremonies Charms, all of which use herbs, blessings, faery lore and Christian symbology for their power.

We need to remember that for our ancestors, it was a transitional time – neither truly pagan nor truly Christian – instead there was an intricate blend of many faiths, including Roman, Greek, Celtic and Anglo-Saxon. People then believed in many deities, they believed in elves, demons and faeries too, and they also believed in God.

Even in our days of the week, the old gods live. Four are named after the deities of the Nordic peoples, who became known as the Saxons – Tuesday is for their god Tiw, Wednesday for Woden (later called Odin), Thursday for Thor and Friday for Freya. We still speak these words, and even our word "love" comes from the Nordic.

"Against a dwarf one must take seven small holy wafers, such as ones make holy communion with," begins the spell against a dwarf or a fever – which dwarves, the workers or smiths, were thought to cause with their smith-fires.

Faeries were said to give the gift of healing to particular people, and it would often be passed down through the generations, with some of these families still esteemed as physicians and surgeons today. They were called by many names – in Ireland they were the faery doctors, and the fae also granted this skill to the cunning men and women of Cornwall, and the wise wives and wise men of Scotland. In Welsh lore, it is believed that the entire body of herbal knowledge was passed down through a family of healers, a gift of the fae to the sons of a faery woman who married a human man from the village of Myddfai. Descendants of this family were still practicing medicine in the 18th century, and there is at least one herbalist in Dyfed today who claims descent from them.

To be granted their healing gifts, sometimes we must seek the faeries out. In the 16th, 17th and 18th centuries, wise men and women would undertake a journey to the realm of the fae in order to bring back the wisdom of healing, of the Sight and of inspiration. It was said in this time that a faery physician must undergo a great trial – they would suffer a terrible illness, come close to death, then be brought back by the faeries, who would have the power to grant them the healing gift while they were close to death, and thus walkers between the worlds.

One such case is that of Anne Jefferies, who worked as a serving woman in a Cornish household in the mid-1600s. She was said to have fallen into a fit, and slipped in and out of consciousness for more than a week, remaining weak and unable to walk or work for some time afterwards. When she was told later that she had suffered a fever and been unconscious, she denied it, declaring that she had been carried away by the faeries, who had gifted her with special powers while she was between the worlds. In 1645, this was not a safe thing to declare, given the religious climate, but Anne was determined to heal with her newly given faery touch. And she set about doing so. Her first healing was to relieve the pain of gout from her mistress, and this success spread the word far and wide, and Anne found herself a renowned cunning woman, healing with her energetic touch, and able to predict the future.

She was arrested and tried for witchcraft, and while she was not ordered to be executed, perhaps for fear of faery retaliation, it was decided to hold her prisoner, and give her neither food nor drink. But the faery folk brought her their offerings, and she was released after one year, without ever having been fed by those who held her. While she was released, and said to be in robust good health, Anne retired her practice, and sadly never spoke to others of the faeries again.

Shakespeare, Queen Elizabeth and John Dee

Was Queen Elizabeth, who ruled England from 1558 to 1603, more than a queen of the mortal realm? Could this icon of female power have been a faery queen? It's not as far-fetched as it sounds, because during her long, eventful reign, belief in faeries came surging back in poetry, plays, fashion, fairs, festivals, folk traditions and magic.

Elizabeth was a monarch who at once embodied several archetypes of feminine power – the longing her people had for the Virgin Mary (she was a Virgin Queen), their need for a Warrior Queen (her speech to the troops in the field, protecting the shores of Britain, was in part inspired by Queen Boadicea's speech before going into battle with the Romans circa 60CE), their desire for a figure of Beauty and Inspiration (she was known for her love of pageants, dancing and fashion), and a Mother Goddess (she called the English her children, and said she would do anything for her people).

It was during her reign that Edmund Spenser wrote the epic poem *The Faerie Queene*, devoted to Elizabeth, and William Shakespeare penned his famous play *A Midsummer Night's Dream*. Set in Athens, it features Oberon, the king of all fae, Titania, his faery queen, their servant Puck (who was based, strangely enough for a character dwelling in Greece, on British lore's Robin Goodfellow, a mischievous spirit of the land and personification of the Green Man), Bottom, Snug and various other faery beings. Set on Midsummer night, the feast of the faeries, the play expresses the imagination of the Elizabethans, who regarded their monarch, Elizabeth, as the faery queen. This magical play is still performed on summer nights in the open air, evoking magic and drawing a faery audience who giggle at the idea of watching the humans watching the faeries!

While this contradictory, iconic queen – part faery, part warrior, part diplomat, part religious icon – reigned over a land torn apart by the reformation of the Catholic faith and dominated by plots and intrigue, faith in the fae flourished again. Her coronation date had the hallmarks of magic, as John Dee, the great wizard and astrologer who was her Merlin, cast the queen's horoscope to choose exactly the right day for her crowning, becoming and remaining one of her most trusted advisers throughout her reign.

The Reformation and Reverend Kirk

Upon her death in 1603, the peril of being a Virgin Queen, or at least one without an heir, was revealed. Elizabeth's greatest threat during her lifetime had been the Scottish monarch Mary Queen of Scots, a fervent Catholic who'd campaigned to take the English throne from her. When Elizabeth died, Mary's son James, who had been declared king of Scotland as a child after Protestant rebels forced his mother to abdicate, was crowned King James I of England. It was the last thing the far more tolerant Elizabeth would have wanted.

At this time, Scotland was a fearsome place, a nation whose devotion to the creeds of Calvinists and Presbyterians was expressing itself through religious persecution and witch burnings. Figures vary, with historian estimates saying 10,000 women were burned, and others claiming the victims numbered more than a million.

We'll never know the true count, but we do know that Scotland, once a land bristling with faery folk, had changed. Since the Protestant Reformation began in the 1500s, the influence of the notorious John Knox, a fearsome fire and brimstone preacher whose hatred of the Catholic Queen Mary had done much to bring about her downfall, held sway. He ensured that her son James grew up believing in and fearing the infamy of women, witches, faeries and spirits. In 1589, in the first week of James's marriage to Anne of Denmark, six women were accused of stirring up a storm against her ship, and burned as witches. Taking this as their cue, the wise wives and wise men of Scotland grew secretive and cautious. Consulting with the fae was now punishable by death.

The faeries, and the gods and goddesses, were now, by law, "devils". And thus began the story that the fae were "fallen angels", the ones who had defied God, and been banished to earth. It helped, of course, that King James was responsible for a new translation of the Bible, which had colourful and instructional passages, such as the following from Leviticus 20:27. *A man also or woman that hath a familiar spirit or that is a wizard, shall surely be put to death: they shall stone them with stones: their blood shall be upon them.*

It was against this background of witch hunts, devil-seeking and bibles with proclamations to kill that Reverend Robert Kirk, the minister of Aberfoyle, wrote *The Secret Commonwealth of Elves, Fauns and Fairies.* Published as a pamphlet in 1691, it had an enormous impact on the folk beliefs of Scotland, and when it was reprinted in 1893 its words were held to be truth. Today it remains one of the most consulted references on faery lore and behaviour, quoted in novels such as the enchanting *Wicked Lovely* series by Melissa Marr and referred to by modern faery scholars.

Kirk had been involved with the trial of a witch, Alison Pearson, who had been accused of trafficking with the faeries and consulting with the spirits of the dead. His pamphlet was actually a courageous endeavour in many ways, for while it condemned the faeries, it also documented his fascination with them. It was said he'd been taken away by them and given his knowledge of them – good and bad – by the fae themselves. "They have," he wrote, "a middle nature betwixt man and angell... with light, interchangeable bodies somewhat of the nature of a condensed cloud, and best seen at twilight."

How did he know? Robert Kirk had been investigating the fae for some time, had even gone to Faeryland, it is said, and was reporting back to the Godly people about their wiles and evils. Then one evening, clad in his nightshirt, he walked up the local faery hill, one of his favourite haunts, for his last corporeal faery encounter. He collapsed there, and was found the next day by his wife, who was pregnant with their child, and declared dead. Another story claims all that was found was his nightshirt, and that he had disappeared without a trace, never to be heard from again.

He has a grave in the local churchyard, but this was not the end of Reverend Kirk's dispatches from Faeryland. He appeared some time after his funeral to his cousin Graham, declaring that he had not died, but fallen into a trance and been abducted by the fae, who were holding him captive in the Hollow Hills. He confided the means of his escape from Faeryland – when his child was christened he would appear, as he had been given permission to bless his child. At this moment, Graham was to fling a knife over him and break the faery spell, which would permit him to return to his parish.

But when the good reverend did appear at the christening feast, poor Graham was so shocked at the sudden materialisation of his dead cousin that he forgot to throw the knife – and Robert sorrowfully faded from sight and was, finally, silenced.

Why would he have been abducted? Perhaps the faeries found him dangerous. Perhaps they thought his propaganda was a peril to their very survival. After all, he had attacked the faeries outright, with phrases such as: "They transgress and commit Acts of Injustice and Sin... for the inconvenience of their succubi, who tryst with men. It is abominable." Were the fae he was dealing with malevolent? Did he go voluntarily, enchanted by a faery queen, seduced by their joy, sensuality and laughter, something that seems to have been missing from this dour man's earnest existence. Whatever the cause of the faery abduction, his relatives, to this day, wait with a knife at every one of his descendants' christenings, ready to fling the blade that will cut the faery enchantment's cords.

Perhaps Kirk's greatest legacy is as the originator of so much faery myth – he is the source of the legends of changelings and the dangerously enchanting power of their food. If not for his *The Secret Commonwealth* pamphlet and apparent abduction, he would have been known simply for translating the psalms from Latin to Gaelic.

But instead, through Kirk we can trace back the source of so much of the fear that taints interactions with the fae to this day. We need to thank him too though, for amidst the bitterness of his words there are those where even he could not fail to see the wonder of the faery world he beheld. For the man who wrote: "Seers or men of the Second Sight have very terrifying encounters with the faeries they call Sleagh maith, or the Good People," is the very same man who claimed that they were half-human, half-angel. And *The Secret Commonwealth*, published first in 1691, again by Sir Walter Scott in 1815 and finally in 1893 with a foreword by Scottish folklore collector and author Andrew Lang, has proved as long-lived as the Fair Folk themselves.

Despite the influence of Kirk's work, and the popularity of the witch hunts of the day, not everyone in Scotland was a faery foe. Many were faery friends, but had to be secretive about their allegiance. Not so the powerful MacLeod clan, whose 700-year-old castle still stands in Dunvegan on the Isle of Skye to this day.

Mighty Dunvegan Castle is isolated enough to have protected the MacLeod clan from much of the witch hunts and persecutions.

Their power and wealth built walls around them too, that not even the fierce inquisition could smash down. But perhaps the real reason the MacLeods didn't suffer for their faery faith was what they had in their possession – the faery flag itself.

How this magical flag, which can still be viewed at the castle, was given to the clan is a source of mystery, but there is a beautiful story that's been handed down about the way the clan came to have the flag of faery, this flag of three wishes and great power.

According to the women of MacLeod country, the flag was gifted to the clan in the 1700s. This story, passed down in a lullaby that is still sung today, says that one night, a faery of great beauty visited Dunvegan Castle, passing through armed guards and locked doors, until she came to the room where the MacLeod clan heir was asleep in his cradle. She dropped to her knees, according to the astonished and terrified nursemaid, and crooned a lullaby. And the nursemaid never forgot its haunting tune. This song, when sung over and over, has the power to bestow protection, long life, good health, great love and sweetness of temperament.

This MacLeod heir grew to be a fine man, so the story goes, and wed a faery woman, despite knowing that their time together would not be forever. After twenty years they parted at the faery bridge of Dunvegan, and she passed to him their newborn infant son, wrapped in the flag of faery. She whispered to him that if ever the clan had terrible troubles, the flag was to be waved three times, and the faeries would come to the aid of the MacLeods who had so loved the fae, and who now carried the blood as their own.

Called an bratach sith, the flag can only be unfurled by the clan chief, and only when there is great peril to the clan. It has been waved twice, and Winston Churchill called upon the MacLeod clan chief to bring the flag to Dover during WWII, from where the MacLeod chieftain could wave it a third and final time if Britain was invaded by sea. Though it was held at the ready, it did not need to be unfurled. Gold and red in colour, and made of silk, the flag is now tattered and torn, a faded glory, but its magical powers may still be intact, awaiting their awakening in a time of great need.

Two modern-day descendants of this Scottish MacLeod clan are acclaimed faery artist Sharon McLeod, from Queensland, Australia, and artist and photographer Carolyn Colmore, who lives in Waitakere, near Auckland, in New Zealand.

"My connection to the MacLeod clan is through my father's side," Carolyn explains. "Years ago I developed an interest in my lineage, and followed up the MacLeod part of it. Most of my bloodline is English, Scottish, French and Maori. On the Maori side there's an interesting legend about the Patupaiarehe, a race of fair-skinned, red-haired faeries that inhabited our forests and mountains but were hardly ever seen. Some of the Maori people are throwbacks to them, having red hair and green or blue eyes.

"I think with the connection I have, the bloodline fits with my beliefs, feelings, visions and other things about myself that I have discovered spiritually. It's been hard to stay grounded as I explored all this history – it's just amazing, truly amazing stuff. I have kept many things to myself though, perhaps because of the fear of what other people may think," she admits.

Carolyn had many dreams about Dunvegan Castle as a child, before she knew of the MacLeod blood she carries. "They started when I was about eight years old, although I was four in the dream. I remember passing though many rooms, with very light stone work, almost white, very old but in good condition. It had these wide staircases I walked up, and there were lush, rich red and gold draperies, nice things you may expect in a well-kept castle.

"I walked through gardens with stone archways, square and very open all the way through, so you could see the scenery and plants, all growing up the columns and twisting around the archways. And the grass seemed to meet the edges of the stone walkway under my feet, which accentuated the surroundings and embraced it for you to behold, rather than taking nature over and having it as a feature.

"Knowing about the royal and faery blood is pretty humbling. As a descendant, am I protected by the flag? I am most definitely protected by something, there is no denying that. I'm not sure if it's the flag's power, but I have been saved many times and in many different ways!" Carolyn says.

There remains one more waving of the faery flag, which is still at Dunvegan Castle, on display, there awaiting the next threat to the Clan MacLeod. During both World War I and World War II, young men of the MacLeod clan, and indeed many Scottish servicemen, carried a depiction of the flag, which was particularly favoured amongst the Scots of the air force. And it's said that not a single pilot carrying their treasured picture of the flag was shot down.

The Celtic Twilight

Across the sea in Ireland, prevailing all throughout this beautiful sacred island's history of shadows and light, the faery faith has glittered. Perhaps this is because the Tuatha de Danaan, it is said, were among the first inhabitants of the Emerald Isle.

Ireland is a fae nation, with legends suggesting that most of the six million people living there today carry faery blood. Irish people around the world are renowned for their passion, their storytelling and musical gifts, as well as a tendency to enjoy being intoxicated.

In the seventh century the Synod of Whitby in England effectively banned many of the practices of the Celtic Church, which had combined faery faith, druidry, indigenous shamanism and Christianity. In the 17th century, Oliver Cromwell's troops converted masses of Catholic and faery-believing folk to Protestantism, and sowed the seeds which would turn into Ireland's bloody 18th, 19th and 20th century religious and political troubles.

In the 1700s, Britain sent many Irish convicts to its American colonies, with others going as free settlers. After the American War of Independence began in 1775, the Irish convicts were sent to Australia. Thousands more fled Ireland as a result of the devastating Potato Famine of the 1840s. And so the faery faith travelled the world, and the faeries went to the new lands. Today many Australians and Americans claim Irish descent, and a connection to the fae.

In 1892, *The Christian Doctrine* was published in Irish Gaelic and in English, and distributed throughout Ireland. In it was a round condemnation of faery faith. "The lucht pisroeg are enchanters who possess fios sigheog, or knowledge of the fairies," it stated. It prohibited "any attention to witchcraft, to charms, to dreams, or to any words or signs for a purpose to attain which they have no efficacy or virtue from nature, or God, or the Church." Saint Patrick's hold on the island had driven out, it was believed, the moon faery Aine and her sister, the sun faery Grian, who Patrick claimed to have exorcised, replacing them with the Virgin Mary and the Christ.

The Irish people's deep belief in faeries could not be eradicated, so the Church's best alternative was to put word about that the faeries were angels sent to earth from heaven because they wouldn't take the side of either Lucifer or Archangel Michael. They were neither good nor bad, so it was said that on earth they could choose to take the side of good or evil. But despite the Church's attempts, the faeries remained in the hearts of the people. Offerings were still left for them, stories were told of them, and wise women and men continued administering their healing arts.

It wasn't easy to be a faery doctor. Biddy Early was one of Ireland's treasured faery healers, and her memory is revered to this day. Biddy grew up on a remote farm in County Clare in the 19th century. She claimed she saw and spoke with the faeries as a child, and was later given by them, she said, knowledge of all the plants, and the ability to commune with them and hear what they could be used for.

Biddy healed family, friends, neighbours and animals at first, but word spread, and soon she was not only sought after by people seeking her healing powers and knowledge, she was also embroiled in what would become a long-running spiritual war with the local priest, who believed she'd gained her powers from the devil.

The Church was never able to fully eradicate the practice of the faery doctors. Most performed their craft in the country, or kept one step ahead of the authorities, or were protected by the local people. Or perhaps they were protected by their own, the faeries themselves.

While some thought the faery doctors were simply herbal healers, others, like the poet WB Yeats, felt they were the priests of the faery faith. He considered faery doctors like Biddy Early to be worthy of great respect, and interviewed more than a hundred faery doctors with Lady Wilde, Oscar Wilde's mother. He learned from them that there were lines running through the land, which the faeries walked and kept healthy, and that the fae were willing to share their knowledge and help the human race and the animals. The faeries, Yeats came to believe, did indeed hold the secrets of the plants, the trees and the energy lines of the land itself.

Yeats concluded that the faery beliefs had blended with the Christian beliefs, although they predated them, and thus they were able to exist harmoniously side by side with them.

In 1893, a year after *The Christian Doctrine* was published, *The Secret Commonwealth* was re-published, and widely distributed for the first time. Lady Wilde's exploration of the faery faith, *Ancient Legends, Mystic Charms and Superstitions of Ireland*, was also released. So, although Saint Patrick claimed Aine and Grian had been driven out of Ireland, it seems the old magics and the faeries were stubborn, and had held fast to their haunts, and were returning to the wells, the springs and the hearts of the Irish people.

Edwardian Fae and the Cottingley Case

In 1904, JM Barrie's stage play *Peter Pan, Or The Boy Who Wouldn't Grow Up* was performed for the first time at the Duke of York's theatre in London, and Tinker Bell's mischievous faery energy was unleashed upon the world! Perhaps her influence called out to the faeries to arise and come out of their hiding places, for in 1917, two young girls, cousins Elsie Wright, 16, and Frances Griffith, 10, took photos of the faeries they played with in their garden in the village of Cottingley, England. Elsie's mother Polly took the pictures to a local spiritualist meeting, and news began to filter through the countryside of the enchanted woods at Cottingley.

The Cottingley case caught the imagination of a nation battered by the shocking casualties of World War I, giving hope to those who had lost sons. Among the believers was one who had lost his own child, Sherlock Holmes creator Sir Arthur Conan Doyle.

In 1920 he wrote a feature story about Elsie and Frances's photos for *The Strand Magazine* entitled "An Epoch-Making Event: Fairies Photographed". With this grand announcement, the Cottingley Fairies saga began in earnest, with heated debate about whether the five photos were genuine. Many people saw them as confirmation of the fae's existence, and in 1922 Conan Doyle published his book *The Coming of the Fairies*, based on the Cottingley Fairies and other accounts of faery sightings.

As the Cottingley Fairies were embraced throughout England, anthropologists began uncovering the faery lore of previously "undiscovered" tribespeople. In 1932, Danish explorer Knud Rasmussen spoke to Inuit people (often called eskimos) about their faeries. They called them Little People, in their language "aua", and described them as helping their shamans to bring back knowledge for hunting, for ceremony, and for other magics. The shamans described them to Rasmussen as tiny females who were no bigger than a loaf of bread, and who wore pointed caps, bearskin trousers and high boots. They had very pointed, upturned toes and, they said, seemed to walk only on their heels.

From the late 19th century until now, Pan, the Arcadian god of fauns, elves, faeries and fields, of the groves and the shepherds, has been an increasingly common figure in literature and art. He's appeared in poetry, children's books, novels and music, and of course in the guise of his most famous namesake, Peter Pan. He is the focal point of the animals' worship in *The Wind in the Willows*, whose chapter The Piper at the Gates of Dawn is one of the most beautiful, magical invocations ever written, and the inspiration behind the album of the same name by art rock band Pink Floyd. Pan has also been a movie star many times over, and a character in many novels, including Tom Robbins' *Jitterbug Perfume*.

Pan has emphatically returned, and behind him flow the faeries, taking up permanent residence in our hearts, our imaginations and in the changing magical and spiritual landscape of the 21st century.

Faery Culture Today

As we've seen, when the faeries were banned by religious doctrine, they broke through to us via the imagination, creativity and our love of nature. Artists, writers, poets, dreamers, dancers and musicians are often conduits for faery energy breaking through the veil and again imbuing the world with enchantment.

The Flower Power children of the hippie era captured and evoked faery energy with their music, dancing, freedom, peace marches and the flowers in their hair. Their activism and vocalising of the shift in energy brought the protection of the earth directly into politics and the mainstream. Environmental causes gathered steam in the late 1960s, which soon led to the birth of Greenpeace, the founding of Earth Day and other eco campaigns, which are now in danger of being appropriated by clever companies capitalising on going green. It is up to every one of us to ensure that the fae's needs, and nature's beauty, remain at the forefront of our decisions and choices.

As people became more peaceful, alternative and aware of the environment, the faeries began to be seen again. At first, as they so often do, they appeared to artists. In 1979, Brian Froud and Alan Lee's groundbreaking book *Faeries* was published. Brian was also the concept artist and designer on the magical films *The Dark Crystal* and *Labyrinth*, and he created the Lady Cottington series, inspired by the Cottingley Fairies, which includes *Lady Cottington's Pressed Fairy Book*. Several films, novels and TV shows also took inspiration from Elsie and Frances's photos of the fae.

In 1981 the girls admitted they had photographed paper cutouts of faeries, but in a poignant interview not long before she died, Frances insisted that the fifth photo was genuine, and that she and Elsie had most definitely seen faeries in their garden. She maintained her belief in the faeries to the end, and her daughter and granddaughter still continue this faith, along with so many others.

Today in the United States, the Feri Tradition, a blending of folk magics developed by Victor and Cora Anderson, has influenced modern-day witches like Starhawk and T Thorn Coyle. In the UK, Alicen and Neil Geddes-Ward teach Faeriecraft, a melding of faery faith and witchcraft from a Celtic perspective. And in 2006, Jessica Galbreth, faery artist and champion, founded Fairy Day.

"It's for everyone who believes in the magic of faerytales," Jessica says. "It is for those imaginative souls who dare to dream impossible dreams. It is for the children of the world, wide eyed and open to the magic that surrounds them. It is for adults too, who long to capture a bit of the magic they remember from their own childhood."

In 2008, Doreen Virtue, best known for her angel teachings and writings, founded the World Fairy Festival, held in early May each year. Ten per cent of all proceeds raised from the workshops and events held in conjunction are donated to environmental charities.

Today people believe in faeries more than ever. We are at a point where our belief in them is evidenced by organic foods being available in supermarkets, by the love we shower upon the earth, by their appearance in magazines, fashion collections and a Paris Hilton perfume, by festivals and musicians' songs, and especially by the conservationists working to save forests, or manoeuvring boats through the southern oceans to protect the whales. Faeries are here, and more powerful than ever! And when you tune in, that last great adventure, of seeing them with your eyes open, will happen.

It is not true that they die if we do not believe in them. What is true is that we experience a death of the soul, of our selves and of our true wildish nature when we do not believe in them. Faeries are eternal. As can we be too.

Selina's Faery Magic

Born on the night of a full moon, for which she was named, Selina Fenech is an Australian artist who paints beautiful faeries, goddesses, mermaids and other enchanted creatures. She uses watercolours and acrylics, with inks, pencils and even digital elements added to best capture the magical images in her mind. She illustrated the stunning *Wild Wisdom of the Faery Oracle* deck, and her art has been published in books and magazines worldwide. It is available in original and print form as well as on t-shirts, calenders, stationery, figurines, coffee mugs and jewellery. Her beautiful work, along with other artists she promotes, can be viewed at www.SelinaFenech.com.

I remember as a little girl, reading faerytales over and over and over, and being enchanted by the stories and artworks in the pages. But really, when I think about it, there aren't many faeries in faerytales! I'm not sure if I discovered faeries, or if they discovered me. I know I started drawing dryads and earth goddesses and elves when I was about 10, but I honestly can't remember where they came from, or what inspiration led me to draw them. They just started coming out onto my paper.

From then on my love affair with all things fantasy began. I started reading fantasy novels and watching fantasy movies. I had a desperate desire to be taken away to a fantasy world full of magic, to live those adventures. It wasn't until I was about 16 that I started researching and seeking out actual faery lore, and learning more about faeries in particular. And from then on I've been absolutely hooked! Surrounding myself now with faeries and fantasy, and painting images of them, is my way of escaping into those fantasy worlds I dreamed of as a kid.

I connect with faeries through my imagination. I'm always asking "What if...?" questions to them in my mind. What if they were a faery queen?

What if they were in love? Then I let my imagination play, and that's when I see the faeries that I paint.

Faeries are important on so many levels. They remind us that the world is a living thing that needs our care. They bring us tales of morality. They bring smiles to little girls who are believing for the first time, and smiles to women, who are reminded of the happiness they felt as a child. They tell us that magic is real and is everywhere, even in the mundane. They show that wings aren't always needed to fly. And they let us have a little bit of that magic we all crave.

I guess you could say I'm a faery agnostic. I believe in them as a metaphor for all that is magical and mysterious in our natural world, but I also know that just because I haven't been lucky enough to see one myself, that doesn't mean that they don't exist. I have had many people tell me that with what I paint in my artwork, I simply must see faeries. And maybe I do, but have only seen them in my mind, not yet through my eyes.

Because I haven't yet seen a faery with my eyes, I'm left to play my "What if...?" games in my mind. And the inspiration that comes from that is never ending. I'm on a quest to capture the image of faery on paper. I don't believe I've quite gotten it yet, and maybe I never will, but the inspiration that comes from that quest is wonderful. There are so many aspects of faery to explore, so many types of faery, so many "What if...?" questions to ask. I could paint faeries all my life and never be bored with them.

I want to live my life like it's a faerytale, and I want my artwork to make other people feel the same. I love that for a person of any age my faeries can bring back the magical memories and feelings of adventure from their childhood – and I hope they also create new memories and dreams of magic!

Courts of the Fae

"And I serve the fairy queen,
To dew her orbs upon the green.
Farewell, thou spirit, I'll be gone;
Our queen and her elves come here anon."
William Shakespeare, A Midsummer Night's Dream

Faerylands and Their Inhabitants

It was Lughnasadh morning. After a night of sweet heavy rain, the sun was shining. Just outside my front door, on the slender, velvet-green ribbon of grass that lines my street, two faery rings had sprung up. I looked at them for a while, seeing the dew collecting on the creamy white and golden brown mushrooms of one, and the silvery spotted toadstools and crooked circle of the other. I heard the faeries speak, and tell me this:

These are our meeting places. The circle is our time to talk. To discuss. And this time, the Seelie and the Unseelie Courts have come to you, to share.

Right outside my house? In the middle of the city?

Silence...

Okay then, I thought. It seems they have decided to camp here for a while. It's a long way from the hallowed halls of Faeryland, or Annwn, or the Hollow Hills, or Elfhame, or the Alfheimre, or any other faery kingdom. Instead, the fae of the Seelie and Unseelie Courts were in the middle of the nature strip in the city, unless a particular trickster faery was pulling my leg!

But then, stranger things have happened. I knelt down, and gazed at the tiny clumps of mushrooms amidst the tangled tree roots. It was all so very small from my human perspective. I wondered how the denizens of Faeryland had fitted inside the mushroom and toadstool rings, and whether perhaps the twisted roots of the liquid amber trees that had filled with rainwater overnight were their faery wells and bathing pools. And if it was the faeries of the courts here, had they shapeshifted? The Seelie and Unseelie are often human-sized, sometimes even larger, appearing like super-humans, unnaturally tall, fair, wingless and shining.

I pondered whether they had tinied themselves down and winged themselves up for their convention in the inner-city Sydney mushroom and toadstool meeting rooms. Because they are able to do that – transform themselves from the tall, shining ones of ancient lore, and shrink down, down, down into the diminutive winged fae so beloved of the Victorian era. It's how they've stayed safe for so long in a world so hostile to nature and magic.

I thought too of how they had said that both the Seelie and the Unseelie were meeting – together! I was a little surprised, as legend has it that the two courts are not exactly best of friends. But interesting times, like the ones that we live in, make allies of even the most habitual of enemies. So I went inside to continue writing, wondering if their meeting would filter through to me, or if their meeting outside my door was in any way an accident.

Faery Courts

The faeries of the Seelie Court are understood to be bright, delightful and blessed, and are considered to be shining and radiant with light. Some call them the Summer Fae or Light Fae. Those of the Unseelie Court are said to be rather different – tricksy, rebellious, volatile, invisible, unseen. They are the Dark Fae, the Winter Fae.

The legends and lore of these two courts of shadow and light seem to have Gaelic roots. In Scotland the words "sligh", "slee", "sith" and "seelie" are all varieties of names for the fae. "Sligh", from which "seelie" is derived, is Scots Gaelic for "bright and delightful, joyous", and is also the root of the word "silly". Think of that next time someone calls you a silly so-and-so – it puts a whole new flattering spin on what could be rather uncomplimentary!

The Seelie and Unseelie faeries may have originated in the ancient northern lands, but they have for many thousands of years been making their way around the world, riding energetic waves and hitching on human transport, migrating to the Americas, to Australia, to Africa and to the islands of the Pacific. There are also many Seelie and Unseelie fae in New Zealand, a land full of people of Scottish descent. Of course, there are indigenous fae in all these areas too, and like we humans, the faeries are still working out their relationships today!

So even if you are not in a land that is Gaelic, Celtic or Pictish, it is possible to see and sense the Seelie and Unseelie wherever you are in the world as they are multi-dimensional, and all it takes for you to glimpse them is the ability, and the willingness, to slip between the worlds. The Seelie, and all faeries to a degree, can change shape, and manifest to us via a borrowing of our energy in order to grow "denser". The more developed our Sight however, the less this interaction or energy exchange need take place.

If you have a drop of faery blood, you can and will see and experience them. If they are not in your ancestry this lifetime, they may be more difficult to "hear", and your faery interactions could seem a little like straining to hear music carried on the wind. Yet if there is a past life connection you can connect, whatever your ancestry and the DNA your own blood carries. Such is the paradox of the fae.

The Seelie and Unseelie Courts are the names of the two structured courts of the faeries. All faeries are wild, and have a more instinctual nature than we over-domesticated humans, but the Seelie and the Unseelie are quite different to the wild ones who tend the flowers and nature, who are more tribal and clan-like, more free and wild in their faery clans and villages.

The Seelie and Unseelie are more organised, aristocratic and socially-minded than other fae. They have certain hierarchies, which is very un-faery-like! Most faeries rejoice in freedom and yet work very well in groups, very naturally and harmoniously. They do not enjoy rules and being part of a social order, and do not seem to need a "leader". But the faeries of the Seelie and the Unseelie Courts are different – wild yet organised, with a kind of "royalty" and a definite lineage and protocol. They have always been different to the pure nature spirits, although they too are changing with the demands of this evolving world...

The Seelie Court

The Seelie are also known as the Blessed Court. They have been called the Good Folk, and the trustworthy fae, and it is quite certain that they are the more traditionally friendly of the courts when it comes to dealing with we strange humanfolk. They are not so determined to bring change about, unlike their breakaway kin, the Unseelie, who are often characterised as "bad" and untrustworthy.

But of course these words and labels need examination. "Good" and "bad" depend on the context, and there are times when the rebellious, restless and disruptive energy of the Unseelie, with their nonconformity and questioning attitudes, is going to be healthier for us all. Because they both have power, the influence of the two courts is held in balance, and they are rarely in dispute. The members outside my door told me that they hold meetings and an annual discussion every Lughnasadh, where the breaking of faery bread takes place in stone circles, groves and, yes, even on city streets.

I wondered, since the Seelie and Unseelie fae are often taller than humans, how they could possibly sit on the toadstools. Then, as if the faeries had just rolled their eyes at me, I remembered that they are able to shapeshift – to grow larger or smaller at will. So yes, they can vanish, and they can meet wherever they want to.

The Seelie fae are very honest. They take the giving of promises most seriously, and do not understand humanity's ability to make promises then break them. So, if you make a pledge to the Seelie, it is wise to intend to keep it, and to do so. In this way, the Seelie remind us to be in integrity, to be committed to our deepest principles, and less swayed by the easy path and the quick way.

They do not do deals, and they do not help in exchange for something else. They simply help, then show you how you can be of assistance to them, so you need not be afraid of being indebted to them. But if a member of the Seelie Court has helped you, the universal law of energy exchange means it is wise for you to do something for them in return. They do not ask much, after all, and it is not so difficult to give. We need only empathise with them and ask what they would like, for them to send us a clear message.

For example, the Seelie fae will often point out to me something small that needs to be done environmentally. To remember to recycle my old mobile phone, as the coltan in mobiles is mined in areas of the world that are in danger of disappearing. Great forests are being torn down for this resource, so the more that is recycled, the less needs to be mined. They remind me to recycle all that I can, and to be respectful of how I consume and use resources.

If you have asked them how you can help, it is very important to follow through and complete the task. The Seelie never break a promise – they simply do not. It seems not to be in their make-up to be able to. They are careful to keep their word, and they never say yes unless they are committed. They may say nothing, but this is not to be understood as, or confused with, agreement.

Their distinguishing feature is virtue, although not in the sense of the Christian virtues. There are nine faery virtues – honesty, justice, compassion, courage, hope, faith (to see the invisible world) integrity, laughter and joy. They are generous, believe in free will, have strong ethics, are patient and peaceful, demonstrate great kindness, and enjoy a hearty, passionate love of life.

The Seelie are here to be intermediaries between nature, the animals, the elementals and the humans. They do their best under trying circumstances. They are diplomats, and moderators, and many are exhausted, which is why humans are being asked to step in, and step up, and be more accountable. Those of us with faery blood are especially undergoing this waking up process, and perhaps we too may be members of the Seelie Court.

Seelie fae traditionally rode horses, but they too change with the times, and now they move about in cars, or catch public transport, and you could even end up sitting next to one on a jet. They are not fond of iron, but can now handle exposure for several hours, going into "sleep mode" to minimise the impact on their system. Sea Seelies ride dolphins and whales, and can also travel without an animal companion. Sometimes they even shrink their size down and ride about on dragonflies or butterflies as their faery steeds.

Tall and extremely fair, these faeries are very long-lived, with the average lifespan for both the Seelie and the Unseelie described in this Gaelic traditional rhyme.

> *Nine nines at the breast,*
> *Nine times unsteady, weak.*
> *Nine nines on foot, strong,*
> *Nine nines able, strong.*

Nine nines strapping, grown,
Nine nines victorious.
Nine nines bonnetted, drab,
Nine nines beardy, grey.

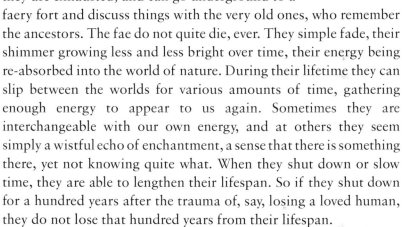

This, people far better with numbers than I have said, gives a lifespan of 729 years. This breaks down to a number, again, of nine – a number very sacred to the fae.

Seelie can also "sleep" for a time, when they are exhausted, and can go underground to a faery fort and discuss things with the very old ones, who remember the ancestors. The fae do not quite die, ever. They simple fade, their shimmer growing less and less bright over time, their energy being re-absorbed into the world of nature. During their lifetime they can slip between the worlds for various amounts of time, gathering enough energy to appear to us again. Sometimes they are interchangeable with our own energy, and at others they seem simply a wistful echo of enchantment, a sense that there is something there, yet not knowing quite what. When they shut down or slow time, they are able to lengthen their lifespan. So if they shut down for a hundred years after the trauma of, say, losing a loved human, they do not lose that hundred years from their lifespan.

Safe haven is a principle held to by both the Seelie and Unseelie Courts. They can offer you the cloak of enchantment and protection, which can make you less visible, if you need to escape or move about without being seen. A cloak of enchantment is for many reasons best made of a natural fibre, which can hold energy more efficiently and longer term than synthetic fibres.

The Unseelie Court

The Unseelie fae are less controlled and far darker than the bright and well-behaved Seelie. They are wild, anarchic and unpredictable, and they think of themselves as liberators who hold the faery keys to the prisons of conditioning, development and technology, and the hundred locks and bindings of the human world. They are unimpressed with humanity's rules and regulations, and do not see the point in being so rigidly controlled. They are anarchists, though they would roll their beautiful eyes at that word, and will provide you with the help you need to awaken from being controlled.

The Seelie will assist, always, and gently, but the Unseelie will come in and completely work over your life in chaotic, adventurous ways. Many faery faith scholars recommend that you never seek out the Unseelie – they will find you. All faeries create beauty and love, but the ways the Seelie and the Unseelie go about this are very different. They are not "good" and "bad", it is just that it is easier for us to divide them into these roles because of our own perceptions, and how we experience their magic. Yet it is best to ask a goddess such as Brigid, Dana, Morgan, Rhiannon or Elen of the Ways to intercede with you regarding the Unseelie.

For those of you wondering what a member of the Unseelie Court could be like, watch the delightful film *Drop Dead Fred*, where Rik Mayall plays an anarchic, sociopathic yet ultimately healing and loving faery, Fred, who appears as an oppressed young woman's imaginary friend. Thanks to his chaotic and destructive urgings, she breaks the shackles of her repression and, via her Fred-inspired mishaps, finds herself, frees herself, leaves an abusive man, stands up to her controlling mother and comes closer to the possibility of finding someone who loves her for her own true self.

With his destruction, fiery temper, insults and mayhem, Fred is undoubtedly a member of the Unseelie Court, and one whose rebellious, defiant energy brings hope, joy and freedom.

Can a member of the Seelie Court become a member of the Unseelie? Yes indeed, this can occur when it is necessary for change to take place, when one or the other is too rigid in their approach. The courts are ever evolving. At the present time they're focused primarily on convincing humans by whatever means to take care of, and feel at one with, this beautiful planet we find ourselves on.

The Wanderers and Guardians

It was the early 20th century mystic, revolutionary and poet WB Yeats who brought the terms Trooping and Solitary into faery lore. These faeries usually avoid human contact, having their own missions to carry out, but there are also those domesticated faeries who inhabit the world of people – living, often undetected, side by side with us – such as the brownies. Sometimes they remain invisible to humans, co-existing peacefully. Sometimes they are detected by those humans with the Sight, but most times they can pass for human for a very long time indeed.

Recently, my faery friends tell me, fae such as the house brownies and hobgoblins have recognised that they need to infiltrate places where people actually are these days, so they have taken up residence more firmly in our workplaces and daycare centres, as the people they need to reach and influence are spending less and less time at home, and more and more time at work. Faeries will do interesting things in the workplace – they will work on switching off air-conditioning systems, turning off fluorescent lights and setting off fire alarms to give everyone some time outside in the natural light.

It is not always pleasant for the faeries to go to work with us. Some cannot stand entering toxic workplaces at all. Yet they continue to help us deal with harmful workplace energies. My beloved dragonfae companion of several years, Cecelia, saved me from carrying a toxic cloud of energy around by eating out the toxins from my aura that accumulated every day at my former Tower-like workplace. Cecelia always left me at the entrance to the building in the morning, but she was always there, waiting outside for me, at the end of every difficult day. I did not see her inside, ever. But there she would be at the end of my working hours, and she would leap into my auric field, munching and regurgitating the toxins, the daggers and so on. Sweet Cecelia, thank you!

But not all faery beings are like these ones, who cannot enter harmful places. Some are more like humans, less sensitive, more resilient, and longer lived. I suspected for a while that Cecelia was quite young, due to her small size and her sensitivity.

You may even be working with a faery right now. Look at those around you in your office. Do you see anyone with faery traits? Someone with pointed ears, who sings out loud, is bejewelled, has a chaotic workspace, and rings out with laughter and mischief.

Keep an eye out for the mischief makers and the merry folk who make working life fun, who see the delightful side, and who seem to have a wonderful energetic effect on the office. They, like the angels who are nurses, caregivers and sometimes flight attendants, are wonderful beings to be around. So too, at home, look out for the brownie who will assist you with your housework, and the hobgoblin who will help light your stove.

Solitary Faeries : the Guardians

Solitary faeries live in the place that they are caring for – most often a well, a glade, a meadow or a forest. There are many solitary fae who care for the energy of a sacred place, and who can only be seen fleetingly, or if you have a special connection with them. They are said by some faery scholars to be dangerous, but this is not what my experience has taught me. It is more that these places are wild, and thus there is some discomfort in our reaching them.

Solitary faeries are very powerful. They usually work alone, but sometimes they meet with other fae to decide on the best course of action, and they are also associated with Nemetona, the goddess of groves and healing springs. They can make it difficult for logging to occur, for roads to be built or for development and construction work to take place on the piece of the world that they safeguard.

Some do still live in the cities, and it is here that you will see the wild world reclaiming the concrete and tar, although they are very tired from their constant efforts. It is not known whether solitary female fae seek out fae men to have children with. Some do have children, but these are usually fostered out, and will only be brought back to live in the wild or sacred place when the time is right, which is when their long-lived faery parent is tiring and getting ready to fade and return their essence into the heart of the world.

Trooping Faeries : Wanderers of the Leylines

The trooping faeries are, it is said, the aristocrats of the faery world – the ones who often pass their blood on to humans, and who can intermarry and intermingle with us. They are so-named because they travel in long processions. They are the wanderers, and are akin to the elves of *The Lord of the Rings*, who went to the shoreless seas of the west. Most trooping faeries travel west in the northern hemisphere, and east in the southern, following the flow of energy.

They are hundreds-fold, and are led slowly and tirelessly, resting only at the ancient special power spots – beneath the trees declared sacred, where the awen flows still, or in areas sacred to the gods and goddesses who work with them. On rare occasions they may take time from the journey and rest in the ancestral halls of healing that are beneath the mounds of the Hollow Hills.

Humans, like the one in the legend of Tam Lin, a man captured by the faery queen and made to troop with her court until his mortal love could rescue him, can and do join these processions, and travel between the worlds for miles, sometimes emerging from Faeryland in a place altogether different to the one in which they began their journey. At other times we are simply observers.

In 1919, young Harry Anderson of Wisconsin, USA, was walking along a country road. In such a sparsely populated area, with its dairy farms and large fields of cattle, Harry could have expected to walk alone. But he did not. According to Harry, at twilight he was joined by 20 small men, walking earnestly and in single file towards him on that summer night, illuminated by the moon's light.

They were all bald, bare-chested and dressed in leather knee pants and suspenders. They were, Harry claimed, mumbling as they passed him, and didn't even glance his way. Stunned and frightened, Harry bolted for home, and told his Scandinavian parents what he'd seen.

Had Harry slipped between the worlds? Had his ancient Scandinavian blood sang to him, and had he been visited by the Trooping fae, or elves, in honour of his ancestry? Did he see them as a precursor to developing the Sight? We do not know, for Harry spoke little of them again, fearing ridicule. But that night he revealed what he saw, and it haunted him all the days of his life. And perhaps he joined them, after he too passed from this world.

The Faeries of the Wild Hunt

The Wild Hunt, a group of faery huntsmen racing in mad pursuit across the earth, just above it or even through the skies, careers along the old roads and byways, the leylines of the earth and the ways of Elen, the Palaeolithic British horned goddess who is the keeper of the roads and passageways of this world and the next.

Throughout the places where the veils between the worlds are thin, and through the gateways of the eight sacred festivals, come thundering the faery horses of the Wild Hunt. At the head is the faery king Gwyn ap Nudd, riding in the midst are lords and ladies of the Seelie and Unseelie Courts, and in front of them flies the white hart, or stag, their quarry. They ride on and on, through countryside, cities and towns, never stopping.

This is their role, to ride through these energetic byways and passageways, to reinvigorate the leylines, to bring vitality back to this realm. The Wild Hunt helps the faery energy flow through this world and the next, stripping the over-civilised energy clean again, bringing back the wild world and the fierce vital energy that we all crave. This is their hunt. The hunt for the sacred white hart, who is showing them the ways that need clearing.

The Wild Hunt may rarely be seen, but when it is it always inspires awe. It is not a faery activity of recreation or play, but of the dynamic chase between dark and light, of the changing of the seasons, and of the urge to seek out the sacred and to remind the planet that her sacred paths are being cleared and kept well.

The hunt recharges the energy of the more fixed faery kings and queens, who cannot troop and travel as their nature wishes to. But they can tear across the countryside, and feel the wind in their hair, travelling faster than any human ever could, their horses' hooves not touching the ground, flying and riding and crying out for the joy of the hunt in the night!

The Wild Hunt has its origins in Faeryland, but like so much of the realm of the fae, it has been transported into our popular culture, and appears in literature, folklore and faerytales. Once it was said that seeing the Wild Hunt was a precursor of doom, but that foreboding tone and attitude was, at times, attributed to anything fae. It's more fitting to assume that its appearance suggests it is time to clear your energy, to sweep and tear across the land, to give in to the wild magic of the self when the hunt comes to visit, or passes you by, showing you the possibilities of your life.

And if the Wild Hunt should stop, and seem to recognise you? Then you know your faery kin have found you again, across all the miles, and years, that separate you.

The red-eared hounds of Annwn lead the way, chasing the scent of the white hart, which is a being of the forest who is seen only by faeries, or those who have the wise blood singing in their veins. These fae-related people have crossed water, and mountain ranges, and spread all around this bright world.

In the United States, the Wild Hunt has been seen many a time, and its fierce and beautiful fae are known as Ghost Riders, who dress as cowboys or outlaws. In the Nordic lands, it's referred to as Woden's Hunt. And in Wales it is called Cwn Annwn, and as Annwn is the realm of the faery king Gwyn ap Nudd (pronounced gwin up neeth, or nuth), we can safely say that it is Gwyn himself who leads the wild hunt.

A few people today have seen the Wild Hunt, in the most ordinary of circumstances. Donna Morgan is a spiritual woman who makes essences, energetic mists and healing tools such as wands. Totally unexpectedly, Donna saw the Wild Hunt one day from her then-home in Jervis Bay, in New South Wales, Australia – a world away from the British homeland of the Wild Hunt, but only a moment away from the call of her faery blood.

"I was sitting outside in the garden just soaking up the winter warmth, because southern NSW gets really cold some days," she remembers. "I don't think I had even started fully on my magical path then, but I have always been a nature person and I guess deep down I always knew that there was more.

"I remember drifting into a space where I was wondering how the garden would look come spring, when I saw a flash of movement. At first I thought it was the cat, but then I realised it was misty, and I was looking through a mist or veil of sorts. I could hear noises – I couldn't make them out at first, it was just faint sounds then yelling, getting louder, and followed by shouting, like excited fun. There were lots of footsteps, then the sound of galloping. I thought for a moment that the horse across the road had gotten out, and I almost got up to check, but something held me in that space. And then I saw a white stag leaping past," Donna explains.

"The sights and sounds were so real that I remember ducking, because I thought I was going to be knocked over. Then suddenly there were men on horseback flying past me. They looked like us but not quite like us. They had long, tangled hair flying in the wind, and some had leaves and pieces of plants stuck in their hair and beards. Some had long braids and others had hats or bands around their foreheads holding their hair back from their eyes," she says.

"I felt a rush of excitement, almost orgasmic it was so exhilarating. Then I could smell earth, like composting leaves under a warm sun. There was the scent of fresh honeysuckle and faint wood smoke. I will never forget the eyes of the man on the largest stocky horse. His eyes shone with excitement – they were so clear that I almost melted into them. Green pools so deep with wisdom and loving, yet also making me wary and a little afraid. He felt so familiar, like I had met him before in another time. The connection was powerful and strong – and then in a flash they were all gone. All of this happened in the space of maybe five minutes, yet it was so powerful that I can still feel the echoes of it today."

Faery Royalty

"They are said to have ariscraticall Rulers and Laws, but no discernible religion," wrote Reverend Robert Kirk in *The Secret Commonwealth of Elves, Fauns and Fairies* in 1691.

Lady Charlotte Guest, as she collated and translated medieval Welsh manuscripts for *The Mabinogion* in 1838, wrote: "He is no less a personage than the king of faery. Very numerous indeed are his subjects and very various are they in nature. He is the sovereign of those beneficent and joyous beings who dance in the moonlight."

It's natural that in a time of kings and queens, courts and royalty, people imagined faery society would be structured in the same way. Or maybe we just aren't so different, after all.

Today, we have given over the powers of enchantment and glamour to people who we may never meet, and who often do not participate in making the world a better place, nor even a more joyous place. Think of the vacuous pop stars, page three models and silly heiresses, who contribute nothing to society, and yet are the ones the young people today try to emulate.

However, many faeries are actors, performers, singers, musicians and dancers, those who inspire and uplift us, and who find their home in expressing creativity and imagination. They are often very small away from the stage, just as they are huge on stage – displaying a variety of the shapeshifting skills of the fae.

Faery powers and talents can draw riches, and fame, and as long as they do the good work – keeping a dream alive for us all, be it through writing, entertaining or designing – we all have access to the realm of enchantment that is the true fae nation.

We often make stars of even the people who are teachers of wisdom, and the star system can be very harmful, and create personas and false egos, fantasy and bitter disappointment when human beings do not live up to our expectations. Cults of personality are very different from following a path. Be sure to work with the fae with respect, and with self-respect. That flowing exchange of energy can bring great things. We can all venture to Faeryland, and bring back the blessings of the court to the mundane world, if we dare!

Shhh! Faery Secret

Faeries love to listen to poetry. They like WB Yeats, William Blake, Edgar Allan Poe, Dr Seuss and Lewis Carroll, and they truly appreciate you speaking to them in rhyme, so craft a poem for them and read it aloud.

The Faery Court

Meeting the faery court was once an overwhelming experience, as many humans believed faeries to be evil, or of the devil. Now that we are evolving away from the fearful ways of the past, we are embracing our relationship with the fae again. And this means we are sometimes gifted with a journey to the faery court, where we may meet a king or queen, as did this faery-human, Petal Vandeheer, a faery seer from Perth in Western Australia.

"The first time I met Titania, the queen of the faeries, was the week of my 21st birthday. With the fluttering of my eyelids I was summoned to the Seelie Court throne room for an initiation. I was given gifts and responsibilities," Petal explains.

"These faeries are posh, and you can only talk to them in ye olde English rhyming poetry," Petal elaborates. "Titania has blonde hair and green-blue eyes – I've seen them aquamarine in sunlight and silver white when she does magic. She has a yellow/pink/golden aura and wears a long peach dress. Sometimes it has long sleeves, sometimes no sleeves and sometimes short cap sleeves, but it's always raw silk, a long dress with an empire line.

"But while her dress is always similar, her crowns, tiaras and jewels seem to be how she expresses herself for whatever the occasion. The girl is bling! As I get older it is more and more intimidating to be called to her throne room. If you're young, meeting the queen is exciting, but as you get older and respect grows, being summoned to Titania's throne is full on. She has her royal court guards and yes, I have seen Oberon, the faery king, but never have I seen him talk, only whisper softly to his queen. I've been summoned twenty times to the throne room, but I've seen Titania one-on-one a hundred times, as she likes to drop by and check on my progress and give personal encouragement.

"The Seelie Court festivals are fun and more relaxed, but in the throne room you have to bow and curtsy, bring gifts from deep within, and not speak until spoken to. Australian faeries are somewhat casual in comparison," Petal says.

What wonderful experiences! These journeys to the courts and the throne room can happen very spontaneously, as they did for Petal. For others, they may take place during visions, and can be inspired by scrying, meditation or trance. Our dreams can also be the vehicle for such visits. Or they can occur suddenly at a moment that has great meaning for us, such as a 21st birthday, or at a time when the veils between the worlds are thin, as they are during the eight Celtic festivals or sabbats.

Belinda Annesley, a pagan skincare consultant from Hervey Bay in beautiful Queensland, travelled between the worlds to the faery court at a sacred time of the Wheel of the Year. Here she describes her wonderful Otherworldly visitation.

"On the night of February 1, 2010, Lughnasadh in the southern hemisphere, I woke up from a dream. I could smell wood, and trees like pine. I was in the faery court – it was outside and they were getting ready to travel. I had never thought of the courts before, and asked which one I was in, the Seelie or the Unseelie," she says.

" 'Seelie, Unseelie,' they sang to me in my head. Perhaps it was a riddle. I don't know if it was both of the courts, but wherever I was did not feel bad. They did feel dark, but they were nice, and not airy-fairy. I was with them preparing for travel, and the energy was warm, smothering and active. I remember an antler mask the most clearly, but there were many others around me, and they were excited and getting ready for something.

"My dream ended with me placing the antler mask on a man. I can't remember him, just the mask, and so many other beings, who were surrounding us and were so excited. And then that's when I woke up," Belinda recalls dreamily.

Faery Elders and Faery Royalty

Gwyn ap Nudd

"Hound-hoofed is my horse, the torment of battle,
While I am called Gwyn, the son of Nud,
The lover of Creudilad, the daughter of Llud."

From the Black Book of Carmarthen, a collection of
Welsh poetry and historical folk tales created in 1250CE.

Did Belinda see the crowning of Gwyn ap Nudd in her dream-like vision that took her to the faery court? The symbol of antlers is a strong faery tradition, and they have often been depicted on the head of the horned god, who is known as Cernunnos, or Herne, or sometimes as the faery king Gwyn ap Nudd.

Gwyn ap Nudd simply means "Gwyn, son of Nudd". In Welsh, the word "nudd" means the Milky Way, so Gwyn's father is a sky god. When we say the land of Nod, we are referring to dreamtime, and to this faery king's realm. Nudd is also the name of a place in Wales, the sacred Vale of Neath. Gwyn is thus a faery king of the earth (his antlers), the below (the Hollow Hills of the Vale of Neath), and the great above (the celestial realm of the Milky Way).

The king stag is also a sign of great potency, and Gwyn's own horns mean he is the king stag of his people. His official territories stretch from Wales in the west through to the east of England and far north into Scotland. His domain on Glastonbury Tor was considered so powerful that it was officially exorcised by the church in the seventh century. The entrance to Gwyn's domain is still very much a real place on the Tor, where we can sit, meditate and journey with him into the labyrinthine caves beneath, exploring the tunnels and crystals, the healing halls, feasting rooms, ballrooms and even the bed chamber of Gwyn, if he so desires, and if we so dare.

His kingdom is the realm of Annwn (pronounced ann-oon), which is the dimension of Faeryland itself, all over the world, throughout the cosmos and between the worlds. He is a traveller, an eternal one who will live forever. Shining with light, he illuminates our knowledge of ourselves, and of the realm of the fae, and its endless interactions with us, the human kin of the faeries.

This handsome, strong and regal lord is a leader of the children of Dana. He is immortal, unlike many of the Seelie and Unseelie, with their 729-year lifespans, and even some of the longer-lived faery kings and queens. He is different. Undying. Related to the gods and goddesses, such as Arianrhod, the mother goddess of fertility and the full moon, Gwyn is the link between the celestial and terrestrial, the cord between the goddesses and the fae, and the bloodline that links humanity and animals. He is a multi-dimensional power source and energy field, whose time is rising once again.

Call on Gwyn ap Nudd for: Protection, connection to your family ancestry, travelling far and wide, learning the magics and wisdoms of the old ways, mapping out the stars, celestial territories and links, and for times of difficult transitions, for working with your shadows and your light, and bringing them into balance.

Invoke your inner Gwyn ap Nudd by:
☆ Remembering your spirit's immortality.
☆ Creating a special place where you can meditate undisturbed and journey between the worlds.
☆ Extending your power and influence in bright and good ways.
☆ Connecting deeply to the earth, reaching out to the stars and knowing you belong there too.

Oberon

You will recognise Oberon when he comes to you, as he is a king who is handsome, yet quite unlike the idea of fae men being elvish, lengthy and long in limb. He is stocky, thickly muscled and short. Unlike the elvish, who he descends from, and who resemble graceful dancers more than warriors, he is very strong, akin to a Viking in his appearance. He is Germanic in his ancestry, and has very strong ideas about protecting, providing and ensuring your survival.

He is not a king who will spend a great deal of time wooing and loving – he is a leader, a protector of his people, and someone who will do what must be done for the good of the whole faery kingdom. He is very ethical, and will make the very difficult choices that ensure this will occur. He does not complain, nor does he explain, but he has deep, passionate feelings that can be seen when you look into his eyes. He is the faery king to call on when resources seem to be dwindling, and when challenges for the basics in life are coming thick and fast. He can hunt, ride, fight and care for you. He will do so, and you will know how very worth living your magical life is.

Call on Oberon for: Issues regarding family, health, your legs, keeping yourself grounded, and issues to do with food, appetite and feeling safe. He is a protector faery king.

Invoke your inner Oberon by:
☆ Protecting yourself. Taking care of your needs. It is your responsibility in this life to have them met, so work out what you can do, right now, to be more comfortable, safe and protected.
☆ Grounding yourself, and eating healthful foods.
☆ Reminding yourself how safe you truly are.
☆ Understanding that your ancestors are looking out for you.
☆ Dancing, and thanking the earth for supporting each footstep.

Aine

Aine's gentle silver light and cleansing powers have moved gently across whole countries in the mists of the moonlight. And as moonlight is everywhere, so is Aine's cleansing, healing energy. Aine is an Irish faery queen, whose domain is the moon, and thus all that falls under moonlight. The light of the moon provides a crystal cleansing, and her domain is specifically that of healing and regenerating the sacral or sexual regions for both men and women. Wherever there is moonlight, there is Aine, and she can gift you with her ability to see clearly when all seems dark about you.

It is said that when Saint Patrick arrived in Ireland in the fifth century to force Christianity on the people of the faery and druid faiths, he exorcised Aine, at the same time as he was asking his God to protect him from "the spells of women and druids". But how can one banish the light of the moon, or the stars in the sky? This beautiful faery queen's influence has remained, and to this day women seek her reflection in the sacred pools of Ireland.

Aine, whose name means "radiance, glow, bright", was born in southwest Ireland. She has incarnated as a human woman several times, and was married for a time to a human, the legendary Irish chieftain Fionn MacCool. She can bring happiness in love, prosperity to families and to lovers, and can eradicate the guilt people so often feel in sexual relationships, about enjoying their sensuality fully.

Her name is pronounced awn-ya, and she is described in folktales as "the best-hearted faery woman who ever lived – lucky in money and love". It is said that she slept within the Hollow Hills during the times when Ireland was safe, arising to help during English military leader Oliver Cromwell's invasion in the 17th century, and ensuring that her people safely ventured all over the world during the great waves of Irish migration in the 18th and 19th centuries.

Call on Aine for: Healing sexual issues, guilt around femininity, dissolving any residual or conditioned thinking regarding women being "sinful", and reclaiming your worth and your right to love fully, to prosper and be happy. Having total control over who and what has access to your body. Her speciality is cleansing these energy woundings from your light body under the moonlight.

Invoke your inner Aine by:
☆ Celebrating your sensuality. Dissolving the guilt or conflicted feelings you may have over your beautiful body, your sexuality and your feminine parts.
☆ Wearing sensual clothes.
☆ Swaying your hips when you walk.
☆ Remembering your innocence.
☆ Having a delicious moonbath.
☆ Remembering that you are in *total* control of your body, and who you share its wonders with.

Grian

Grian, pronounced gree-arn, is the Irish goddess of the sun, a faery queen who brings life to the world, and breathes loving power and productivity to all. She is associated with bringing to life your dreams, firing up your enthusiasm, igniting your own internal sun, and being bright, strong, warm, loving and powerful. In visions Grian can appear to be part fire dragon, part faery, part goddess, and she is often seen with bright flames and small dragonfae beings gathered about her. She is heat, and life, and the ignition of dreams.

She is the one for whom the ancient temple and archaeological site of Newgrange in County Meath is named – it is New-Grian, or Grian's place. At the winter solstice each year, Grian's rebirth as the solar goddess brings back life to the land. Her first great act is to bring her sword of light into the centre of the womb of the earth, represented by the narrow beam of sunlight that illuminates the centre of the Newgrange passage tomb on this day.

Call on Grian for: Times when you require empowerment, or you're self-sabotaging or avoiding taking action on your dreams. For activating dreams into reality, and completing concepts. For staying motivated and excited about life and yourself, for believing in your power, asserting yourself, protecting your own boundaries and expanding your energetic influence in peaceful ways.

Invoke your inner Grian by:
☆ Smiling without moving your lips.
☆ Remembering a natural talent, and setting it free.
☆ Expressing your power in healthful ways.
☆ Being warm and staying strong.

Ambrosia

This delicious faery queen offers us all the exquisite sensations of love, and brings these to us directly through our senses, especially through taste, touch and smell. Ambrosia is the food of the fae, the life-sustaining, vitality-filled food of love, and she opens our hearts, purifies us of suspicions and brings us a plate brimming with unconditional love. If we eat of this divine faery food, we too can love, and never feel the hunger of a heart full of unrequited longing.

Ambrosia's name comes from the Ancient Greek drink of the gods, a liquid of immortality. She is very old, and seems able to regenerate. Her power wanes in areas where pesticides and GM food crops are decimating the bee population, and the bee is one of her emblems. Honey is her food, and honey and mead are the traditional treats consumed for a lunar cycle by honeymooners.

When we eat honey, or use it to dress a wound or scent a candle, or use beeswax to light our way and ionise our atmosphere, Ambrosia's gift is with us, and our hearts open to the great beauty and love of the world, and we love her back. Ambrosia's magic can also keep us healthy, well and youthful. She can purify, as she did to Hera the goddess of love and marriage, and increase our attractiveness, as she did for Penelope, the wife of the Greek king Odysseus.

Call on Ambrosia for: Unconditional love, healing hurt, anger and disharmony in relationships, sweetness, vitality and the strength to love again. Work with her by using honey and oils to scent your home or self, and attract love and prosperous abundance into your blessed life. She will also assist in directing you to the right foods to help regain physical "weight" balance with your body, by releasing that which is not love. According to the epic Greek poet Homer, she is the divine exhalation of the earth. She will make your skin glow, your hair shiny, healthy, fast growing and glossy, and she nurtures babies in the womb. The Melissas are faeries who have passed down her traditions and take these gifts to lovers, and today the Goddess Temple in Glastonbury is run by beautiful helpers called Melissas.

Invoke your inner Ambrosia by:
☆ Offering a sincere compliment.
☆ Remembering that you are love.
☆ Drizzling honey on your toast – or on your lover's body.
☆ Giving yourself a honeymoon – even if it only lasts for an hour.
☆ Adding honey to your food, and using it as a treatment for any burns or wounds on a physical and an energetic level.

Morgan

As a faery, a human and a priestess who dwelled in Camelot and in Avalon, and as a shapeshifter, and one who could speak with the spirits, Morgan la Fey is about communication between your aspects of self. She is Priestess, Lover, Sister, Mother, Mentor, Rebel, Politician and Diplomat, so she is able to help you express what needs to be said in balanced and thoughtful ways, or in passionate, stirring ways if you need to inspire people.

Of faery and human blood, Morgan exists now dimensionally, still coming through in her bloodline in human form. Morgan is about speaking your truth, and speaking from an empowered, clear and diplomatic place. She is the antidote to the "what do I say?" moments. It is important to work with her when you are struggling to find the right way to work through a situation.

Morgan usually appears as a small, dark-skinned and dark-haired woman, but she is very able to work with glamour – the art of the subtle alteration of appearance. And so she can increase her height and her size, and even change her hair and eye colour. She is a grail keeper, and is able to bring you that which you thirst for, and help you drink the knowledge of the sacred red and white springs of Avalon, which are your bloodline and your spiritual lives and ancestry, often known as past lives.

Morgan means "woman of the sea", and so she is also associated with salt water, oceans, waves and deep knowledge – and can increase your ability to communicate about this, without becoming overwhelmed and unsure of what to say. She has a beautiful voice, and can help you to find yours too.

Call on Morgan for: Connecting with your voice, overcoming the fear of speaking up, speeches and writing, being able to communicate in many different situations, loving to communicate and being understood, and having a presence or charisma when you have something important to share. She can help you avoid choking up with emotion, deal with PR-related activities and heal wounds caused by words. Your words hold magic, and work spells, simply in the tone and the style you choose to speak in, so be aware!

Invoke your inner Morgan by:
☆ Speaking with gentle clarity and power.
☆ Remembering that you know what to say, as you have said the words before.
☆ Singing out loud, for the sheer joy of it.
☆ Relaxing your jaw, breathing deeply, making sound.
☆ Expressing your anger and fury by taking yourself somewhere safe, and allowing the rage to be sung through you until you feel calm and centred again. And never allowing it to stay within you – always letting it move through and be released.

Mab

Queen Mab (Maedbh or Maeve) is an Irish faery queen who is very much a protector of the ancient ways. She has the gift of the Sight, which she learned and worked with from the druidess Fidelma, and has foreseen much of what is to happen. She gifts certain humans with the Sight so they can become helpers of faery kind and of humanity too, for our fate is interwoven. Many say she is the energetic blueprint for the Irish Queen Maeve, a warrior queen who ruled fiercely, who was a great beauty with a lusty appetite for handsome young men, and an intoxicating woman of great power.

But this faery queen Mab is older and deeper than the legends of Maeve and her real-life historical counterpart. Because of her influence and power, and ability to lift the veils between past, present and future, and see between the dimensional worlds and warn us of consequences, Mab is often seen as quite dark. Perhaps it is rather that she has seen the possibility of disaster unfolding, tells us the truth, and is doing all she can to help humanity and faery kind through to the next stage of our evolution. Mab often works with dragonfae beings, and has incredible gifts of clairvoyance (clear seeing), clairsentience (clear feeling), claircognisance (clear knowing), clairaudience (clear hearing) and even clairgustance (clear taste). Work with her when you wish to develop any of these senses, but most especially your Sight and your knowing.

Call on Mab for: Knowing the implications of present action for seven generations forward and back from the present moment, and learning more of what the fae would have us do. Also if you wish to develop your gift of foresight, and to tune in and tune up your clairvoyance in particular. She is a wonderful guide through the magical world, and helps creative people send their message through poetry, song, writing and even films. She is a queen of glamour, and can help you develop that faery gift too.

Invoke your inner Mab by:
☆ Allowing your Sight to show you the faeries.
☆ Scrying using water, sky, fire or crystals.
☆ Using your favourite oracle or tarot cards, and allowing the images to become doorways that open into the Otherworld.
☆ Seeing, with your physical eyes closed, the invisible world.

Lady Viviane

Viviane is one of the great Ladies of the Lake of Inis Witrin, or Avalon, who incarnates through many beings, and whose energy is found within the landscape at certain sacred sites, most particularly where water meets land. These places, known as liminal sites, are where the Lady Viviane can come forth.

Her domain and her gift is Unity, and helping us to understand that the borders between worlds are not so vast and great as we would think. She is a rainbow bridge between worlds – life and death, us and them, men and women, fae and human – showing that all our differences can be loved and appreciated, not used to divide and create hatred, when her magic and energy is present.

Lady Viviane's ancestry is Palaeolithic, dating back to the last Ice Age. When the melting of the ice sheets began, and the land was divided from the water, there she was, at this birth of the warm world. She works with water, crystals and lineages of sacred women. She also appears to wizards, such as the great druid leader and wizard Merlin, as a lover and bearer of future children carrying faery blood. Other legends say she hearkens back to Atlantis and even further into the past, to the days of Lemuria, where the watery world met the land and we first went between both worlds.

Viviane often appears as a very tall, slender, quite regal woman. She is almost godmotherly, grandmotherly, and although she appears ageless, her energy abounds with infinite wisdom and deep, true kindness. She is a fair and just judge, and is a wonderful being to seek assistance from with issues regarding boundaries and spaces. Yet she simultaneously helps us feels united and infinite, and creates common ground with others who may appear to be different to us with our sometimes limited consciousness.

Call on Viviane for: Help when you must decide what belongs to you, what is your responsibility and when there are issues of justice. She can also assist when you are looking for the right place to live, for easing flood or drought, for staying safe and "hidden" if you are feeling endangered, and for finding a wise mentor and teacher.

Invoke your inner Viviane by:
☆ Seeing the pattern behind the world.
☆ Allowing the cosmic web of life (or wyrd) to be revealed.
☆ Connecting with someone who seems different to you.
☆ Remembering that we are all infinite aspects of One.

Whether you have never been to Faeryland and are longing to, or you are a regular visitor with a personal and strong relationship with a faery king or queen, be sure to remember to give thanks for all the signs you receive from the faeries. Eating delicious foods, breathing and sleeping well, respecting and engaging with our vivid dreams, and making time for spontaneous fun, play and entertainment, are all ways in which the realms, courts and royalty of these magical beings include us, and bring us great blessings each and every day of our lives.

Lady Amaranth's Faery Magic

Fantasy model Lady Amaranth aims to create whole worlds through the medium of photography. She has worked as a model for many gothic and fantasy clothes designers, and appeared in several international magazines. Through her work she wants to create beauty that will not fade with time, to capture a grain of sand before it falls and the moment has passed. She is also a writer, promoter and web designer, and brings a sense of beauty to everything she does. She grew up in South Africa, but returned home to the UK as an adult, and now lives in London. You can find her little piece of the web at www.LadyAmaranth.com.

I discovered faeries when I was very young. I was an indigo child living in a world of my own creation. At a young age, where everything is inexplicable, the impossible can be your reality. I chose to build my reality with the strands of dreams, and wove into it the beautiful creatures that filled my story books. Growing up in a little town in South Africa, where I spent most of my childhood barefoot amongst the tall grasslands, these faery folk played alongside me. I loved nature, and the freedom I felt when immersed in it, along with the pulse of the natural world beneath my feet and within my grasp, was personified by these beings.

Today I believe in the fae metaphorically, not literally. I believe in energies, in manifestations of spirit which can reside in nature. But these are more felt and "known" than visual materialisations of the little winged beings. Sadly the cold, harsh reality of adult life has cut my ties to the faery realm, and no matter how many times I try to reclaim them, the cynical adult in me laughs at my folly. It is for that reason that I choose to adorn my life with the beauty and mystery of goth and the fantasy of enchantment. Each time I create a character for a photo shoot, I let my inner child run riot, and

Photo © Gothicindulgence.

remember the beauty and wonder of untainted eyes.

Yet the faeries inspire my work in almost every aspect. The Otherworld is what drives me to create, to bring its beauty to the fore, in an otherwise mundane world. I love the mystery and magic that it promises. It takes me back to when I was running through that long grass and seeing shapes in the shadows, back to the age of innocence and wonder.

I connect with that memory through my photo shoots. Each one is different. For some it's the character that is the impetus, and in that case I'll research the myths and legends surrounding them, gather the tools, clothing and props to get a better feel for them, and immerse myself as one would do if acting out the part. If it's a location that inspires me, I'll visit on a quiet day so I can feel it envelop me, and understand the vibrations of the place and what it is that will complement them.

I've learned through doing this work that not everything is as it seems, and you shouldn't take things for granted. That life is not what you are told it is, but how you choose to interpret it. That everything has a magic and a story of its own, from nature's wonder to man-made grandeur and every stage of decay in-between. And also that beauty is not always obvious, but it's there for those who want to find it.

I think we need faeries today so we can reconnect with our own innocence and bring beauty back into our lives. But beauty not only as one may think it – the external, surface beauty – but a lightness within ourselves and all things, that glowing faery dust that lifts our soul and enchants all that it touches.

Faery Places

"Enchanted worlds still exist because the child within us never dies.
The doorways may be more obscure, but we can still seek them out.
There are still trees that speak and caverns that lead to nether realms.
There will always be faeries and elves within nature because they
will always be dancing within our hearts."
Ted Andrews, American author and mystic

Sacred and Magical Faery Sites

As the spirits of nature, faeries are associated with the wild and
untamed places of our world – ancient woodlands, tropical
rainforests, undisturbed lakes and streams, sacred springs, tangles
of hedgerow and native flowers, bluebell-strewn meadows, moss-
covered stones and ivy-clad oaks, national parks and vast deserts.

The lush countryside of the British Isles is inextricably linked
with these magical beings, for so much of it looks just like what
we picture a faery's home to be. Misty hills and ancient stone
circles. Barrow mounds and cairns, which have long been
considered entrances to Faeryland. Beautiful old trees and sacred
wells, which have become linked with the fae through the tradition
of wishing trees and cloutie wells, where people tie pieces of cloth
or ribbon and leave offerings to seek blessings of the Otherworldly
beings who inhabit these sites.

Then there are the in-between places associated with the fae
through myth and legend – at the crossroads where two paths
intersect, on riverbanks and seashores where earth and water meet,

and on small islands where you must cross over through the mists to reach them – and any other dimension that lurks there – such as the sacred isle of Avalon. Even in cities and towns though there are faery sites, from parklands, beaches and harbours to beautiful Botanic Gardens, ancient trees, and even your own backyard.

There are countless places, and ways, to connect with nature and the fae, no matter where you live. Yet there are also specific sites from around the world that have become closely linked with the enchantment of Faeryland. Of course there are many more – your relationship with nature and the faery realm can make any place magical – but here are a few of the most well-known...

Glastonbury, England

The pretty town of Glastonbury in southwest England, also known as the enchanted Isle of Avalon, is a place of deep magic. Home to the priestesses and druids of old, the sacred oak trees Gog and Magog and an ancient holy well, it is centred around the Tor, a huge grassy hill that has been described as a faery mound, magic mountain, grail castle, land of the dead and gateway to Annwn, the Otherworld ruled over by the faery king Gwyn ap Nudd. Many tales recount his adventures, as well as those of the humans who feast and frolic within his walls beneath the Tor, returning home years later either full of wisdom or driven to madness by their time in his realm. When Christianity came to England a church was built on top of this faery hill to close the entrance to Faeryland, but an earthquake destroyed it, and today only a small tower remains.

The landscape of the Tor and its surrounding apple orchards, water meadows and wild flowers is so hauntingly beautiful and lush, just like you'd picture the land of the fae to be. At the base of the Tor is Chalice Well and its spectacular gardens, watered by the sacred spring and full of vivid colours, cute little creatures and nature spirits you can tangibly sense. Glastonbury is also the home of Morgan la Fey (Morgaine of the Faeries), an enchanted being who lived in Avalon, which could only be reached by crossing the surrounding waters and being able to part the mists of this Otherworld dimension to reach its heart. Even today, with the waters long gone, some people can pierce through the mists and catch a glimpse of this magical realm.

Cornwall, England

In the southwest of England is an ancient place of shadows and mists, where Otherworldly beings seem closer to the surface and a belief in faeries is common. Cornwall, on a peninsula that juts dramatically into the wild ocean, is the mythical birthplace of both King Arthur and Merlin the Magician, and is still considered by many residents to be separate from England, one of the Celtic nations – along with Wales, Ireland, Scotland, the Isle of Man and Brittany – with its own identity, Celtic language and culture.

There are many stone circles and ancient burial mounds, long believed to be entrances to Faeryland, and people still make offerings to the nature spirits at the sacred wells of Madron and Sancreed, both beautiful, peaceful sites. At Sancreed the well is deep within Mother Earth, reached by descending a series of stone steps, while at Madron the well is above ground, a pretty spring with a ruined chapel nearby. Both wells are shaded by a wishing tree, where clouties, small strips of cloth and ribbon, are tied to the branches to pay homage to the faeries and request from them love, healing and wealth.

Cumbria, England

The region of Cumbria, in the northwest of England, is a desolate yet beautiful area that encompasses Lake District National Park, one of the prettiest parts of England. The Hardknott Pass, which winds between dramatic mountains, is overlooked by Mediobogdum, an old Roman fort that was reputedly built over the site of a faery kingdom that still remains in an Otherworld dimension imposed over the "real" land. Outside the town of Cockermouth is Elva Hill, which has long been associated with the faeries, and the remains of a late Neolithic stone circle. This region boasts many beautiful, powerful stone circles, including Long Meg and her Daughters.

Nearby is the Castle Rock of Triermain, which from a distance looks like a ruined castle, but up close is revealed as a craggy outcrop on a hillside. According to legend it was once a castle where King Arthur and his faery wife Gwenhyfar stayed with their fae friends. And in Beetham there's a set of steep, narrow steps carved in a hill, and it's said that anyone who can climb these faery stairs without touching the sides will have their heart's desire granted by the fae.

Findhorn, Scotland

In northeast Scotland, not far from Inverness and its Loch Ness Monster, is the spiritual community and ecovillage of Findhorn, which began as a commune in the 1960s. It gained international attention when founders Peter and Eileen Caddy and their friend Dorothy Maclean claimed that it was their communications with plant spirits, called faeries or devas by some, that allowed them to grow lush gardens with larger than normal vegetables (20kg cabbages instead of 2kg) and tropical plants not native to the area, despite the stormy, bleak weather and barren, sandy soil.

They discarded common gardening principles and instead asked the plants what they needed, communicating telepathically with the spirit of each one to discover how far apart to sow their seeds, when to prune them, how often to water, and the way to merge their own energy with the plant's to improve its growth. Today you can visit the community, which has the lowest ecological footprint in the industrial world, or stay there for retreats and workshops.

Aberfoyle, Scotland

The village of Aberfoyle, northwest of Glasgow, lies on the banks of the Laggan River in the shadow of Craigmore mountain, a liminal place with an air of mystery and tranquillity. It is known as the main faery site in Scotland because of its association with Reverend Robert Kirk, who was born there in 1644. He was the minister of the town, yet he also wrote about the enchanted realm, and he used to walk every day to nearby Doon Hill, also known as Fairy Knowe, which has been considered a faery hill for centuries, and which the reverend claimed was a portal to Faeryland.

Pilgrims today climb the hill and tie ribbons or pieces of white silk on the branches of the largest pine tree, to implore the fae for their wishes to be granted. Some also run around the tree seven times in the hope that the faeries will appear to them. Robert's grave is in the church grounds, yet according to legend his spirit is contained in the tallest pine atop his beloved faery hill.

Aberfoyle, now a forestry village, was also a favourite place of Mary Queen of Scots, who spent time at the nearby Inchmahome Priory as a child, and returned there regularly during her royal reign in the 1540s. The publication of Sir Walter Scott's poem *The Lady of the Lake* in 1810 also increased the number of visitors to this beautiful region. Faery hills dot the Scottish countryside – look at the place names on any map, and if you see anything containing the words "sithean", "sidhein" or "sith", it is likely to be a grassy mound, knoll or hill that is associated with the faeries.

The Isle of Man

This small island in the Irish Sea, located between England, Wales, Scotland and Ireland yet not part of the UK, is made up of rolling countryside, rugged cliffs, ancient megaliths and hidden coves. There are lush glens too, with clear waterfalls, deep rock pools, bluebell meadows and pretty woodlands. It has a long tradition of faeries, who are referred to here as the Little Folk or Themselves.

On Castletown Road on the east coast is Fairy Bridge, where locals say hello to the faeries who live under it before crossing, for fear they'll cause accidents if they are scorned. Some taxi drivers have even been known to refuse to take a person across it if they don't politely greet the fae. Spanning Middle River is Real Fairy Bridge, which has similar superstitions attached to it. There is also a strong belief in bugganes, ogre-like creatures that live underground and have been reported to punish people on behalf of the faeries, glashtyns, handsome men who shapeshift into water horses and drag girls out to sea to drown them, and a ghostly black dog that has long haunted Peel Castle, itself said by some to be the site of the Arthurian Avalon.

Llyn y Fan Fach, Wales

In a dramatic valley of the Black Mountain in Carmarthenshire, Wales, in the Brecon Beacons National Park, is beautiful Llyn y Fan Fach, a magical lake long associated with the fae. Legend tells of a beautiful faery woman who lived with her kin in an enchanted realm beneath its dark waters. One day she met a local man who fell in love with her, and they were allowed to marry on the condition that she would return to her underwater home if he hit her three times.

They lived together happily for many years, and had three beloved sons, but one day the man patted his faery wife on the back

to hurry her along, a year later he tapped
her on the shoulder to stop her crying at a
wedding, and finally he tapped her a third
time to stop her laughing at a funeral –
at which point she left forever. Yet she
often visited her sons, teaching them all
her healing lore, and they later became
known as the Physicians of Myddfai,
renowned for healing with faery skill.

The Emerald Isle

Ireland has long been associated with magical creatures, from
powerful deities to faeries, leprechauns, nature sprites and
elementals, who flit through the forests and dance in the sunshine
and the rain, sometimes helping humanity, sometimes playing tricks
on them. Legends tell of fiery, feisty faery tribes, such as the Fir
Bolg, the Daoine Sidhe and the enchanted Tuatha de Danaan, who
inhabited this magical land long before humans arrived, and
who are said to still live within its ancient mounds and forests.

There are round banked enclosures known as raths or faery forts
scattered around the country, and the fae are thought to have
constructed temples such as the Dingle Diamond in the hills of the
Dingle Peninsula, a stone structure aligned with the summer solstice
sunrise to recreate the mystical marriage of sun and earth that
occurs on that day. Ireland's ancient monuments are often associated
with the fae, and many are said to be portals to their realm, where
they withdrew when they could no longer deal with humans.

Grange Stone Circle, County Limerick

The largest and one of the most beautiful stone circles in Ireland is
Lios na Grainsi, the Stones of the Sun, near Loch Gur just south of
Limerick. It's known as the Fort of the Faeries, and is believed to be
a gateway to the Otherworld. It's made up of 113 stones, all
touching, with the biggest one standing more than four metres high
and weighing 40 tonnes. Twelve of these massive stones are
distributed at key points around the circle, with two of them
flanking the imposing entranceway on the northeast side.

A narrow, stone-lined passage leads to a break in the surrounding embankment, where two guardian stones stand, opening up to the richly fragrant, lush grassy circle within. One pair of stones and the entranceway are aligned with sunset on the cross-quarter day of Samhain, which falls in early November in Ireland, and another is aligned with sunrise on the summer solstice – the feast of the faeries. On this morning the sunlight streams through to illuminate the exact centre of the circle, but on any day it is magical, whether it's sparkling with dancing sunbeams or shrouded in cold, swirling mist.

Maeve's Cairn, County Sligo

Another Otherworld place is Maeve's Cairn atop the sacred mountain of Knocknarea, also known as the Hill of the Moon. This northwest region is WB Yeats country, a beautiful, dramatic landscape of green mountains, black lakes and wild ocean, a perfect faery realm. Maeve's enormous mountaintop cairn – a mound of stones piled up as a memorial over a stone burial chamber – is 55 metres in diameter by 10 metres high, and dates back to 4000BCE. It's said to be the legendary resting place of Maeve, who is variously Mab, queen of the faeries, Queen Maeve, the Irish warrior queen, or Maedbh/Maeve the goddess, embodiment of the land and fertility.

It is covered in stones of varying sizes, as people traditionally bring one on their pilgrimage up the hill and add it to the pile when they reach the top, as an offering to Maeve to request luck and love. On a clear day you can see the cairn from down below in Sligo town as a bump on top of the hill, but on other days, when the thick rain is falling or the misty fog is swirling, you can climb the hill and stumble on the tomb itself before catching a glimpse. It's so mysterious and mystical and Otherworldly up there, as though a space between the worlds has opened up and you can enter this other dimension.

Further south is Knocknashee, a massive limestone plateau known as the Hill of the Faeries, similar to Knocknarea in geology, shape and mysterious, magical atmosphere. And at the bottom of the hill is Carrowmore megalithic cemetery, constructed circa 4000BCE, which is also a place of magic. It's a field of stone circles, ancient burial mounds, passage tombs, dolmens and yellow buttercups, all laid out in a spiral pattern, with most of the sites pointing to a giant dolmen – some think it's a portal – in the centre.

Glendalough, County Wicklow

South of Dublin, nestled in the Wicklow Mountains, is the valley of Glendalough, meaning Glen of Two Lakes. It's renowned for its well-preserved medieval monastic settlement, which was founded in the sixth century by the hermit priest Kevin, who lived in a cave above the lake and was later canonised. But it was sacred in Celtic times too, and has long been considered a place of faeries. Farmers used to drive their cattle through the lakes at Beltane in a purification ritual, and there are also stories of a peist, or worm creature, living in the lakes, which indicates leys of earth energy running through the site.

Today Glendalough is also popular for its breathtaking beauty. Hiking trails criss-cross the area so people can enjoy the forests, river and lakes, and the Glendalough Oakwoods, a forest of old oaks with an understorey of holly, hazel and mountain ash that's carpeted with bluebells, wood sorrel and anemones, is also aligned with the fae.

Hill of Tara, County Meath

Northwest of Dublin is one of Ireland's most sacred sites, long associated with its high kings and royalty as well as with Otherworld beings. The beautiful grassy landscape, dotted with earthworks, mounds and ceremonial enclosures, has a magical, mysterious air to it, and a weight of history that adds atmosphere and power.

The small Neolithic passage tomb known as the Mound of the Hostages, with its tiny gated entrance into the mound of earth, looks like a faery place – the kind the Tuatha de Danaan are believed to have retreated to. It's aligned to sunrise at Samhain and Imbolc, the first days of winter and spring, so it has layers of magical significance.

Also within this archaeological complex is a hill fort surrounding two ring forts, and the Lia Fail, the Stone of Destiny, a one-metre-high standing stone considered by some to be a fertility symbol, and others a part of the inauguration of the high kings – according to legend, if the ruler was worthy the stone would roar its approval. There is also a faery tree and two wells with Otherworld connotations.

In the *Artemis Fowl* book series the Hill of Tara is used as a travelling point by the faeries, and in OR Melling's enchanting *Chronicles of Faerie* novels, two girls sleep within the Mound of the Hostages in the hope that it will act as a doorway to Faeryland.

Navan, Northern Ireland

Across the border in Northern Ireland is the ancient monument of Navan Fort, a ceremonial area atop a beautiful hill in gorgeous wooded countryside, located in County Armagh. Once known as Emain Macha, the seat of the kings of Ulster, it was the spiritual, political and cultural centre of its day, and remains a magical, mystical pagan place today. Sacred since 5000BCE, this massive circular earthwork and its holy pool has similarities to the Hill of Tara and Glastonbury Tor. You can still see the indentation in the very centre of the mound where a massive oak pole once stood, which linked the Otherworld with the earth plane and the heavens, a faery tree of sorts. Navan is one of Ireland's oldest and most significant sites, although it's far less visited than those south of the border.

Also in Northern Ireland are the Beaghmore Stone Circles, a Bronze Age complex of seven circles, each with its own cairn and stone row, nestled in the glorious Sperrin Mountains of County Tyrone. They record the movements of the sun and moon and mark particular lunar, solar and stellar events, with three of the stone rows pointing to sunrise at the summer solstice, and another aligned to moonrise. The whole site used to be surrounded by faery forests of oak, rowan, birch and hazel, although now it's all fields.

Australia

The land Down Under is a huge country, and there are many places that have become entwined with the fae. In the Blue Mountains west of Sydney, particularly around Leura, the bushland is wild and untamed, with beautiful waterfalls and crystal clear streams, tangled undergrowth and a powerful, tangible earth energy. In Sydney itself there is Nutcote, the beautiful harbourside home of May Gibbs, author and artist of the magical Snugglepot and Cuddlepie books. The garden, which runs down the hill to the harbour, is filled with beautiful flowers and native shrubs, hedges shaped like caterpillars and statues of gumnut babies and banksia men.

Tamborine Mountain, inland from Queensland's Sunshine Coast, is another magical place, with its waterholes and leylines, and Tasmania and Western Australia are also filled with lush rainforests and national parks that would perfectly suit the fae.

New Zealand

Beautiful New Zealand is filled with faery sites, as the world discovered when it became the location of the *Lord of the Rings* films, with its dramatic mountain peaks, grassy hobbit mounds and mysterious woodlands of the elven folk. There are acres and acres of ancient forests, and due to its geographical isolation, many kinds of trees that don't grow anywhere else on earth.

In the centre of the North Island there are lush fern tree forests, as well as dramatic Tongariro National Park, with its ancient Maori sites and faery forests, and mist-shrouded Ngongotaha, known to the Maoris as a faery mountain, which overlooks beautiful Rotorua Lake and is reputed to be the home of a race of supernatural beings. On the Coromandel Peninsula and in Northland there are amazing old-growth kauri forests, and in the south there are gorgeous expanses of beech trees and other nature spots, which were the location of Rivendell, the Gardens of Isengard, Buckland Forest, Helms Deep and Lothlorien in the movies.

Across the top of the South Island is breathtaking Kahurangi National Park, Kahurangi meaning "treasured possession". And in the south, Fjordland National Park stretches inland from the jagged coastline, with miles and miles of undisturbed virgin bushland, beautiful hiking trails and a magical atmosphere, which made it the perfect location for some scenes in *LOTR*'s Fangorn Forest. Nearby is Takitimu, also considered a faery mountain, with its legends of the Wee Folk who have resided there for centuries.

Ha Tien, Vietnam

The tropical country of Vietnam consists of hills, densely forested mountains and miles of coastline. On a beautiful beach in the southwest, near the border with Cambodia, is a remote town called Ha Tien, which translates as "Faeries' River Abode". It is so named because of the legend that every full moon, the faeries come to the Ho Dong lake to dance and bathe. Ha Tien is a beautiful old town, boasting several weathered temples, crystal clear beaches and colourful markets, and surrounded by green rice fields, jagged limestone outcrops dotted with pretty caves and grottoes, waving sugar palms and sacred mountain peaks on the horizon.

Broceliande Forest, France

In Brittany in western France, near historic Rennes and not far from the stone alignments of Carnac, lies mythical Broceliande Forest, home to the legends of King Arthur and the Lady of the Lake. The beautiful forest, filled with lush beeches and oaks up to a thousand years old, is a place of magic and mystery, filled with enchantments and trees that whisper in the wind. Parts of it are said to have been bewitched by Morgaine of the Faeries, particularly the dramatic Val sans Retour (Valley of No Return), where she imprisoned any knights who came by in revenge for her broken heart.

There are many magical locations within the forest, which is called Paimpont on maps – the lake called the Mirror of the Faeries, where the Lady of the Lake resides; the tomb of Merlin the Magician, where ribbons, flowers and baby booties are tied; Viviane's Fountain of Eternal Youth, which promises immortality to those who drink from it; the castle of the Lady of the Lake; and the Arbre d'Or, the golden tree, a huge chestnut covered entirely in fine gold.

Delphi, Greece

Beautiful, mystical Mount Parnassus in central Greece was home to the Corycian nymphs, three faery sisters named Corycia, Kleodora and Melaina, who embodied the spirit of nature and place, and were associated with the Muses of love and inspiration. Corycia gives her name to the sacred Corycian Cave and its healing spring, which nestles in the woodlands and rocky crags of the southern slope of the mountain, and was also at one time a place of worship for the nature spirit Pan.

According to legend, the union of Kleodora and the god Poseidon resulted in a son named Parnassos, who founded the city of Parnassus and gave his name to the mountain where his mother lived. And Melaina had a child with the god Apollo, that she named Delphos, who some believe is linked with the town of Delphi. Once considered the centre of the world, today Delphi remains a sacred site with spiritual and magical importance. It was the location of the Oracle of Delphi, the most important oracle in the ancient world, and the Temples of Apollo and Athena, which today, even in their ruined state, still have a power and presence that touches the heart.

The Black Forest, Germany

The home of so many faerytales, as well as the famous Black Forest chocolate cake, this stunning wooded mountain range has long been rumoured to host a race of faeries and elves. Covering the southwest of Germany, the trees in this sprawling ancient forest grow so closely together that they block out the sun, hence the name. Within its borders are mountains and valleys, tiny thatched-roof villages, wide rivers and gentle streams, wineries, mineral springs and health spas, and a body of enchanting folklore recorded by the Brothers Grimm.

Stretching 200km long and 60km wide, the forest is made up of oak and beech woods on the lower slopes, with fir and pine taking over higher up, their heavenly scent lifting the spirits and cleansing the soul. Thousands of miles of long-distance trails wind beneath the trees, through the valleys and around the glittering bodies of water, perfect for walkers, horse riders and the faery folk.

Iceland

One of the most remote places in the world, Iceland is a small but dramatic island in the North Atlantic Ocean, just south of the Arctic Circle. It's punctuated by spectacular fjords along its coastline, and has several active, energetic volcanoes and geysers. Its people are influenced by its Norse heritage, and although much of the land is covered by snow, ice or sand, and the forests are few and far between, there is still a long tradition of faeries.

A large part of the population today still believes in elves, lovelings, gnomes, dwarves and other huldufolk (hidden people), which are thought to live under stones and rocks, inside caves, on craggy hillsides or in the beautiful fly agaric mushrooms, the big red ones with white spots that have inspired faerytale writers and artists for centuries. There's even an elf school, Alfaskolinn, in the capital city of Reykjavik, which teaches students and visitors about these enchanted beings and the qualities of each different type of huldufolk.

Mount Shasta, California, USA

Described as California's Mystic Mountain, Mount Shasta is considered a spiritual hub and the home of everything from aliens and ancient Lemurians to faeries. Peter Caddy, co-founder of Findhorn in Scotland, later moved to Mount Shasta and began a teaching centre there. Several people claim to have seen beings going in and out of the caverns in the mountain, and one woman reported watching 11 tiny blue faeries dancing in a clearing at dusk.

"They were perhaps one foot tall, and seemingly transparent. The blue colour was electric, seeming to pulsate or flicker, the wings were larger than the faery bodies themselves and were delicate and lacy," she said. As well as being incredibly beautiful, with miles of forest, lakes and mountain trails, the area of Mount Shasta also includes pretty Faery Falls near Lake Siskiyou.

Perelandra, Virginia, USA

An hour's drive southwest of Washington DC, in the foothills of Virginia's Blue Ridge Mountains, are the beautiful, mysterious gardens of Perelandra, a centre for nature research named for the CS Lewis fantasy book. This gorgeous energy garden, surrounded by open fields, woods and streams that help protect and amplify the magic within, is made up of eighteen concentric circles of herbs, vegies and flowers, all radiating outwards from a giant quartz crystal. No chemical or organic repellents are used, yet the plants flourish, there are never pest problems, and visitors claim that even the moles that live in the area do as they're asked.

Owner Machaelle Wright says she started working with nature in a conscious way in the mid-70s, when she began communing with the nature spirits of the land in a similar way to those at Findhorn. She attributes the success of the garden to a co-creative process between herself, nature spirits (faeries) and devas (angelic forms), and her ability to communicate with each plant spirit to discover how best to tend it. Perelandra is rarely open to the public, but occasional classes and workshops are held there, and you can ask questions through their website (www.perelandra-ltd.com), see photos, order their healing plant essences, books and other products, and sign up for the newsletter.

Kauai, Hawaii, USA

Like Ireland, where the faeries were driven deep into the forests and the mounds of the earth, hidden from mortal view, Hawaii also has a legend of Little People with magical powers. The menehune, who've been likened to leprechauns, once lived throughout the island chain, but were chased to Kauai, the most northern and most isolated of the main islands, by people and progress. All of the Hawaiian islands are beautiful, lush and full of magic, but Kauai, known as the Garden Isle, has a sparser population and is treasured for its tropical greenery and unspoiled, sparkling golden beaches.

Waimea Canyon in particular seems to be a place of the fae, with its thick, lush forests and deep valleys, and a primal energy that weaves around everyone who enters. The huge Alekoko Fishpond, the island's largest aquaculture reservoir, is also associated with the menehune, who are believed to have built the 300-metre-long dam in a single night, by the light of the moon, for a royal couple who were turned to stone when they couldn't resist peeking at their magical friends. The menehune are also thought to have built a number of heiaus, the old stone temple platforms dedicated to the Hawaiian gods.

Fairyland, wherever you are

And then there's Fairyland, a Facebook application where you create your own virtual faery garden. You and your faery alter-ego grow a variety of herbs, which you use to create healing elixirs, as well as beautiful flowers that bloom into bees, butterflies, peace doves, hearts or planets. The real-life faeries in this realm water each other's gardens, help new faeries with tips and advice, and leave out platters of food to entice dragons, unicorns, rabbits, birds and endangered animals to visit and be spotted by their friends.

In addition to making beautiful friends from around the world, spending time in Fairyland also supports Nature Conservancy (www.nature.org), as each plant you harvest online contributes to ad dollars going to the organisation, which protects ecologically important areas for nature and people, has saved more than 120 million acres of land and 8000 kilometres of rivers worldwide, and operates more than 100 marine conservation projects globally.

Karen's Faery Magic

Karen Kay is the editor-in-chief of the UK's *FAE* magazine, and has worked for the BBC and environmental publications. She's been a punk singer and session vocalist, and is now pursuing her own music, as well as producing meditation CDs and film scores with her partner Michael Tingle. Karen is based in Penzance, in England's beautiful, mystical Cornwall, and is the founder of the 3 Wishes Faery Festival and the Faery Ball. You can visit her, and find links to all her magical projects, at www.KarenKay.co.uk.

I don't think that I discovered faeries – I think faeries discovered me! And they thought: "Here's someone who will do our work and raise our profile in the human realm!" On a more serious note, I was first introduced to the faery realms by my grandmother Chris. She loved flowers, especially roses, and we spent many an afternoon wandering around her beautiful garden enjoying the fragrances and colours of the roses. That was my first connection with the flower faeries. I used to collect the rose petals and make faery perfume at a very young age. And when I was about 15 I got a tattoo of a faery on my shoulder, and she has been watching over me for my entire life.

I find it quite easy to connect with the faeries, as they are only a thought away. I can connect with them wherever I am, whether it's in my office, in the garden or when I'm relaxing in a nice hot bath. I'm also receptive to their communication with me, although it often tends to be on their terms.

However, you do have to take control sometimes, otherwise they'll have you running around in circles. They don't really understand the constraints of the human realm, so I often have to explain to them that, being half-human, I can only do so much in a day. Having said that, they often keep me up working through the night too!

Photo © Lee Searle.

One of the most important things to do when attempting to communicate with the fae is to be open-hearted and to keep your intent pure. You cannot fool the faeries, for they can read your true intentions. I would say I definitely have a heart connection with them.

The relationship between faeries and humans, I believe, is symbiotic. We need them as they are the guardians of the land, the plants, trees and flowers. And the faeries need humans to help them on a practical level, picking up litter, planting seeds, saving trees. The beauty of working with the faeries is that magic really does come into your life if you let it.

I tend not to use the word "believe" when referring to faeries, because belief implies that they may not exist, whereas if you "know" they exist it becomes a reality. For me faeries are real – quite simply, there is no doubt in my heart or mind that they are a very real race residing in another realm that coincides, and on occasion merges with, our own. Their work and role is integral to the wellbeing and continuation of our planet.

The faeries inspire me every day in my work as a magazine editor and event organiser. In fact, they inspire me in virtually every aspect of my life, not just work – which is really play for me. They often wake me up with wild and wonderful ideas, which I follow, and they bring magic and beauty into my life. My creativity is inspired by the faeries, and they will often plant bizarre ideas in my head, which more often than not end up being some of my best ideas.

Faeries and miracles go hand in hand, and some of the business opportunities that arise when following their advice are extraordinary. Their magic and love infuse my magazine, and it's a tangible thing, as everyone who reads it says they can literally feel the love contained on every page.

An A-Z of Magical Beings

"Did you ever hear, of the frolic fairies dear?
They're a blessed little race, peeping up in fancy's face.
In the valley, on the hill, by the fountain and the rill;
Laughing out between the leaves, that the loving summer weaves."
Frances Sargent Osgood, American poet

Faeries From Around the World

Throughout history and across cultures, from Africa and South America to China and Celtic Britain, people have connected with faery energy. Often these magical beings are a reflection of the landscape in which they manifest, while others have been taken across the seas with immigrants to a new home, and blended with the nature spirits of a new world. They've been recorded in faerytales and folklore, and while some have faded away in recent times, others have grown stronger in the telling. The faeries we picture – small, beautiful, human-like creatures all shiny and sparkly like Tinker Bell – are a fairly modern western concept. Other cultures have their own magical beings, some dark and malevolent, others kind and sweet. This is a guide to just some of the fae from around the world...

Abatwa: In southern Africa, tiny little creatures called abatwa ride ants, live in anthills and hide among blades of grass. According to legend they can only be seen by children, magicians and pregnant women – and if you do see one, you must claim to have first laid eyes on it from far away, as they are very sensitive about their size.

They are nomadic, shy and peaceful, and live in harmony with the ants – although if they're ever disturbed by humans, they are rumoured to retaliate by shooting them with poison arrows.

Aes Sidhe: The Irish faeries are known as the sidhe (pronounced shee) or the aes sidhe, which translates as "people of the mounds", referring to the earth mounds, ancient barrows and tumuli where these magical creatures reside. They're believed to be the remnants of the Tuatha de Danaan, the people of the goddess Dana, who came to Ireland long ago. They defeated the earlier inhabitants, the Fomorians and the Fir Bolgs, and prospered for some time, perfecting their magical arts. But when the Celts invaded they retreated from Ireland's earthly realm, choosing to live underground in the hollow hills and faery forts they're credited with constructing, out of sight of humans and shrouded by the mists of time and magic. Today these mounds, such as the monuments at Newgrange, are still considered by many to be portals to Faeryland.

Aguane: In the Austrian Alps and across northern Italy live the shapeshifting water faeries known as aguanes. They look like beautiful young women, yet have the feet of a horse. They are guardians of the rivers, lakes and streams, and challenge people wanting to cross these bodies of water. They love children, and are happy to carry them across and save them if they're drowning, but they are suspicious of men and neglectful mothers.

Alux: In the Yucatan Peninsula of Mexico and south into Guatemala, people still leave offerings for the alux (pronounced ah-loosh), the spirits of the ancient Mayan rainforests. Similar to the leprechauns of Ireland, they are small, dwarf-like beings, and although they can be enticed to protect homes or crops with offerings, they are associated with mischief and trickery too. There are also legends of the xtabai (sh-tah-bay), beautiful female spirits who live in cotton-silk trees and entice men into the forests with their song.

Alven: These water faeries of the Netherlands are protective nature spirits that live in lakes, ponds and rivers, and are associated with otters. They are tiny and almost transparent, and according to legend they don't have wings, so they travel in water bubbles.

Being of water they are also linked to the moon, and they love to dance under its silvery light. They are only cruel to humans if they threaten their home or try to destroy nature, especially the night-blooming flowers they adore.

Apsara: These beautiful Hindu and Buddhist water nymphs have been compared to the Muses of Ancient Greece, as they inspire scholars to new heights, and bestow blessings on people at weddings and other life stage ceremonies. Also known as sky dancers, they look after fallen heroes and guide them to the Otherworld, where they soothe their pain. But they have a darker side too, with similarities to the sirens who lure sailors into danger, playing songs on their lutes that can induce madness in those who hear them.

Aziza: These are the faeries of western Africa, who are referred to as the Little People by locals. They live in the forests and are associated with the earth, and although they are shy, they are believed to help people survive, providing good magic and luck to hunters, and imparting spiritual knowledge to those who invoke them.

Bean tighe: This magical Irish being is a kind of faery godmother/ housekeeper, who adopts a family and lives with them quietly and for the most part invisibly, helping the mother with her children and her chores, and overseeing the home. The bean tighe (pronounced banteeg) are gentle souls who love children and want to feel needed by their human family, and they dispense blessings, luck and care in return. Offerings of strawberries and cream were left out for them in the hope of enticing one into the home. Their sister faery is the bean sidhe (pronounced banshee), who wails in mourning when a member of their adopted family dies.

Befana: This old Italian faery loves children, and was traditionally thought to fly through the sky to give gifts to them at Midwinter, to fill them with hope and reassure them that summer would return again. Later she was depicted as a pagan witch-faery, who brought lumps of coal to naughty children and delivered sweets and treats to good ones. Her origin is interwoven not only with Santa Claus but with Befina, a Celtic faery who bestowed blessings and talents on each newborn baby, and predicted its future.

Boggart: These house faeries are not as helpful or pleasant as others of their kind, such as the brownie, and people dread having one take up residence in their home. They are small beings born of the peat bogs of old Europe, reputed to be bad tempered, wear dirty, wrinkled clothes and love to create mess and play tricks on people. They tip over jugs of milk, break crockery, throw food around, leave trails of dust, slam doors, turn out lights and tangle electrical cords. They also love to torment sleeping babies, pinching them until they wake up screaming, and to make dogs howl and cats hiss. In Ireland the boggles are also of the bogs, and they can cause grief to people through their child-like innocence and love of play.

Brownie: In Scotland these faeries are associated with leprechauns and hobgoblins. They are portrayed as small brown men who work around the home and in the barns and fields of farms in exchange for small gifts or food – porridge is a favourite. They live in a secret part of the house, appreciate their privacy and hate being seen, tending to work through the night when the household is asleep. They often attach themselves to one person in the family, who can confide their woes to the brownie and get good advice back. They dislike lies and cruelty, and may cause mischief if they are treated badly – and in extreme circumstances they can turn into a boggart.

Clurichaun: These solitary Irish faeries are wine-loving male creatures who take up residence in hotels, inns and wine cellars. They guard the contents of bottles and kegs from leakage, spoilage or theft, and are even thought to improve the taste, all in return for a small share of the contents. They bring luck and prosperity to any alehouse – but their merry demeanour vanishes if they feel mistreated, in which case they'll spoil the wine, make a huge mess or leave altogether, with nothing able to entice them to return. In other stories they are related to leprechauns, and have the power to shapeshift, travel in the blink of an eye and help humans.

Curupira: In Brasil, the faeries manifest as the curupira, male nature spirits who guard the Amazon rainforest and protect the animals from hunters who want to kill for sport. Likened to Pan through their relationship with the trees and their benevolent nature, they are eco faeries who assist all people to be more environmentally aware.

They have flaming red hair and wear green to blend in with the trees, and their feet are attached back to front to keep hunters off their trail. In the *BeastMaster* series a female curupira was the guardian of the wild beasts and gave sacred powers to the hero.

Dakini: In the Himalayas there is a group of Otherworld beings variously described as cloud faeries, sky dancers and celestial women, their name, dakini, means "she who traverses the sky". These winged manifestations of energy love to dance, and are believed to have magical powers. They are protective, and are considered by many to be a form of guardian spirit or faery godmother. They are often invoked to impart wisdom, lightness and joy.

Deva: In Persia, the devas are tiny faeries that appear as small spheres of light – their name means "shining one" in Sanskrit – but in the west they are the spirits of nature, which live in trees, lakes, flowers and other parts of the natural landscape. At Findhorn in Scotland they were defined as the very essence of each plant, which could communicate with people to let them know what their species required to flourish. Deva has also come to refer to a magical being similar to an angel, that is aware of human thoughts and can communicate with people telepathically to aid in enlightenment.

Djinn: In the Middle East, the djinn is an elemental of both fire and air, which can shapeshift from invisible to visible, and from serpent to human, and many things in between. In Persian tradition they live on Mount Kaf, the sacred mountain that is home to the gods. Elsewhere they live in an Otherworldly dimension, and can be invoked and manifested into our world, where, if trapped in a bottle, they can be summoned at will to do the bidding of their master. In the west they're immortalised as the genie of *Aladdin* – powerful, prophetic and able to grant wishes, but sneaky too, and very literal, requiring careful consideration of the phrasing of the wish.

Domovoi: These faeries bring good fortune in Russia and Slavic countries, where it's believed that every home has its own domovoi, a house spirit that takes on the appearance of the owner and works while the family sleeps so no one suspects it's a supernatural being. They are the guardian of the home, helping with chores, spreading good fortune, maintaining peace within the family and acting as an oracle. They are kept happy with offerings of milk and cookies, and live in the kitchen, often behind the stove. If a family moves house, they usually invite their domovoi to go with them.

Dryad: In Greek mythology the dryads are the wood nymphs who live in the wild forests and protect nature and the earth. They are closely related to hammadryads, whose lives are intrinsically tied to the tree they dwell within, and who die if it is chopped down. Dryad comes from the Greek word "drys", meaning oak. In the Celtic lands dryads are considered the life force of the trees, particularly those sacred to the druids, such as oak, thorn and ash. They are beautiful, ethereal faeries, wispy and insubstantial, elementals of the air who encourage people to protect the natural environment.

Duende: Throughout Spain, South America and many of the Spanish-speaking nations around the world, duende describes a sprite or other faery-like being, similar to brownies and leprechauns. The legends speak of short men who act as protectors of the forests (and sometimes turn sinister, luring young girls into the woods), as well as small women who live in households, cleaning the home, doing chores and occasionally getting up to mischief there.

Shhh! Faery Secret

Some help with household chores, but you must set a good example and acknowledge their help – faeries work with us best when praised, given lots of attention and love, and helpful suggestions on how to improve.

Dwarf: In Europe dwells a race of male beings who look like little old men even when young, with long grey beards, wrinkles and stooped shoulders, made famous in the faerytale *Snow White and the Seven Dwarfs*. They are helpful to any humans who come across them. Linked to the earth and nature, they are miners and protectors of natural resources and treasure, smiths and craftsmen with a talent for forging magical weapons and gemstone-encrusted jewellery. There is a superstition that they turn to stone if exposed to the sun, which is rooted in the fact that they spend their days underground.

Elf: Different cultures have different interpretations of the term elf, which is sometimes used interchangeably with the word faery. In England they are commonly perceived as cheeky young boy faeries, in northern Europe they are similar to leprechauns, wingless artisans who are cobblers and spinners, helpful and friendly to humans, and in other folklore they are considered the spirits of the dead who return to assist a family. In Norse legend they are tall, human-like supernatural beings, divided into the beautiful ljossalfs, elves of light, and the uglier swartalfs, dark elves. JRR Tolkien's grand and elegant race of gorgeous elven beings, with their powers of prophecy and second sight, are based on these light elves, although elsewhere they have been diminished in size and power, such as Santa's hard-working little helpers.

Encantado: In Brasil these spirit beings live in an underwater realm. They are believed to have magical abilities, such as the power to control storms, inflict illness or death and enchant humans into doing their will. Some encantados can shapeshift into pink boto dolphins, and there are legends of these dolphins turning into men to seduce young women and father magical children. Even today, some South American people claim descent from encantados, which translates as "enchanted one", and they are believed to be able to bestow wishes and luck upon people.

Fauns: In Roman mythology, fauns were the spirits of the untamed woodlands, protectors of the aspect of nature where they are located. They are often described as similar to the Greek satyrs – human-like, with the lower body of a deer and the hooves and horns of a goat, a la CS Lewis's Narnia character – but more gentle and kind. They played music to entice the forest nymphs to dance, and bestowed blessings on farmers, gardeners and vintners. The 16th century physician and philosopher Paracelsus described them as mystical spirits with power over the elements, and they have been connected to women's erotic dreams.

Fenodyree: On the Isle of Man, fenodyrees are magical beings akin to brownies. They work hard for their human family, mowing (the name translates as "nimble mower"), harvesting, herding and threshing, and expecting only food and drink in return. Shy like many of their brethren, they usually work from dusk until dawn, remaining out of sight of humans, but getting through more work than a mortal could, as they're considered bigger on brawn than brains. They're very loyal, but it's claimed that a fenodyree will leave instantly if they're given clothing, either because they think it's not good enough, or that it will make them physically ill.

Feufollet: The southern parts of America have their own legends and magic, especially in the bayou areas that spawned voodoo. Glowing lights and balls of fire called feufollet, French for "Cajun faeries", were seen hovering over the swamps and dancing through the trees, and were believed to be faeries that would guide (or sometimes lead astray!) travellers. In Europe these spirits of the marshland are known as will-o'-the-wisps, in Sweden lyktgubbe ("the old man of the lamp"), and in places where they're thought to be the spirits of the dead they are called treasure lights or corpse candles.

Folletti: These pretty Italian faeries are elementals of the air, tiny and light and almost invisible, energies that dance on the currents of air and soar across the landscape. They don't associate much with humans, being of another dimension, but they have a cheeky, happy nature, and are friendly if they are encountered. They're believed to shapeshift into butterflies when the mood takes them, while the males have a reputation for kicking up dust storms and changing the weather for their own amusement.

Fossegrim: These Scandinavian water faeries live in lakes and streams, waterfalls and fjords, and are made up partly of water. They can shapeshift into handsome young men who attract women with their beauty and their sweet songs, although there are rumours that some lure people with their music then drown them, much like the female sea sirens of old, while others scream a warning at dangerous stretches of water to prevent accidents. Tales abound of fossegrims who married mortal women, but they waste away if they have to move too far from their watery home, and most unions end in separation when the fae goes back to his water source. Other stories tell of people taking offerings to them in the hope of learning their heavenly songs, which are said to be so hauntingly beautiful that they make the trees dance and the waterfalls stop.

Gan: In southwest North America, the Apache people traditionally communicated with the gans, or mountain spirits, holding elaborate ceremonies where they interacted with them through ritual dance, dressing in elaborate costumes with body paint and weaponry. The gans were reputedly sent to teach the Apache people the arts of civilisation, and are noble, kindly spirits who speak with the medicine men of each community.

Ghillie dhu: These ancient Scottish faeries are guardians and protectors of the trees, especially birch, and dress in the leaves, branches and moss of their woodland homes. Their numbers have dwindled as the forests have, although they've always been secretive and remained out of sight of humans. Those that remain have a reputation for malevolence, especially if anyone threatens their trees, and there are stories of the ghillie dhu binding people up with forest vines and foliage and taking them to Faeryland.

Gnome: These are the earth elementals, and because they live close to the earth they are denser than the winged air elementals. Their name is a contraction of the Greek "genomus", which means earth-dweller, and they are linked to the land itself, the guardians of sacred sites, mountains and forests. According to some, gnome is simply another name for dwarf, and like those small creatures, they are the patron spirits of mines, quarries and treasures. They live in caves, amongst the roots of ancient trees and in forests. They protect the plants and animals of the earth – hence their use in gardens today, symbolised by the ceramic garden gnome – and are believed to live for a thousand years or more. Renowned 16th century physician and philosopher Paracelsus categorised the elementals, choosing gnomes to represent earth, salamanders for fire, sylphs for air and undines for water, but each of the elementals manifest with different names in different places.

Goblin: These are strange, gnarled little creatures, of the earth and its darker places, and the name is thought to derive from the Greek word for evil spirit. According to some they have no home, for they are restless spirits, travellers who wander through the deepest forests and wildest places. Popular throughout European folklore, goblins have no great liking of humans, and are prone to mischief-making, tricks and the weaving of bad luck for anyone who encounters them. They are malevolent and dark-natured, and will reportedly band together to enslave other magical creatures to do their bidding. They have been described as dwarf-like in size, with huge ears and noses, and green or brown skin to blend in better with their environment. In many tales they are hideously disfigured, which could explain their temperament. JRR Tolkien's orcs are based on the goblin legends.

Gumnut baby: In Australia, the faeries of the native bush were depicted by May Gibbs as the bush babies, a kind of local version of Cicely Mary Barker's flower faeries. Her gorgeous little characters were spirits of the wilderness, dressed in the plant they depicted, such as Snugglepot and Cuddlepie, the gumnut babies who wore the gum nuts of the eucalyptus tree, and their female counterparts who were clothed in the flowers of the gum, as well as wattle and boronia babies and even evil banksia men. They were the humanisation of the Australian bush, and like all good faeries they liked music and dancing, and were protectors of their home forests and the natural environment.

Hantu hutan: In the lush jungles of Malaysia, the indigenous people remain in awe of the hantu hutan, powerful spirits of the forest who they respect and fear in equal measure. They leave offerings for them, and say a prayer to them requesting protection every time they enter the forest to find food or shelter.

Hobgoblins: These benevolent earth faeries are old and wizened in appearance, considered ugly by some, and look like small, hairy old men. They are kind and caring to humans. Traditionally they were known as hobs, and were attached to the home, doing chores at night while the household slept or helping out on the farm. It was thought that if you gave a piece of clothing to a hobgoblin he would leave, which is the source of JK Rowling's house elf Dobby, who was freed from servitude to a wicked master when Harry Potter tricked the man into giving the creature his sock.

Harry and his friends understood the giving of clothes as an emancipation from slavery, but the hobgoblins take it as an offensive gesture. (Dobby's name is linked to dobie or dobby, a house faery from the north of England.) In other traditions hobgoblins are returned to nature, living within the earth and capable of mischief in their dealings with humans. Tolkien described hobgoblins as a larger, stronger and more menacing form of goblin, but later admitted he'd got them the wrong way around – hobgoblins are kin to the goblins, but smaller, harmless and more caring.

Ille: In Iceland there's a group of earth elementals called illes, who live in caves, forests and within the earth. They have a reputation for helping people – unless they're crossed, when all hell breaks loose – and a love of precious metals. They are one of the huldufolk, the "hidden people" or light faeries, who have inspired an industry of elf tours and maps of the hidden world. There are 13 different kinds of huldufolk, ranging from tiny flower elves, called blomalfar, to some who are as tall as people. Even today, belief in the fae is high, and contractors move building sites or redirect roads if it might cause the destruction of an elf site. Bulldozer breakdowns, equipment failure and accidents are attributed to angry elves, and even the government consults with mediums to ensure they're not inconvenienced. Like most fae, they are considered to exist to preserve nature.

Jimanino: In Mexico and Central America, these are seasonal fae, connected to nature and the cycles of the Wheel of the Year, which they are believed to help turn. They are active at the eight sabbats, coming out to dance in celebration of these seasonal midpoints, and they are an important part of the Festival of the Dead, which is marked at Samhain, the first day of winter. They look like pudgy, cherubic children with wings, and are thought to be Spanish in origin, travelling over to the new world with the colonists and taking up residence in a new landscape.

Jogah: The Iroquois people of the American northeast believe that all of nature is interconnected. Their faeries were known as jogahs, and embodied all the aspects of nature, aligned with the rocks, rivers and the earth itself. Others ruled the underworld and controlled the beings who existed there. These small nature spirits helped the tribespeople grow plants for food and increased the fertility of the earth, and watched over them in a benevolent way.

Knocker: Helpful sprites known as knockers have been associated with Cornwall, in southwest England, for centuries. They live within the earth, and have a special relationship with the miners there, who work underground mining tin and other minerals. To find a vein of ore, the miners listened for the sound of the fae's little tools as they knocked on the rocks. They left offerings to the knockers, who also warned them about floods and mine shaft collapses, and when Christianity came to the region, the miners refused to make the sign of the cross underground so as not to offend these tiny nature spirits. In Wales such faeries are known as coblynau.

Kobold: In Germany the tree sprites are known as kobolds, and they're similar to fenodyrees and leprechauns, dwarf-like creatures the size of small children. They work for households if offerings of food or milk are left out, and become loyal to the family if they're treated well. Kobolds were the inspiration for jack-in-the-box toys, as people went out to the forests to try to capture one in a wooden box, thinking it would give them control over the being.

Korrigan: The Celtic-influenced region of Brittany in western France is home to a group of beautiful white-clad faery women who are elementals of both water and earth. They live in woodland groves, cool grottoes and sacred springs, rivers and water fountains, and love to dance among the stone circles and alignments of the area, which they've long watched over. They're associated with the druidesses of the area, and are believed to have built the mythical city of Ys, off the coast of Brittany, which now lies under the sea. According to some they have a reputation for trickery, leading travellers astray when the mood takes them, and their love of mortal children has seen them blamed for changeling substitutions. Others believe they are the spirits of former druidesses, cursed by the early Church and condemned to wander the earth forever.

Leprechaun: Ireland is home to many magical beings, including the well-known leprechaun. These small fae creatures look like old men but are the size of a small child, and dress in green with a red hat.

They are often solitary and live in forests, but will sometimes attach themselves to a home and do chores in return for food – in this aspect they've been immortalised in the form of garden gnome statues. They have long been associated with good luck and for bestowing blessings on those who treat them well, and they are reputed to know the location of a pot of gold, which they'll reveal if a person can get around their trickery. Like their surlier cousins the clurichauns and the far darrigs, they like to play practical jokes.

Lorelei: These European water elementals have their origins in the German river sprites, who would sit on cliffs and sing a haunting melody that drove sailors to distraction – and often straight into the cliffs to their death. Also known as sirens, and the basis for many mermaid legends, these beautiful nymphs spread out from their home in the Rhine River, near the cliff area also called Lorelei, to encompass all bodies of water. Like the male fossegrims they're protectors as well as harbingers of death, and if approached in a respectful manner, might help humans.

Lunantisidhe: These pretty, shy Irish nature faeries live in the wild places, and are particularly allied with blackthorn trees, which they protect and are in turn protected by. They don't like people chopping down their trees or cutting off branches, especially at the cross-quarter days, and they mete out punishment to anyone who causes wilful destruction to a blackthorn. In Ireland stories abound of blackthorns being chopped down to build a warehouse or store, and the bad luck that results for that business. When the Irish need a branch for their shillelagh, the wooden walking sticks also used as weapons (and iconic as a leprechaun's staff), they make a request of the lunantisidhe and leave an offering before taking it. The lunantisidhe love dancing outside at night, especially under the full moon, when they will leave their tree to pay homage to the lunar goddess for whom they are named. They are environmentally conscious like most faeries, and hope to teach people to treat nature with respect and use only what is necessary.

Lutin: In France there is a small, friendly goblin-like creature known as a lutin, a household spirit. They are usually male, and have a mischievous nature like a pixie. They're fond of children, who they'll entertain for hours, and horses, which they'll take care of for farmers (although they have been known to plait their manes into strange twists to amuse themselves!). They'll sometimes help out around the house, but they don't like mess, and will leave if a home is too untidy.

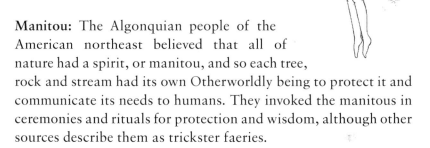

Manitou: The Algonquian people of the American northeast believed that all of nature had a spirit, or manitou, and so each tree, rock and stream had its own Otherworldly being to protect it and communicate its needs to humans. They invoked the manitous in ceremonies and rituals for protection and wisdom, although other sources describe them as trickster faeries.

Mazikeen: These shapeshifting Jewish faeries are described as either winged creatures with the power of enchantment and divination, or tiny invisible demons corresponding to the Arabic djinns. Also known as shideems, they are believed to be the offspring of Adam or Eve when they lay with spirits after leaving Eden, and they are placed somewhere between humans and angels in rank, with the ability to fly, prophesy and become invisible like the angels, and the mortality of men. Like other faeries they love to eat, drink, dance and make merry, and they're thought to marry and have children, and live in traditional family groups.

Menehune: In Hawaii the faeries are known as the menehune, happy little forest spirits who are shy of being seen by people. They eat bananas and fish and look after the wild places of the islands, and are fond of mischief and practical jokes. According to legend these Little People would help humans by building fishponds and walls and working the fields by night, then hide during the day. Some believe they were a magical race related to the leprechauns and faeries of Ireland, and that they intermarried with the Hawaiians and live on to this day. Others think the term menehune was the word for a people already living in the islands when the first Polynesians arrived, who were chased into the shadows by them. Either way, Hawaiians believe in their power and magic.

Mogwai: Western faeries aren't the only ones with a mischievous side – in China there are beings called mogwais, which have supernatural powers they often use against humans, playing tricks or even causing them harm. People make offerings to them, sometimes burning money in their honour, to try to stay on their good side.

Naga: In Hindu legend there are nature spirits known as nagas, which can shapeshift into a human or serpent appearance. They live underground or in rivers and lakes, being elementals of both water and earth, as well as inhabiting other dimensions. They are considered the guardians of sacred wells, springs and other water sources, and offerings are made to them to bring rains in times of drought, fertility to both the land and its people, and luck and prosperity. They are environmentally conscious, retaliating against people who harm the earth, and bestowing blessings on those who work to preserve it.

Nunnehi: The Cherokee people of southwest North America had their own spirit beings, called the nunnehi. They could take on the appearance of men and women, sometimes shapeshifting into a specific person to confuse or soothe, and were kind to children. Legends tell that they guided the Cherokee people to safety in times of strife, and they were considered protector spirits, who would warn their people of danger and foretell future happenings. They're believed to be immortal, never having been born and never dying, but waiting in the forests and mountains of the land until needed.

Nymph: In Ancient Greece the nature spirits were known broadly as nymphs, beautiful young women who watched over the rivers, forests, mountains and valleys of the land. The naiads became closely associated with bodies of water such as sacred springs, streams and lakes, while the nereids were the sea nymphs who oversaw the oceans and whose songs protected sailors, and the dryads were of the trees. They were the genius loci or guardian spirit of a place, and were bound to it and protective of it. They were believed to bestow fertility on the country and its people, and were also associated with goddesses and magic. They were so beautiful that the gods often took them for wives or lovers, and mortal men proclaimed their love too – it is from the passion they instilled in men that we get the term nymphomaniac.

Oakman: New Forest in England, and other wild woodland areas, is inhabited by unfriendly creatures known as oakmen. They make their homes in the saplings that grow out of fallen oak trees, and unlike the faeries who frequent sacred groves, these dwarfish beings are mischievous and sometimes dangerous, offering poisoned food to passing travellers. They are guardians of the forest and its animals, and wear little toadstool caps and clothes made from leaves.

Ole Luk Oie: These Danish faeries are guardians and judges of children. They are tiny winged beings, somewhat transparent, whose clothes change colour according to the light. They visit children at night, blowing faery dust over them to ensure they sleep well. But they carry two umbrellas – one that they open over good children, which has beautiful pictures painted on the inside to inspire sweet dreams, and the other blank, which is opened and held over naughty children so they don't know the bliss of dreaming. Hans Christian Andersen immortalised these faeries as Ole Luk Oie, god of dreams.

Oosood: One of the Serbian nature spirits has a special role, as the birth faery who appears to each child a week after they're born, to predict the child's fate and bestow blessings for a joyful life. They are visible only to the mother of the baby, and only on that day. In return for the magical gifts, the new mother gives food and flowers. Oosoods are related to the fate faeries of other cultures, although they usually manifest as three or more faeries, whereas the oosood comes alone. This concept is immortalised in the faerytale *Sleeping Beauty*, where the fae come to offer blessings to the baby princess.

Peri: In Persian mythology, the peris are beautiful winged creatures with magical powers, similar to the western concept of faeries. They survive by inhaling beautiful perfumes, and are described as "good" faeries, in contrast to the djinn, who are considered by some to be "bad" faeries. Although they don't live in the mortal world, the peris do visit, and they can be seen or heard by humans when they allow it. They're believed to have descended from fallen angels, and been excluded from heaven unless they can earn their way in with good deeds. Lower level demons lock them in iron cages to prevent this, echoing the superstition that faeries hate iron. Perihan is the queen of the Persian faeries.

Pixie: Today the term pixie is often used interchangeably with faery – Santa's helpers are sometimes elves, sometimes pixies, and Disney's Tinker Bell is described as both a pixie who uses pixie dust and a faery, depending on the scene. Yet in the western regions of England, particularly in Cornwall and Devon, pixies are separate beings, with pointed ears and pointy hats. They have magical powers yet no wings to fly, and they love dancing, music and playing with children. These pixies – or piskeys – are of the earth, living on the desolate moors or in the ancient woodlands, keeping to themselves for the most part, yet helping people in need. Later the Christian church explained them as the souls of children who died unbaptised, and they have also been linked to the small-statured Picts of Celtic times. In *Harry Potter* a cage of mischievous Cornish blue pixies are let loose so students can learn how to defeat them.

Qacina: Among the Hopi people and other Native Americans of southwest USA, the spirit beings are known as qacinas, and they live within the earth and the mountains. They represent the different aspects of nature, and also incorporate the spirits of their ancestors. Medicine people communicate with them to ask for blessings for the community in the form of abundant crops, good weather, healing and protection, and people make offerings to them and dance to invoke them.

Queen: Faery queens are those beautiful, powerful women who rule the enchanted realms, such as Titania, the regal faery of Shakespeare's *A Midsummer Night's Dream*, Oonagh, queen of the Tuatha de Danaan, and Maeve, a melding of Irish goddess and fae being who transformed into the faery queen Mab. In Danish folklore the Snow Queen is the dazzling faery queen of the ice realm, who glamours mortal men to fall in love with her and do her bidding. In some legends the faery queen is a mortal woman who is kidnapped – or goes willingly – to wed the faery king, and in others she is the warrior woman who protects her kingdom and the magical beings within it.

Redcaps: Celtic legends of the redcaps recount a bloodthirsty race of small magical beings, who look a little like brownies but feed off the energy of evil events and play dangerous pranks on passersby. They inhabit ruined castles, and it's claimed that they kill the humans who stray into their realm to dye their caps with their blood. Other stories are kinder though, describing them as solitary beings who bestow good luck and blessings on those who can see them.

Rusalka: Of Russian origin, the rusalkas are beautiful female nature spirits associated with both water and earth, who take their power from water. They love to dance in the moonlight, and often entice young men or children to join their revelry. They're attributed with healing powers, and they bless the land with fertility and protection, and aid nearby human communities. In return people leave ribbons tied in birch trees and small offerings. Rusalkas are said to be able to shapeshift from their invisible form into young, innocent women or older warrior queens, but if they move from their watery home their power diminishes. In Slavic legend the rusalkas are the spirits of young women who drowned, fated to remain near the waterway where they died and haunt it until their death is avenged.

Salamander: These are the fire elementals of Paracelsus's classification, vibrant faeries associated with fire, flame, volcanoes and heat. They live within fire itself, and are aligned with creativity, inspiration and action. They can appear as lizard-like creatures or as balls of flame-coloured light, as they are expert shapeshifters, and they're considered the strongest and most powerful of all the elementals. Yet they can be quite child-like at times, and create action without any thought of the consequences.

Satyr: In Ancient Greece, the male nature spirits were known as satyrs, and were linked with the god Pan. They were spirits of the woodland, associated with fertility, and considered brothers (or lovers) of the nymphs. Initially they were depicted as naked men with pointed ears, horse tails and full beards, wreathed in ivy or vines to show their affiliation with the forests, but later they were melded with the Roman Faunus, and developed into half-man, half-goat beings. The female equivalent was the maenad, a wild spirit of nature and the forest, who appears today in the Sookie Stackhouse novels.

Sylph: These are the air elementals, the beautiful, luminescent and winged creatures most often portrayed in art and literature as faeries. They are delicate yet strong, with the highest vibratory rate of the elementals, and live to be a thousand years old. According to legend they can earn a soul through good deeds. They live on mountaintops and in high, desolate areas, and travel around as the very air itself, invisible to humans, yet able to shapeshift into physical form when they want to be known. Some believe their role is to inspire people, like the Muses of old, and help them create and compose.

Tengu: These Japanese nature spirits are winged beings that live in the forests and on mountain peaks, and are guardians of the landscape. They can reportedly shapeshift into animals to escape detection, as they are very shy, private beings who try to avoid any contact with humans. They can appear as a traditional anthropomorphic faery carrying a feathered fan, or as either a bird or a half-bird, half-human creature. They are very protective of the earth, and of any humans they do encounter.

Tien: In Vietnam, the fae are called tien, a word that encompasses nature spirits, angels and other immortals. They are associated with moonlight and night-time revels, and encapsulate the spirit of the land and the balance between humans and nature.

Tomte: Pre-Christian Scandinavians believed in leprechaun-like beings that the Swedish called tomtes, the Finnish named tonttus and the Danes referred to as nisses. They looked after the family home, guarded against bad luck and helped around the farm, although they were shy, coming out only at night. They were loyal and hard working, yet easy to offend, and people left offerings of food (especially porridge with fresh butter) to appease them and compensate them for their work. After the coming of Christianity they were demonised, and jealous neighbours would accuse successful farmers of consorting with the tomte, a very serious, and dangerous, allegation.

Troll: Often depicted as ugly and stupid, these European creatures are excellent shapeshifters, and perhaps take on their scary, hunched form to frighten people away from their homes. Like dwarves and goblins they live and work within the earth, in underground palaces or caves in the mountains, and legend claims they turn to stone, or transform into frogs, when exposed to sunlight. They are associated with treasure, and known as master metalworkers, creating beautiful jewellery and sacred weaponry. They are also herbalists and healers, and like other fae creatures they love music and dancing. They are the guardians of bridges, highways and crossroads, and fiercely protective of their wealth and their dwelling places, guarding nature from any threat.

Tunder: In Hungary the faeries are known as tunders, and they are beautiful, sweet-natured female fae with wings and magical powers. They're well loved by those who encounter them, and offer healing and other assistance to humans, who regard them as protectors of orphans and the poor, who they bestow gifts and blessings upon. They work with herbs and cast spells and enchantments, possess jewels and pearls with magic powers, and their tears are believed to have great healing properties. They live in remote areas, but can fly to nearby communities to help people. They love singing, dancing, music and moonlight, and gather at night in forest glades.

Tylwyth Teg: To the Welsh, the fae are referred to as the Tylwyth Teg, the Fair Folk, as they have golden, shining hair and radiate an inner light, and are helpful and kind when the mood takes them. Yet they're also mischievous, and are regarded with caution, for although they reward some humans for good deeds, there are stories of them swapping their sickly children for healthy mortal babes, and a belief that they create faery paths that can bring death to those who walk them. They are renowned for their shapeshifting ability, and live in isolated places of nature, such as densely wooded areas, lofty mountain peaks and small islands in the middle of lakes. They're predominantly nocturnal, coming out at night to dance in the moonlight within their faery rings.

Undine: These are Paracelsus's water elementals, the sprites and faeries associated with water. They live in waterfalls, forest pools, lakes, rivers and oceans, and have enchanting voices that bewitch sailors. They are graceful faeries, human in appearance when they manifest into form, but often transparent and insubstantial, simply a part of the water in which they live. They're concerned with the preservation of their home element, and all the plants and animals they share it with. According to legend, an undine is able to gain a soul by marrying a man and bearing his child, which forms the basis of the classic Hans Christian Andersen faerytale *The Little Mermaid*. In German lore however, it requires her to give up her immortality, a dilemma that JRR Tolkien gave to the beautiful half-elf Arwen in *The Lord of the Rings*.

Vidyesvaras: This is the name of the faeries, nymphs, nature spirits and angels in Hindu legend. They are linked with the Pan-like deity Pasupati, a nature god who oversees the wild places of the earth. They have powers of prophecy and much wisdom. They usually shun human contact, feeling no need to meddle in worldly affairs, but if someone seeks them out they will offer guidance. Associated also with the god Shiva, the vidyesvarases are portrayed with ten arms and four faces, and are thought to do his bidding.

Vila: In Croatia, the faeries are known as vilas, shapeshifting spirits of the forest who can manifest as various animals or as beautiful young women who love to dance. They have healing powers, which they pass on to mortal women, and are protectors of nature. They've been immortalised in a song about the faery of Velebit, who lives in the Velebit mountain range in Croatia, which is part of a beautiful nature park that includes caves, lakes and forests. Within the park is a special area of largely unexplored wilderness, where access is allowed only for research purposes – the perfect place for nature spirits. Vilas were recognised in the *Harry Potter* series, as Fleur Delacour, the Triwizard champion of Beauxbatons, is part vila. In Slavic countries the vilas are wind and storm spirits, capable of calling forth hailstorms, rain and whirlwinds. Depending on their natural habitats, people speak of land, water, wood and cloud vilas.

Wila: The Polish fae are called wilas, female nature spirits who live in the wilderness. They have healing powers and will sometimes help humans, so offerings of cakes, fruit, flowers and ribbons are left out for them at faery trees, wells and caves. They also have a reputation for mischief, which is another reason for the offerings. According to legend, they can shapeshift from beautiful maidens into swans, and if a person plucks a feather they will be able to control the wila and her magic. They have beautiful voices, like the sirens of the sea, and despite their beauty they are fierce warriors. Faery rings of mushrooms or grass are believed to be the result of their dancing, and it's considered very bad luck to step on one.

Xana: In the Asturian legends of Spain, the xanas are pretty faery nymphs who live in rivers, forests, waterfalls, caves and fountains. They offer the pure water they're associated with to thirsty travellers, and reward humans they like with gifts of gold and silver – yet they also have a reputation for attacking people they dislike. They brush their hair with combs made of sun or moonbeams, and have beautiful voices that bewitch people through their haunting songs.

Yaksha: According to Hindu and Buddhist mythology, yakshas are nature spirits aligned with the elements, particularly the earth, as they live underground, within mountains and in trees and tree roots, caring for the environment, making plants grow and looking after buried treasure. In most legends they are benevolent and kind, although they've also been portrayed as two natured, cannibalistic and ogre-like, as keen to waylay or devour someone walking through their woods or crossing their lake as to help them. In southern India the female yakshas are portrayed as vampire enchantresses.

Yokai: This Japanese term encompasses many preternatural creatures, from faeries and goblins to ogres and humans who can shapeshift into animals. They can be evil, simply mischievous, or working for good. They have spiritual, supernatural powers, so are regarded with caution and superstition, and there is a belief that extremes of emotions, such as jealousy, can transform people into yokai ogres.

Zana: In Romania, the magical creatures of the woodlands are called zanas, which means beauty. They're a bit like the faeries in the story of *Sleeping Beauty* – they bestow upon newborn babies great gifts like the art of wisdom, health, beauty, kindness and luck, but if they're offended or upset, they will call down a curse on the child that will haunt them all their life. They are also associated with the Graces of Greek and Roman legend, goddesses of charm, beauty, nature, human creativity and fertility.

Izzy's Faery Magic

Izzy Ivy is an English visual artist and clothes designer with art in her blood. She has a degree in theatre design, specialising in unconventional costume and puppet making, and her company Zizzyfay creates beautiful faery, goddess and bridal outfits. Izzy is passionate about bringing the mythical into the mundane through her creativity and aerial dance, and travels a lot – she currently lives in Australia as she is solar powered and can't stand the British winters. Her exquisite creations can be found at www.Zizzyfay.com.

I discovered faeries at the bottom of the garden with my grandma as a small child. We fed them milk and honey, and in return they filled my dreams and art pads with their presence. Then life got complicated and they left my immediate thoughts, but 15 years later I found myself surrounded by them, working in a shop of magical relics from the world of the fae. Becoming a children's party entertainer dressed as a faery made me realise how natural it felt, and how dramatically the attire helped me connect.

Faeries bring a lot of joy into people's lives – many of whom do not believe they actually exist. A lot of people like to dress up as faeries at fancy dress parties, and I've never seen anyone dressed as one who doesn't have a smile, which is infectious.

I feel faeries are halfway between literal and metaphorical. They show themselves in many forms – I sense them as balls of intense energy which is usually felt rather than seen, and their presence is often only apparent after they've gone. In my work I know when they're on hand because of the serendipities that occur. My best designs are usually the ones that the faeries have interfered with in some way. And I think they show themselves in ways we can get our head around. They're generally depicted as little humans because we understand concepts easier if they're personified.

I feel a strong connection with the fae – that I am one of them, in one form or another. And I love meeting other faeries of the incarnated kind, as I experience a sense of deep understanding, unspoken connection and a feeling that nears on going home. I meet a lot of incarnated faeries, some who are aware and some who are not. That's one of the best things about designing these clothes – I attract like-minded souls.

In my magic I work a lot with the four elements, personified as elementals. I think faeries appreciate it when we work with earth energies to manifest what our soul seeks, so they like to give a helping hand. They help us realise we are all free spirits, if we choose to recall what our wings look like, and help us remember why we are here and what beautiful talents we can offer to the web of existence, thus inviting us to let go of the fear of unfurling our wings and start to be the unique individuals we are.

They bring us a sense of freedom, and a deep connection with nature and natural forms such as plants and insects, as well as their ethereal qualities and sense of fun. They don't take themselves seriously, yet they have a sense of knowing who they are. Their pagan roots and connection with the female form – not as magazines tell us it should be, but as shimmering natural manifestations of powerful goddess energy – inspire me greatly.

They also remind us to look at nature more carefully and put in context the beauty that is often taken for granted. And I think they're helping facilitate us to a higher level of personal evolution through forcing us to deal with our dark corners, and do it with a sense of light-heartedness, love and compassion. They may not always seem like they're helping us, but when the story starts to unravel a deep sense of transformation and freedom can occur.

Famous Faeries

"Some day you will be old enough to start reading faerytales again."
CS Lewis, *British author of* The Chronicles of Narnia

Faeries in Film and Literature

Faeries have long inspired writers, appearing in early French literature, the classical works of Shakespeare and Tolkien, as well as modern epics such as the Sookie Stackhouse and OR Melling novels. They appear in movies and art too, from Disney blockbusters to indie films, as well as becoming part of our culture through mythic figures such as the Tooth Faery and Santa's elves.

Faeries come through to us via the imagination, and some of the world's greatest imaginations have tapped in to the power of the fae with their stories. So many books, stories, movies and television shows have given us beautiful sights – and insights – into the magical world of faeries. Perhaps sometimes a movie isn't just a movie – perhaps it is an enchanted portal, a gateway through which faery energy can enter our world and communicate directly with us.

At the very least these artistic endeavours spark our own imaginations, entertain, amuse and delight us, and allow us a glimpse into a world of infinite possibility, extraordinary magic and the dizzy heights humanity can reach through the art of storytelling and other expressive channels.

Here are some of those most powerful faeries, our favourite faeries, and their portals through which you can have your very own faery film festival or magical book marathon!

The Tooth Faery

The first faery most people encounter is the Tooth Faery, a mythical being who swoops in whenever a child's tooth falls out. The tooth is left in a glass of water by their bed or under the pillow at night, and the Tooth Faery takes it away, leaving money or a small gift in exchange. The Tooth Faery, who has the power of flight and a purse that never empties, was invented to reassure children concerning the potentially frightening event of losing a tooth, and reward them for their courage. Rituals marking the progression from infant to child signified by the loss of milk teeth have taken place since ancient times, although the Tooth Faery is a fairly modern concept, prevalent mainly in Australia, America and the UK. In France, Italy and most Spanish speaking countries it is a faery mouse who swaps money for each tooth, as the mouse, whose chompers continue growing throughout their life, symbolises strong, healthy teeth.

The Faery Godmother

In the faerytale *Cinderella*, a kind young girl is mistreated by her stepmother and stepsisters and forced to serve them. She endures everything with a sunny disposition and a positive attitude, until she is tricked out of her chance to go to the ball and meet the handsome prince. When she breaks down in tears, her faery godmother appears in a flash of sparkles. This loving magical being transforms her life with her magical powers – with the flick of her wand a pumpkin is turned into a coach, mice into horses, a horse into a coachman, Cinderella's dog into a footman and her rags into a beautiful dress. But she is warned that she must be home by midnight, because the spell will be broken when the last stroke of 12 chimes out. Faery godmother roles are popular throughout folklore, but they are unlike the traditional view of the fae, being devoted to helping their human protege rather than leaving them to take care of their own affairs.

The Other Faery Godmother

Princess Fiona's faery godmother in *Shrek 2* is kind of like the anti-faery godmother – she seems all sweetness and light, with her sparkling wand, her violet hair and her laughter and promises of help, but in truth she is a wily junk food addict intent on helping her son, the egotistical Prince Charming, steal Princess Fiona away from her beloved ogre Shrek. One of the loveliest things about the Shrek universe is how it turns traditional notions of dark and light on their head – and the faery godmother, played by British comedian Jennifer Saunders, is a wonderful example of a goody-goody who is not at all as she seems. It was also fantastic that this animated tale was the biggest grossing film of 2004, proving that we all need a little magic in our lives.

Claudine Crane

In Charlaine Harris's *Southern Vampire Mysteries* book series and its TV spin-off *True Blood*, telepath Sookie Stackhouse has her own faery godmother, Claudine, who saves her life several times in her battles with rogue vampires and two-natured beings. Claudine and her brother Claude are breathtakingly beautiful faeries with pointy ears, lustrous dark hair and model-looks, who are hugely attractive to humans (and vampires!). Claudine is working her way up to be an angel, and she uses her magical faery powers to keep Sookie safe, materialising at will to prevent accidents and rescue her from danger, as well as providing guidance, advice and friendship. But others of her kind are not so sweet, and in the ninth book there is a terrible war in the faery realm that spills over into the mortal dimension, sparked because some magical creatures want to close the portals between Faeryland and our world forever. And how sad that would be!

Flora, Fauna and Merryweather

In Disney's 1959 film *Sleeping Beauty*, beautiful Princess Aurora is cursed at her christening by an evil sorceress to die on her 16th birthday, and it is the Three Good Faeries who save the day. Although Flora, who wears red and pink, and Fauna, in green, have already bestowed their blessings on the child, blue-clad Merryweather is able to change the curse from death to sleep, which the princess can be awakened from by true love's kiss. The three faeries then disguise themselves as peasants and bring the young princess up in a tiny cottage in the woods, in order to keep her safe from harm. These small, sweet but bumbling faeries are more human than most, but while they ban themselves from using their magic to avoid detection, they are able to make dresses from scratch, manifest a feast, clean the house and change their own appearance with a flick of their wands. In the 17th century faerytale by Charles Perrault and the 19th century Tchaikovsky ballet, on which this film was based, several good faeries turned up to the christening to bestow blessings on Aurora, and they were far less involved in the human world than Flora, Fauna and Merryweather.

Tinker Bell

Probably the most well-known faery of all is Tinker Bell, who sprang to life from the imagination of JM Barrie, the Scottish creator of Peter Pan. In his 1904 play *Peter Pan, Or The Boy Who Wouldn't Grow Up*, which turned into the novel *Peter and Wendy*, Tink was a faery whose special talent was mending pots like a tinker, and whose speech was a tinkling bell, hence her name. She loved Peter Pan and was jealous of, and mean to, Wendy, although she redeemed herself in the end. (The author later explained that because faeries are so small, they can only feel one emotion at a time, so when they are angry they act on it, unchecked by consequences or compassion.) She could help humans to fly by sprinkling them with faery dust, but she died at the end of the novel, so she wasn't immortal. Tinker Bell has appeared in many adaptations of the Peter Pan story, including the blockbuster *Hook*, portrayed by Julia Roberts, and been depicted in paintings, artwork and sculpture.

The Disney Fairies

Tinker Bell has recently been resurrected by Disney, who have made her their mascot and the centrepiece of the Disney Fairies franchise. She was just a supporting character without a voice in their 1953 film *Peter Pan*, but she now stars in her own movies – including *Tinker Bell and the Lost Treasure* – and has become a sassy, brave, kind and well-meaning faery. And in 2009 Tink even got her own star on the Hollywood Walk of Fame! This delightfully impish faery lives in Pixie Hollow, Never Land, with her faery friends, such as Silvermist the optimistic water-talent faery, Fawn the mischievous animal-talent faery, Lily the practical garden-talent faery, Iridessa the helpful light-talent faery and Vidia the loner flying-talent faery. Each faery has her own unique talent and personality, so young girls (and the not so young!) can relate to the one most like them. In addition to movies, the Disney Fairies brand includes children's books, dolls, dress-up costumes, a website, magazines, and fun, magical merchandise.

Princess Holly

One of the most adorable little faeries around today is Princess Holly, from the animated TV show *Ben and Holly's Little Kingdom*. She is the daughter of King and Queen Thistle, and she has two little twin sisters, Daisy and Poppy, who are terrible at magic. Her best friend is Ben Elf, who has no wings and has to ride a gorgeous ladybird to fly with Holly. They all live in an enchanted kingdom filled with faeries, elves, insects and other cute creatures, which is reached by going through the bramble woods. Nanny Plum (who has the cutest wand ever) can speak most animal languages, and is instructing Holly in magic – with sometimes disastrous, always amusing, results. It's such a sweet show, and as captivating for adults as it is for the preschoolers it was created for.

Morgan la Fey

Morgaine of the Faeries holds a special place in myth, legend and literature. Today she is best known as the priestess of Avalon and half-sister of King Arthur in the beautiful book *The Mists of Avalon*, but in early accounts she was a supernatural being rather than a mortal, hence her name, Morgaine of the Faeries. In historian Geoffrey of Monmouth's 12th century opus *Vita Merlini*, he claims that when Arthur was badly wounded he was taken to Avalon, the underworld Faeryland, to be healed by Morgan, the most powerful of the nine magical sisters who resided there. Morgan was an Otherworldly healer to Arthur in other accounts too, while in early French literature she was mentioned as the mother of the faery king Oberon by her lover Julius Caesar. In Italy she was referred to as "the mistress of the faeries of the salt sea", and in Welsh epics she was queen of the faeries. It's only in more recent stories that she's become human, although her magical powers remain, and she's described as having mismatched faery eyes and gifts of prophecy and the Sight.

The Faery King and his Court

One of the most captivating and beautiful book series about the fae is *The Chronicles of Faerie* by OR Melling, which draws on Irish legends and history to recount the magical events that occur when the human and faery worlds intersect. The first book, *The Hunter's Moon*, follows the adventures of two mortal girls as they stumble into Faeryland, one of them far more willing than the other.

The faery king takes one of the girls and uses all his powers of glamour and concealment to keep her from being rescued – but has she been abducted or gone willingly for love? In the second book, *The Summer King*, a young girl must save Faeryland from destruction – for its demise would impact on our world too, since in this series they are so entwined that neither can survive on its own. In the third book, *The Light-Bearer's Daughter*, a young woman whose faery-loving twin died mysteriously the year before, must go on a quest to save all that she loves, meeting many enchanted creatures along the way, and finding her fate wrapped up with a faery king's. And in the conclusion, *The Book of Dreams*, all the previous characters must band together to save Faeryland and the mortal world from being tragically separated, a state in which no happiness can exist. For in this universe, the world of humans and the world of faeries have hung like two shining apples on the tree of life – separate but joined together, one providing dreams and the other, dreamers. The four books have a strong environmental theme, without being preachy, and captivate readers with the magic of the faery realm, the strength of humanity and the beauty and transformation that results when people interact with the fae.

The Flower Fairies

In the early 20th century, English artist Cicely Mary Barker created the Flower Fairies, a series of characters who popped up in books, paintings and merchandise. They were tiny magical beings (all under 20cm tall), who live in their individual flower and are charged with caring for it. Their powers lay in looking after nature, for whenever a seed sprouted, its own baby faery was born alongside it to look after it, and the two grow and flourish together. There's Buttercup, who loves skipping through summer meadows and singing in the sunshine, Wild Cherry, a shy and delicate faery to match her blooms, who plays hide and seek in the fruit trees, Lavender, who gives her plant's flowers to other fae so their clothes smell nice, and Rose, a kind, gentle faery who looks after the bees.

The Faeries

In the 1970s, English artists Alan Lee and Brian Froud re-imagined the Victorian imagery that spawned the Flower Faeries and returned these magical beings quite literally to their roots in their acclaimed full-colour art book *Faeries*. They became creatures of trees, twigs and roots, mouldering leaves, ivy and stones, magical beings that emerged from nature in all its wildness, darkness and mystery. These faeries were beautiful yet grotesque, secretive, untamed and almost savage, with a strangely sensual beauty. Gone was the flowery delicacy and innocence of prior faeries – these were nature spirits with a hint of menace, and included cheeky pixies, nasty trolls, twisted sprites, gnarled old dwarves and strange goblins.

Elinore

Elinore is a faery-in-training in *Wizards*, a wonderful animated feature made in 1977 that has some of the most interesting depictions of faeries ever filmed. She engages in sex and some violence – she's a daring faery with a dark side, who nevertheless does a great deal of good. The movie centres around Faeryland, which is being torn apart due to humans creating an apocalypse. There's an awesome wizard named Avatar, a faery queen called Delia, lots of other sweet and sour faeries, talented shapeshifters, scary mutants, graceful elves and grumpy dwarves, and a beautiful faery forest and sanctuary. It's a diverse, shadowy and wild film, and a cult classic for good reason!

Shhh! Faery Secret

Some famous people believe in faeries, including singer Tori Amos and members of the British royal family. Princess Margaret always stopped at faery trees and honoured the local faeries when she visited Ireland.

Lady Galadriel

In JRR Tolkien's epic *Lord of the Rings* book series, Galadriel is an incredibly beautiful royal faery woman, who rules a kingdom in Middle Earth. She's 7000 years old, warrior-strong, more than two metres tall, with glorious hair that captures the radiance of the Two Trees that brought light to the land. She is telepathic and very powerful, and her magic is reflected in her names the Lady of Light, the Lady of the Wood and the Mistress of Magic. She is the most powerful elven ruler in Middle Earth, described as "the mightiest and fairest of all the elves" and "the greatest of elven women". When the Rings of Power were forged, she was entrusted with Nenya, the Ring of Water, which she used to protect her kingdom, and she narrates the prologue in the *LOTR* movies, where she is played by the ethereal Cate Blanchett, because she was the only one with first-hand knowledge of the long history of the rings. She plays an important role in helping the hobbits find and destroy the One Ring, and also in the withdrawal of the elven peoples from the land of men.

Arwen Undomiel

Beautiful Arwen, played by Liv Tyler in the movie version, is one of the mysterious half-elvens in *LOTR*, the granddaughter of Galadriel and the daughter of Elrond, Lord of Rivendell. She has power over the elements and knowledge of incantations, and saves Frodo's life when he's being pursued by conjuring a flood. She also wields the sword of her great-grandmother. As a half-elven, she had to decide whether to be of man or fae, the former requiring her to give up her immortality. She became human through her love for Aragorn, and after many trials they married and she became queen of the reunited kingdoms. She gave up her life, aged 2901, after her husband died, but they had a son and two daughters to carry on the line. Arwen means "noble woman" and Undomiel means "evening star", so this passionate, magical faery is also known as Arwen Evenstar.

The Blue Faery

The 19th century book *The Adventures of Pinocchio*, by Italian author Carlo Collodi, is about a wooden puppet who longs to be a real boy, but can't stop being naughty or telling lies. In the first half of the story his creator Geppetto is the main character, but in the second half it is the Faery with Turquoise Hair (aka the Blue Faery), who acts as Pinocchio's mother and protector, and rewards him for his hard-won goodness by turning him into a boy. She is a spirit of the forest, with magical powers to save and bestow life. In the 1940 Disney movie version, the Blue Faery brings Pinocchio to life, but is less involved in his upbringing than in the original, instead appointing Jiminy Cricket to be his conscience. And she's depicted as blonde, rather than with the turquoise hair of her book counterpart.

Frances and Elsie's Faery Friends

Fairy Tale: A True Story, about Queen Mab and the Cottingley Fairies, is at once beautiful and tender, and a wonderful depiction of how war affects the imagination, and our need for the Otherworld to maintain the good in humanity. The fae in this film are shy, wild and tiny humanoid creatures with lovely wings, and homes made of twigs and moss. They appear to Elsie and Frances, two young girls who believe in them, but move away once the news about them gets out. Watch for the sweet, sad scenes of faeries moving in little twig and moss wagons across big roads! They are also the bearers of good news, and the faery queen Mab comes to the children to let Frances know her father is returning home from war. There are gorgeous costumes, beautiful details, and enough true story to make it a must-see for any faery aficionado.

Christa

The faeries of the beautiful Australian animated film *Fern Gully: The Last Rainforest* live in an idyllic landscape near Mount Warning, just outside Australia's famous Byron Bay. These ecologically aware faeries have the ability to shrink humans down, and one young logger becomes caught up with them when he is shrunk during a logging raid on their homes. Christa, the faery leader who is trying to save the forest, is the one who falls for the human – and it's her human friend who helps her save their beautiful Fern Gully rainforest. A delightful, very funny film, with a wonderful message about the necessity of conservation, *Fern Gully* offers a refreshing glimpse of faeries outside the British landscape.

Kira and Jen

The Faeryland-like realm of Thra in *The Dark Crystal* is just one of the fae-centric qualities of this marvellous film. Its conceptual director, who created much of its imagery and style, is faery artist Brian Froud, and within the world of Thra are many faery-like beings, such as the gentle Mystics and the elfin-like beings known as Gelflings, who are all seeking to restore an ancient crystal's power to unlock their lands from the powerful creatures known as the Skeksis. Kira and Jen are two Gelflings who are the heroes and healers in this beautiful film, which features stunning puppetry and the most inspiring crystalline landscapes.

The nature spirits

The brilliant film *Pan's Labyrinth*, written and directed by Mexican Guillermo del Toro, is a tale of horror and torture – fittingly, as it explores the breakdown of humanity's goodness after the Spanish Civil War ushered in the Franco regime. Against this backdrop is set the interior life of a little girl, Ofelia, who follows a faery into an old labyrinth and encounters a malevolent nature spirit that is insectoid in feel and dangerously unpredictable, who gives her a quest to complete. Although this being is referred to as Pan in the English title of this Spanish film, it was never intended that it be a depiction of the nature god Pan – the literal translation of the title is rather *The Labyrinth of the Faun*. Guillermo del Toro, who will soon direct *The Hobbit* and its sequel, says his "faun" is simply a force of nature – both good and bad, and beyond morality. This film is challenging to watch, depicting as it does the very dark side of humanity and of all nature, but it is also uplifting, and shows the great good humans are capable of. It's one of the most powerful faerytales told in recent years, showing the truth of our darkness, and is a must-see for those seeking to understand the potential for good and bad that exists when we incarnate as human.

The Genie

Disney's animated *Aladdin* features a djinn – or, as they are called in the west, a genie – played at breakneck speed by the brilliant comic Robin Williams. His amazing powers are controlled by his master, who is granted wishes that are put to good and honourable use throughout the film. The Genie has many of the traditional djinn talents on top of granting wishes – he can shapeshift, becoming smaller, much bigger or trailing into vapour to fit into his lamp at will. He can change colour and appearance, and can fly on a magic carpet (although it also seems he can fly himself – perhaps it's easier that way?). It's a lovely twist within this film that Aladdin's third wish is for the Genie to be free to go his own way – which he does, with immense gratitude, ready for all sorts of adventures and mischief. Aladdin benefits from their liaison too – finding true love, status and great abundance – and his essential goodness remains uncorrupted by the power the wishes and the Genie bring him. Very Disney, but very charming! It was the most successful film of 1992, proving that audiences young and old love magic and faerytales.

Atreyu

The NeverEnding Story is a beautifully filmed adventure fantasy about a young boy, Bastian, who finds a book that comes to life as he reads it. He finds himself living two parallel existences, both within the book, in the world of Fantasia, and as the reader in the human world. Within Fantasia there is a dreadful force called the Nothing creeping across the land, emptying the world of anything at all, and leaving in its wake... nothing, a terrible blank. Fantasia itself represents the hopes and dreams of the human world, while the Nothing is the result of humanity's greed for power and denial of their dreams. In the real world Bastian must help save Fantasia, while the parallel hero, a young fae-like warrior named Atreyu, braves the swamps of sadness, meets a wondrous luckdragon, suffers a perilous wound and is healed by two gnomes, consults an Oracle and passes through a Magic Mirror gate in his quest to do his bit. Based on the German fantasy novel by Michael Ende that was first published in 1979, this is an enchanting, magical journey.

Yvaine and the World of the Fae

The kingdom (or queendom) of the fae is the setting for *Stardust* (*Being A Romance Within The Realm of Faerie*), fantasy writing royalty Neil Gaiman's graphic novel turned book, which was later made into a film. Within it are many magical beings, including the long-lived witch sisters known as Lilim, who may be part of the lost land of Lyonesse (the story references a sunken land, and three magical sisters, which fits with that particular legend). The heroine is Yvaine, a fallen star who is a living and breathing creature, portrayed by Claire Danes in the film. There is also a tyrannical king, who encourages fratricide amongst his sons competing for the throne of Stormhold, the evil Madame Semele, who seeks the fallen star to consume its heart and thus be restored to youth, and of course there are the fae, who are enslaved by an unscrupulous Lilim. The hero Tristran (Tristan in the film) is half-faery, as his mother is Madam Semele's slave, the beautiful cat-eared faery called Lady Una – a reference to the faery queen Oonagh. The film and the novel are rich with faery markets, enchanted Otherworlds, ghosts and wonderfully nasty villainesses, as well as tough-guy actor Robert de Niro in a hilarious turn as a cross-dressing pirate! The magical world of the fae is also the setting for other Neil Gaiman books.

The Goblin King

David Bowie plays the fabulous (and fabulously sexy) Goblin King in Jim Henson's gorgeously camp movie *Labyrinth*, designed by the artistic genius Brian Froud. Featuring an Escher-like maze, guilt over new babies and wishes that sadly come true, *Labyrinth*'s heroine, 15-year-old Sarah (played by beautiful Jennifer Connelly) wishes her crying baby brother would just go away. And away he goes, courtesy of the goblins. Sarah spends most of the film attempting to win him back from the Goblin King, who has fallen for her. And while some of the songs and the dance routines have dated a little, nothing can quite match the magnificence of David Bowie's tights, revealing ever so much of the rock star's endowments. The film's tension turns upon Sarah's coming into her own power, and denying the Goblin King power over her. Fascinating, visually stunning and rather titillating, *Labyrinth* is well worth seeing, over and over, if only for the contents of David Bowie's tights!

The Fair Folk

Juliet Marillier's magical *Sevenwaters Trilogy* centred around several generations of a family who had long been custodians of a huge, mysterious forest where Otherworld beings dwelled in a cautious harmony with the wise women and chieftains of the clan. These fae creatures remained peripheral to the tests of courage and exercises of magic the family experiences, but in a new fourth book, *Heir to Sevenwaters*, they take centre stage, and much of the action occurs in the realm of the fae. Clodagh is one of the daughters of the Sevenwaters chieftain, but she prefers domestic duties to the herbcraft, healing and seering of her aunts and grandma. Yet when she is left in charge of her new baby brother, the Fair Folk (based on the Tuatha de Danaan) abduct him and leave a changeling made of twigs in his place, and Clodagh must journey into the Otherworld to rescue the baby, prove she was not involved in the kidnapping and re-establish the trust that once existed between her family and the fae. It's a dangerous undertaking, and the young girl risks her own life as she bravely challenges the villainous Lord of the Oak.

Juliet's Faery Magic

Internationally acclaimed author Juliet Marillier writes beautiful, lush stories that are rich with symbolism, myth, magic and adventure, and filled with strong, inspiring characters and haunting Otherworld beings. Her books include the enchanting *Sevenwaters Trilogy*, the darkly beautiful *Bridei Chronicles*, the faery delights of *Wildwood Dancing* and the mysterious, romantic *Heart's Blood*. Juliet was born in New Zealand, lives in Western Australia, and has travelled through the Celtic lands and Old World Europe to research her intricate, historical stories. She is a member of the Order of Bards, Ovates & Druids, and is deeply connected to nature and the nature spirits. Visit her at www.JulietMarillier.com.

For as long as I can remember, I've loved stories of the Otherworld, of enchantments and strange journeys. As a child I adored Andrew Lang's Fairy Books (*The Pink Fairy Book*, *The Green Fairy Book* and so on), which were collections of folklore and faerytales from all around the world. Later I graduated to Lady Gregory's retellings of Irish mythology, the Welsh *Mabinogion*, and of course Scottish folklore with its selkies and Good Folk – so named because to use an uncomplimentary name might offend, and the consequences of that could be serious indeed!

Folk tales from China and Japan, from Africa, Russia and Scandinavia, all broadened my horizons and made me realise that every culture has its version of the Other, the enticing but terrifying mystery that exists out there in the woods, or under the lakes, or in the Hollow Hills.

I don't need scientific proof before I can believe in something, and Otherworld beings are no exception. Whether that belief is literal or not is unimportant. All I know is that the lovely, intriguing and utterly strange creatures who people those traditional stories also make their way into my writing, in one form or another.

Sometimes they are major characters, like Tuala from *The Dark Mirror*, a girl of both human and fae lineage who grows up to marry a future king of the Picts. Sometimes they are close to gods and goddesses, grand, proud and more than a little mercurial in temperament. I love them for their power, their beauty and their ability to survive over eons of time. When I write, I often sense ancient voices helping me along. It is as if the story is coming from somewhere beyond me, conjured by a blend of ancestral memory, instinct and natural magic.

I believe that every myth has its origins in some kind of historical truth. Storytelling truth can be far deeper and truer than plain fact. Why else are those magical women – Nimue, Titania, Morgan la Fey, Baba Yaga – still so well known, hundreds of years after their stories were first told?

In them we recognise and celebrate our own strength. In them we also see the Other – the queen capable of turning a man into an animal with a single sweep of her wand, the crone whose helpers are Night and Day, the fae enchantress who can rob a druid of his craft in a heartbeat. I love them because they are beautiful, powerful and compelling.

The Otherworld, and the many races that inhabit it, are as necessary to me as the human world. They provide me with a sense of wonder, and the knowledge that my own world holds secrets yet to be discovered.

And they teach me that there are realms beyond the reach of our geography, worlds that may be touched through magical practice, through the power of song or story, or by simple means such as tending a garden with mindful hands or brewing a nourishing soup for loved ones. Magic can touch us at any moment – we need only be open to it.

Magical Gardening

"Faery places, faery things,
Faery woods where the wild bee wings.
Tiny trees for tiny dames,
These must all be faery names!"
Robert Louis Stevenson, The Flowers

Creating Your Own Magical Space

One of the simplest ways to connect with the energy of the fae is to create your own enchanted faery garden and welcome these spirits of nature into your life. Filling your backyard or your balcony with flowers, herbs, trees, fruits and vegies, as well as crystals, water features and small faery statues, will invite bees, birds and butterflies to visit you, as well as beings from the enchanted realms.

Spending time outside, nurturing your plants and absorbing the essence of nature, will lift your spirits and fill you with joy, which is just what the faeries want for us. Communing with nature provides a sense of peace and calm, lowering stress, easing depression and putting you back in touch with your inner self. It transports you to another state of being, transforming your mood and opening you up to other dimensions of yourself and the world.

Planting seeds, nurturing seedlings and watching them grow, allows you to be part of the plant's alchemical magic, connecting you to the cycles of the earth and the seasons, and making you part of the cycle of life. Growing herbs and other edible plants also lets you take this energy into you in a very physical, healing way.

Gardening is also incredibly therapeutic. It has become part of the healing program in hospitals, nursing homes, psychiatric facilities, cancer centres, hospices and prisons. It enhances health and wellbeing, lowers stress, increases coping skills and quickens rehabilitation. Gardening therapy is also used to treat depression and for people recovering from strokes or serious car accidents, and for the elderly and those with disabilities. It's not only mentally stimulating and a good form of exercise, but it soothes the soul and brings magic into your life, while connecting you deeply to nature and the nature spirits. The plants themselves also contribute their essential oils to the air, which is very healing, while giving some of their nutrients to the soil, and others to us when we eat them.

Your faery garden will be totally unique, reflecting your own personality and your connection to the spirit of nature. So although some plants are especially linked with the fae, they all have power, and as you're creating a manifestation of your own magic and your own heart, choose those that make you smile when you see them.

It's all about relaxing and learning to be, so don't feel that you have to cultivate a perfect English cottage garden if you live in a tropical environment, because as a personification of nature, faeries will also be attracted to the plants native to your area. And don't be upset if certain plants don't thrive, as some will grow better for you than others, depending on your climate, rainfall, soil quality and pollution. Visit your local nursery and learn about what will grow best for you. And as faeries love the wild places of nature, be sure to let at least a small section of your garden grow free and unrestrained, and cultivate that quality within yourself as well.

Colour Magic

Different coloured flowers will affect you in different ways, and will also attract specific faeries. You can choose a certain coloured flower to create a specific mood, or combine all kinds of different hued blooms for a rainbow effect.

Red flowers represent love, desire, passion, inspiration and vibrance, and will attract the fire elementals to your garden, as well as energetic, playful and take-charge faeries. Plant red roses, peonies, poppies, geraniums, lobelias, hibiscus, carnations and nasturtiums.

Orange flowers represent positive energy, confidence and fiery creativity, and will attract playful faeries who want to dance and laugh and sing with joy. Plant marigolds, nasturtiums, poppies, tulips, flowering maple, lantana, calceolaria, Mexican sunflowers, Chinese lanterns, zinnias and impatiens.

Yellow and gold flowers represent happiness, intellect and clarity, and will attract the air elementals and solar fae. Many of them are used in Midsummer solstice rituals, which adds to their faery association. Plant Saint John's wort, nasturtiums, primroses, daisies, dandelions, dill, aloe, tansy, rue and calendula.

Green flowers and leafy plants represent balance, fertility and groundedness, and will attract the earth elementals such as dryads, elves, gnomes and leprechauns. Plant orchids, euphorbia, hellebore, kangaroo paw, lady's mantle and acanthus.

Blue flowers represent serenity, intuition, tranquillity and peace, and will attract the water elementals and the healing faeries to your sacred space. Plant hyacinths, irises, agapanthus, bluebells, borage, cornflowers, forget me nots, violas, statice, delphinium, bellflowers, gentiana and aristea.

Purple flowers represent spirituality, sovereignty, mystery and magic, and will attract the faery kings and queens to your garden. Plant rosemary, purple morning glory, lavender, thyme, violets, pennyroyal, hyssop, catnip, borage and chives.

Pink flowers represent healing, gentleness, friendship, peace and love, and will attract gentle, kind and quiet faeries. Plant tiger lilies, gerberas, bergamot, valerian, mallow, clover, coriander, yarrow, comfrey, summer savoury, echinacea, astrantia, anemone, camellia, chives, cyclamen, bougainvillea and snapdragons.

White flowers represent purity and spiritual guidance, and are attuned to the energy of the moon and to magic, innocence and peace. They will attract lunar faeries, and encourage night-time frolics and festivities. Plant jasmine, frangipanis, white lilacs, basil, lemon balm, elder, yarrow, feverfew, chamomile and marjoram.

Moon Magic

You can also plant a moon garden, made up of beautiful white blossoms that can be seen at night, bright against the evening shadows and highlighted beautifully by the full moon. Gorgeous white flowers include jasmine, gardenias, white lilacs, Queen Anne's lace, clematis vines, white roses, orange jessamine, Korean spicebush, white alyssum and sweet woodruff. There are even those plants that flower or release their scent at night, such as sweet scented night-blooming jasmine, also known as lady of the night, richly fragrant four-o'clocks, moonflowers, aka moonvine and tropical morning glory, which open at night and wither early the next morning, and angel's trumpet, which has a delicate scent that is most noticeable in the early evening.

Choose the ones you find the most beautiful to look at and the most sweetly fragrant. Moon gardens are gorgeous in the daylight hours too, but they come into their own at night, providing a beautiful, sacred space to work magic or meditate within, and to dance beneath the full moon, just as the faeries do.

You can also use the moon and its phases to enhance your garden's growth, as this beautiful, mysterious celestial body influences not only our moods and emotions, but also the tides of the earth, the moisture content of the soil and the growth rate of plants. As the moon goes from dark to full it's the waxing or growing period, a time of new beginnings, growing vitality and increasing energy. At the full moon it is at its energetic peak, then as it goes from full back to dark it's the waning period, a time of lowering energy, introspection and withdrawal.

These phases are determined by the angles of the moon's position in relation to the earth and the sun as it orbits our planet. The moon generates no light of its own, simply reflecting back the light of the sun. One half of it is always illuminated, and one half is always dark, but what we see depends on the angle between the sun and the moon as we view them from earth.

Each moon cycle lasts around 29.5 days, starting at the dark moon, the point when the moon lies directly between the sun and the earth, and the moon is invisible to us because the side that's reflecting the light of the sun is facing away from us. Shortly after this is the moment of the new moon, when the first tiny sliver of the illuminated side of the moon can be seen. This thin crescent continues to increase as the moon moves from between the earth and the sun, and the angle between them allows us to see more of the moon's reflected light.

After about a week the moon is at right angles to the earth in relation to the sun, and we see a half circle, known as the first quarter moon. This continues to increase, until a week or so later it becomes full, as the moon is now on the opposite side of the earth from the sun, with the earth directly in-between, so the whole of the side that is visible to us is reflecting back sunlight, and we see a round moon in all its shining, golden glory.

After that it appears to decrease in size as it progresses back to the dark moon. It seems to shrink a little each night, until a week after the full moon it is again at right angles to the sun in relation to the earth and we see a half moon, which is known as the third or last quarter moon. From there the crescent continues to get smaller each night, until it returns to the point where it's invisible to us again at the dark moon, and the cycle starts over again.

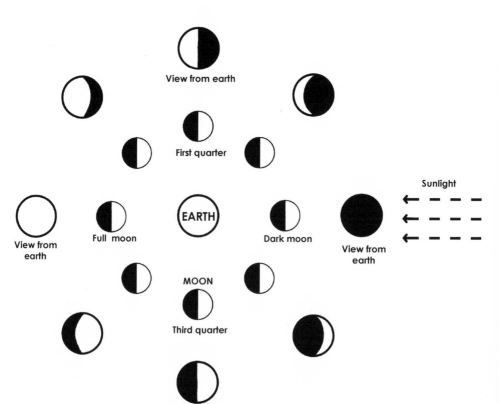

In the southern hemisphere the waxing crescent is a C shape, with the waning crescent a backward C – ☾ ○ ☽ – but in the northern hemisphere it is reversed, and it is from these skies that we get the maiden-mother-crone goddess symbol.

The new moon is a period of heightened energy, new beginnings and vitality, and is the optimal time to plant seeds, both metaphorically, sowing the seeds of new ideas, dreams and hopes, and literally, in your garden. At this time of each month there is more moisture in the soil, as the moon's gravitational effect is strong, causing seeds to swell, burst and grow.

Between new moon and full, as the light and energy is increasing, strong leaf growth takes place, so plants that produce fruit or foliage above the ground, such as flowers and herbs, will thrive. Throughout the waxing period the lunar energy continues to build, so your garden will grow strong. There is an energy of gathering, growing, strengthening, increasing and drawing to you at this time.

The full moon is the high tide of power and energy in a lunar cycle, and the world, and your garden, is filled with energy and potential. The strongest gravitational effect is felt at this time, as the moon and sun pull from opposite sides of the earth. Seeds absorb the most water at this time, and plant growth is rapid. Spend time in your garden, dancing beneath the silvery moon and absorbing the energy of growth and abundance from your plants.

After the full moon, as it starts to wane, and light and power begin to decrease, the energy of the earth starts to draw downwards, increasing root development and growth. Plants that produce below the ground, such as root vegetables and bulbs, will thrive at this time, so plant them between full moon and dark, when the energy is waning and withdrawing. It's also a good time to transplant or grow things from cuttings. Throughout the waning period above-ground plants grow a bit slower, so it's the perfect time to prune, harvest and mow if you want to discourage fast growth.

Lunar phases are printed in newspapers, moon diaries and websites like www.sunrisesunset.com. You can also determine the phase of the moon by its shape and the time it rises, which occurs about 50 minutes later each day, and is explained in the old adage: "The new moon rises at sunrise, the first quarter at noon. The full moon rises at sunset, the last quarter at midnight." There are also gardening-specific moon calendars if you want to explore further.

The Wheel of the Year

You can also plan your gardening according to the festivals of the Wheel of the Year, making your seasonal celebrations both literal and metaphorical. Sow your garden, and the seeds of your dreams, in spring, then watch your plants grow, and your ideas manifest in the world, during summer. Give thanks for your garden harvest, and the things you've achieved, in autumn, then allow the weeds, and the things that no longer serve you, to die off or be released in winter. Then start again with new plants and new dreams as you celebrate the renewal of your garden, and your own rebirth, the following spring, continuing the magical cycle of the seasons and of life.

The winter solstice, which falls on June 21 or 22 in the southern hemisphere and December 21 or 22 in the north, is the longest night and the shortest day of the year. It is the middle of winter, and marks the transition between darkness and light, both literally and metaphorically, as well as emotionally and physically. It's a quiet, reflective time – animals hide away or hibernate, most trees are stripped of leaves, plants die off and seeds lie underground, closed up and cold, as nature withdraws so it can rest and regain its strength before it begins to regenerate. Metaphorically, the energy of this season supports washing away what is no longer necessary and creating a fertile base from which to move forward. In your garden, weed out the dead plants, bring delicate pot plants inside and make plans for which flowers you'll grow next. If you have an evergreen tree such as a pine, which stays lush and green through winter as a symbol of the hope of spring's return, decorate it with faery lights, or faery decorations, and ask the winter faeries to keep your garden safe. For pagans this day is celebrated as Yule, marking the rebirth of the sun and the sun god – the festival that Christmas, which marks the birth of the son of god, is based on.

Imbolc, a cross-quarter day that falls in the first week of August in the southern hemisphere and the first week of February in the north, is the festival of joy and renewal that marks the end of winter and the beginning of spring. The days start lengthening and the light starts returning, illuminating the land as well as our own hearts. It's a time of awakening, renewal and re-emergence, as the earth quickens and nature quivers with the energy to grow again. Metaphorically it's about new beginnings, initiations and rededications, so make a pledge to a new path or a new goal, and write down your dreams or create a manifestation board as a commitment to making them happen. In your garden, the first tentative shoots will appear, buds will unfurl and bluebells and snowdrops will flower, so nurture them well. Bless the seeds you'll soon plant, and weave a wreath of primroses, dandelions and other spring blooms to wear in your hair, or plant seedlings in your garden to call on the energy and life force of the season.

The spring equinox, celebrated on September 22 or 23 in the southern hemisphere and March 20 or 21 in the north, is the point where night and day are of equal length, and marks the middle of spring. It is a time of balance and harmony both within and without, and a celebration of fertility, conception and regeneration as the earth blooms and the memory of winter's barren harshness fades. Seedlings emerge, new crops are sown, the buds on the trees open, birds build nests and lay eggs, and new life is celebrated. (Easter's bunny rabbits and eggs are a symbol of the fertility of the spring equinox – the early Christians converted the pagan festival of Ostara into Easter, and kept many of the associations.) This is the time to sow the seeds of what you want to achieve in the coming year. Write down the specifics of what is required, outline the first action you need to take, then start, because energetically this is a very fertile time, when you can make things happen and create your own reality. Plant a seed or a tree in your garden or in a pot inside, infusing it with your intent and determination, then nurture it along as you nurture your own dream, seeing your own progress symbolically reflected in your plant's growth.

Beltane, which falls in early November in the southern hemisphere and early May in the north, is the festival of love and fertility that marks the beginning of the heat and energy of summer. It's all about fertility, both literally and metaphorically. Your garden will be lush and full of colour, and your dreams will be starting to manifest as the fires of creativity and passion ignite. Beltane is also the festival of the faeries, when they were believed to emerge into the human world to dance, find a lover, impart their wisdom and teach the odd lesson before withdrawing back into the mists. During the long, bright evenings of early summer you can almost see them dancing in your garden, flitting from vividly coloured flower to gently waving leaf. Connect to the energy of the fae by opening up to the faery realm. Meditate in your garden, paint, draw, write about or hang pictures of these magical winged beings, or perform a divination reading with a faery oracle deck, drawing on their wisdom to gain insight into your future and your self. Spend as much time as you can in your garden or near your pot plants, attuning yourself to nature's abundant energy and adding your fresh herbs to food and drinks so you can absorb it all.

The summer solstice, which falls on December 21 or 22 in the southern hemisphere and June 20 or 21 in the north, marks the peak of energy and solar power of the year. It is the middle of summer, so magically captured by Shakespeare in *A Midsummer Night's Dream,* and celebrated as Litha by pagans. In nature it's a time of ripeness and abundance, and your garden will be growing tall and strong. Bury pieces of citrine and topaz crystals in the earth to encourage abundant growth of the plants as well as your dreams. Traditionally it was a time of relaxation, as the crops had been planted but the harvest was yet to come, so rest, restore and enjoy the beautiful weather. This is the perfect time to harvest and dry your herbs for use in winter, as they are at their most potent, having absorbed the sun's peaking strength. Fill a vase with bright summer blooms like daisies, sunflowers, honeysuckle, roses and citrus blossoms to represent the cheeriness of the season, and breathe in their heavenly scent. Plant a sun wheel garden with golden herbs like vervain, Saint John's wort, juniper and rosemary. Midsummer is the second feast of the faeries, so leave an offering for the hidden folk and petition for their blessings in matters of love and life.

Lughnasadh, which falls in the first week of February in the southern hemisphere and the first week of August in the north, is the cross-quarter day that marks the start of autumn and the first harvest festival. The trees turn a rich red-gold-orange-brown-rust colour, and it's a time of thanksgiving and revelry in appreciation of nature's bounty. It's also about the things you grow and create in your own life and a celebration of your successes, so create a ritual of appreciation that is meaningful for you to acknowledge all you have achieved. In your garden, harvest and dry herbs and flowers, make jams if you grow fruit, and gather the seeds to be planted next year to continue the dance of planting, growing and culmination. As the energy begins to subtly slow and the tides of the earth start to ebb, it's also a time to be patient and to trust that everything is as it should be, because there are still harvests to come.

The autumn equinox, which falls on March 20 or 21 in the southern hemisphere and September 22 or 23 in the north, marks mid autumn, and is the second point where the length of day and night is equal. For pagans this is Mabon, a time of crisp, chilly mornings, pale skies and a world aflame with colour as the trees turn a hundred shades of red-gold. The second harvest begins, when fruits, vegetables and remaining crops are brought in from the fields, and the next batch of herbs and flowers are gathered. It's also a powerful time to release what no longer serves you in order to move forward. Many plants grow better, and produce more abundantly, if they are pruned regularly. In gardens and in the wild, old growth is cleared. In your life, cut out anything that's holding you back, draining you or preventing new life and love from flourishing, whether it's work, a person, a belief system, a regret or an echo from the past.

Samhain, which falls in early May in the southern hemisphere and early November in the north (and on October 31 in popular culture, where it is celebrated as Halloween), honours the Wheel of the Year as it turns towards the barrenness of winter, in nature and in our lives, and is a time of withdrawal and introspection. It's the third and last harvest of the year, when anything left in the garden or fields is gathered in and stored for the dark months ahead. Harvest the last of your herbs for use in the winter. At this time the energy of the earth starts to withdraw and nature slows down and begins to wither and die, requiring work in the garden, and inspiring contemplation in your life. This is the perfect time to let go of the energy of the past and of old memories so you can move forward with lightness and strength. It can be hard work at times, filled with sometimes painful self-examination and remembering, but out of this darkness comes regeneration, renewal and transformation, just like in your garden.

Serene's Balcony Garden

A lack of space doesn't have to be a hindrance to creating your very own faery garden. You can plant one in the shade of a rose bush, in a pot (or series of pots) on your balcony, or in a long planter on your windowsill. I live in a city apartment, so I've created a magical balcony garden to bring the energy of nature and the beauty of all the faery flowers into my life.

Start with a large container that has good drainage, in whatever shape you like best. If you can place it in a spot that has some shade, but still leaves it open to being bathed in morning sunlight and dancing night-time moonbeams, that is ideal. You can use one massive pot, and create an entire faery garden in that, or use a few large pots that can combine to create your magical new world.

Once it is filled with good soil or potting mix, create a soft faery carpet for your magical friends to tiptoe through. Plant some fragrant minor or woolly thyme or chamomile in the centre, to provide a soft ground cover that smells sweet and fragrant. It will grow quickly to provide a green leafy carpet, dotted with pretty pink or white flowers in spring. Or grow brass buttons, a gorgeous miniature ground cover that looks like tiny ferns and has mini yellow flowers, making a great forest floor for a wooded faery garden. Or you could use baby tears, a lush green miniature ground cover said to attract elves, or ornamental strawberries, a heat tolerant miniature ground cover that has pretty white blossoms in spring and faery-sized strawberries in summer.

Around the edges, plant a series of small flowers and shrubs, choosing brightly coloured and sweetly scented ones so it's as appealing to you as it is to the fae – and to butterflies, bees, ladybirds and dragonflies.

You could plant a forest of miniature lavender in one corner, and allow it to grow a little wild. Curly chive plants can form a small hedge.

Marigolds will add a splash of fiery colour. Beautifully scented violets, violas or pansies, which have flowers that look like little faery faces, will make you and the faeries smile.

Foxgloves, bleeding hearts, little lady orchids and lady's slippers will also be appreciated as they're believed to provide clothing for any faery visitors, and are beautiful flowers that will make your garden a pleasure to spend time in and around.

Queen Anne's lace, aka wild carrot, can be used for bed sheets (although it is a noxious pest in the US, so avoid planting it if you are there), thistle or milkweed can be used for filling faery pillows, and milkweed pods can be made into cradles for baby faeries.

Lily of the valley and bluebell flowers, amongst others, can be used by the fae to make musical instruments, and the leaves from miniature mint plants make refreshing party drinks.

Toadstools, lichen or moss will also be well used, and will add a sense of magic and fun to your garden.

Next, add a small water feature to your pot. This can be as elaborate as a tiny fountain or as simple as a shell or small dish filled with water, or a pot plant saucer to form a lake. Add a little bridge over it and a cobblestone path made from shells, small pebbles or rose quartz crystals winding through the garden.

Leave some walnut or acorn shells out, along with seashells and other trinkets, for use as faery beds, boats or bowls. Add some furniture, or twigs and stones the fae can use as tables and chairs.

Faeries are attracted to stone circles too, so create a tiny one for them, using your favourite crystals to amplify the energy, pebbles you find on your nature walks, or stones shaped from clay. Add a bit of mirror for good luck, and a faery statue or two so they know they are welcome. You can add doll house furniture too, or buy special faery furniture (try www.thefairysgarden.com and www.thefairygarden.com.au).

If you have room, you can place separate pots right next to your main faery garden pot. Grow larger plants like honeysuckle or jasmine in their own pot, where they will contribute their beautiful scent to perfume the air and their pretty flowers for the faeries to use for clothing and spring festivities. An elder tree in another pot will provide shade, as well as berries and blossoms for food and sacred medicine.

For food, for yourself and the faeries, plant strawberries, cherry tomatoes, small lettuce,

radishes, carrots, cucumbers and any dwarf varieties of your favourite vegies, as well as herbs like basil, chives, thyme, marjoram, calendula and rosemary, which all have beautiful flowers too.

You could use another large pot to create a medicinal herb garden too. Learning about herbal medicine and growing your own fresh plants is an act of love and healing, as you will infuse each plant with your own energy, as well as taking in the unique therapeutic properties of each herb or vegie when you eat it.

You can also make summery faery drinks with homegrown mint, chamomile and lavender. Snip these plants often to encourage them to grow fuller and more abundantly, and also to benefit more often from your yummy, healthy herbs.

Choose light coloured pots if possible, as darker containers will absorb more heat, which can damage the roots of your plants. Plants in pots require more water than those planted in the ground, so keep an eye on soil moisture levels. You can also add crystals to each pot to encourage growth and instil extra energy.

If you're in an apartment that doesn't have a balcony, you can still create a faery garden in your kitchen or on a windowsill. Your plants need a warm, well-lit spot, preferably near a window so they can get fresh air, but where they won't be exposed to too much heat through the glass. A window box or windowsill, where you can open the window when it's hot, is perfect. Plant a herb garden in it, choose some flowers or even start a tiny potted vegie patch. Certain indoor plants, such as peace lilies, purple waffle plants and English ivy, remove toxins from the air as well as attracting faery energy, so have one near your computer or by your bed to encourage peaceful, restorative sleep and magical dreams.

"Where are the fairies, where can we find them?
We've seen the fairy rings, they leave behind them.
When they have danced all night, where do they go?
Lark, in the sky above, say, do you know?
Is it a secret no one is telling?
Why, in your garden, surely they're dwelling!
No need for journeying, seeking afar,
Where there are flowers, there fairies are."
Cicely Mary Barker, Where?

Faery Flowers

All flowers, herbs, trees and plants are magical, but there are some that have become particularly associated with the fae, so any of these will be a wonderful, magical addition to your faery garden. Some are predominantly ornamental, bringing beauty into your life, while others have healing properties in addition to their lovely scent and gorgeous flowers. Remember though, while herbs are natural, they are very powerful, and some can be toxic in large doses, so never self medicate. Even some essential oils are contra-indicated for pregnancy or certain medical conditions, so always consult a herbalist, naturopath or aromatherapist.

Bluebell

One of the most famous of the faery flowers is the bluebell, also known as faery thimbles, which has been closely linked to the realm of the fae for centuries, and has inspired many stories and artworks about the Bluebell Faery. It's said that the faeries ring the bells of these delicate plants to summon their friends to meetings, as well as to make instruments to create their enchanted music, so if you hear a sweet melody coming from a patch of bluebells, there may be faeries dancing amongst them.

In England, the common bluebell (hyacinthoides non-scripta) is also known as ring-o'-bells, wood bells and wild hyacinth. Its pretty blue bell-shaped flowers hang from a central stem, drooping downwards and providing a good hiding place for the faeries, while also attracting bees and butterflies. In spring it grows wild in the forests, blanketing the ground with a beautiful thick blue carpet that identifies the area as ancient woodland, which is home to many rare and threatened species – and no doubt lots of faeries too.

There are several types of bluebells, including the Scottish bluebell (campanula rotundifolia), also known as harebells, and the Australian bluebell (wahlenbergia gracilis). Magically they symbolise love, luck, truth and gratitude, and have an energy aligned with the cleansing power of spring, new growth and inspiration. An old legend states that if you walk through a field of bluebells you'll become enchanted, and be spirited away to the Otherworld by the Little Folk. Making an anklet of bluebells to wear on Beltane Eve can also attract the faeries to you.

Foxglove

Also known as faery gloves, faery petticoats and witches' bells, the foxglove plant boasts beautiful pink, white or purple flowers shaped like bells, hence its association with the fae, as they could be pictured making their homes in the flowers and using the petals as clothing. In Celtic lands it was known as the faery herb due to its magical properties – increasing psychic awareness, revealing what is hidden and protecting from negative forces, as well as encouraging communication with the fae. Simply carrying a foxglove sprig in a talisman is believed to surround you in faery energy.

Today it is known as a magical plant because a compound in the leaves, digitoxin, is a cardiac stimulating substance that has saved the lives of many heart patients, and forms the basis of digoxin, the life-saving heart drug. Yet the plant can be toxic, and should not be taken internally. It was once used as a poison (hence its folk name of deadmen's bells), and to treat congestive heart failure, skin problems such as boils, acne, sores and ulcers, joint pain and swelling, and as a sedative, a diuretic and an antidote to aconite poisoning. But only wise women could administer it, because while in supervised doses it saves lives, it can also be lethal – a warning stated that foxglove "can raise the dead but kill the living," so it should only be grown for its beauty and faery attraction.

The tubular foxglove flowers grow in clusters on a strong stem. The bottom flowers on each stem start blooming in spring, and the others gradually open too until the whole stem is full of blossoms – thriving at Midsummer, the feast of the faeries. The beautiful lily of the valley plant, which has similar properties to foxglove, is also a favourite of the fae.

Primrose

Traditionally known as the faery flower, primroses are a favourite of the enchanted realms, and are said to attract magical beings to your garden. You can also hang a bunch of dried flowers at your front door to welcome them into your home. Primroses are one of the first spring flowers to blossom (hence the name, from the old Latin "prima rosa", or first rose), which makes it an Imbolc herb. It used to be made into a special sabbat wine, and the flowers and leaves were eaten in the belief that they had the power to make the invisible visible, and would help people to see the fae.

There's also a legend that if you tap a faerie rock with a certain number of primroses a portal will open to Faeryland – but if you have the wrong number in your bouquet, you'll be in mortal danger. The primrose's beautiful bright little flowers range from all shades of yellow to white and even pinky-reddish-purple, although yellow is the most common. Ancient peoples considered it a herb of immortality, and it is sacred to the goddess Freya. Primroses are placed on altars and used in rituals to bring love, and are believed to enhance beauty if you add some primrose bath salts or an infusion of the flowers to your bath.

Faery Bath Salts

To prepare for a faery ritual or to strengthen your connection with the fae, soak in a magical bath with your very own faery bath salts. To create a beautiful, natural and magically-crafted bath salt mixture, combine 3 parts Epsom salts, 2 parts baking soda, 1 part table salt and 1 part dried primrose flowers in a large bowl and gently combine. Store them in a pretty glass jar. Add two to four tablespoons to your ritual bath as the tub is filling. You can swap the primroses for any other flower – try jasmine, rose petals, lavender, heather, honeysuckle or any other flower you want to absorb the vibration of. You can also use fresh flowers if you prefer. Just make up a batch of the bath salts without the dried primroses, then when you run a bath, add three tablespoons to the water, along with a handful of fresh petals. Or you can use essential oils – add 10 drops to half a cup of the plain salts mixture and stir well. Test the essential oil on your skin first, as some can cause irritation.

Thyme

This fragrant herb with its pretty pink flowers has long been associated with the fae. An old recipe for a potion to allow you to see into the Otherworld included the flowers and leaves of wild thyme, marigold flowers, rosewater and hazel buds, and was recommended to be taken on Beltane Eve and at Midsummer.

It's believed that wearing a sprig will help you to see the inhabitants of the enchanted realms, and planting it by the doors and windows of your house, or sprinkling the crushed herb there, will invite the faeries to come inside. It's also said that faeries hide their babies under thyme leaves to keep them safe, and in Shakespeare's *A Midsummer Night's Dream*, the faery queen Titania sleeps on a bed of wild thyme thriving on a river bank.

When growing thyme, there are many varieties, which have different coloured flowers and varied sweet fragrances. Woolly thyme creates a sweetly scented ground cover that is heat and drought resistant, orange thyme has a citrus scent, and winter thyme is more strongly aromatic, with narrower leaves. There are others too, so find out which ones will grow best in your garden, and choose the one you like the most.

As well as being a wonderful herb to cook with, thyme has also been used for thousands of years for its healing properties, to treat chest and respiratory problems including coughs, colds, bronchitis and chest congestion, sore throats, wounds, ulcers and abscesses, stomach aches and digestive problems, amongst other things. It was also used in sick rooms as a disinfectant and antibacterial.

It has long been associated with magic and the Otherworld too. The Ancient Egyptians used it in their embalming rituals, and in Europe during the Middle Ages it was burned at funerals to ensure a gentle transition into the next world. It is also placed in dream pillows to aid sleep and ward off nightmares, and an old tradition called for young women to put a sprig of thyme and a sprig of rosemary under their pillow on the night of the full moon, in the hope that the faeries would send them a vision of their true love.

Lavender

This beautiful purple flower is also known as elf leaf, and is believed to attract faeries and elves and help you see the spirit world. In faery lore, the Little Folk make lavender-infused wine for their midnight parties, and they also appreciate the soothing scent of the flowers, so it's a good choice for a faery garden. There are even miniature varieties available that are perfect for balcony planting. It's a hardy plant that requires little water, yet its pretty flowers and soft grey-green leaves are all sweetly scented, and it's one of the most versatile and healing herbs around.

Medicinally lavender has been used to treat many disorders, from migraines, rheumatism and nausea to colds, asthma, depression and nervous tension. The essential oil is used as an antiseptic and healing agent for cuts, burns and troubled skin, and it's also a popular treatment for insomnia and sleep issues, reduces mental and emotional stress and improves meditation and relaxation. Bundles of the dried flowers were once burned in birthing rooms, and the fresh flowers were included in handfasting rituals. You can use dried lavender in a sleep pillow, rub the essential oil on the temples, drop some on your pillow or vapourise it in an oil burner, add fresh flowers to a warm bath, drink an infusion of the plant or inhale the incense. A bunch of flowers, either fresh or dried, will bring the plant's magic inside.

Magically lavender is used in many love spells, and in rituals to bring happiness, peace and harmony to your life. It's an ingredient in incenses that increase inner stillness and peace, can be used to mark out a sacred circle, and also boosts intellect and logic. Traditionally it was burned in the Midsummer fires as an offering to the faeries, so having it in your garden will invite magic – and magical visitors – into your life, lift your spirits and provide a mini medicine cabinet too!

Sweet Woodruff

This lush herb with its delicate white flowers is used by the fae for their midnight revelries, as it reflects the moonlight and adds potent magic to a situation – it's long been an ingredient in magical summer wines for this reason. It is associated with Beltane, and used in rituals and thrown on the bonfires during sabbat ceremonies. And it was sacred to the druids, who used it for protection, both emotionally and physically, to bring luck and in spells for new beginnings.

Aligned with the element of fire, growing it will encourage fire elementals to visit your garden. It is sweetly fragrant and makes a beautiful ground cover, and additionally it guards against garden pests and prevents them nibbling on your other plants. Also known as wild baby's breath, it can be used fresh as well as dried, when it is a popular ingredient in potpourri. Medicinally it has been used to heal minor wounds, soothe stomach and nerve disorders and as a mild sedative. It's a native of Germany's Black Forest, where it is known as the master of the forest, and other faery haunts.

Faery Powder

Creating a herbal powder is a simple way to utilise the magical properties of herbs, and they're easy to make. Simply grind the required herbs, in their dried state, as finely as possible, empowering them with your energy and intent as you do so, then sprinkle it to release its powers. The powder can be stored in a glass jar, and sprinkled whenever you need to call on the energy of the herbs. To see the faeries, make a powder with 1 part thyme, 1 part lavender and 1 part sweet woodruff, and sprinkle it on your altar in the shape of faery wings or a seven-pointed star, which will give you an image to focus on for visualisation, as well as adding the boost of the herbs and their vibrations and influence. Alternatively you could sit outdoors within a sacred circle, its boundaries marked out with the powder, and invoke the nature spirits around you, or simply sprinkle some in your garden to help you connect to the faery energy.

Powders can also be sprinkled around crystals to boost their power, or around the base of a candle before you light it to accentuate the effectiveness of a spell. You could sprinkle a money attracting powder (made from herbs such as cedar, lavender and ginger) in your wallet, on to your money or around your office, a love powder (lavender, cinnamon, rose petals and yarrow) on your sheets, around the bedroom or in a sachet, and a happiness powder (marjoram, lavender and catnip) throughout the house to lift your spirits. A pinch of ground orris root, which is the root of the iris plant, will fix the scent of your powder, as well as adding its own special properties – orris is a lunar herb, so it's widely used for divination and dreamwork, and connecting with the Otherworld.

Heather

This hardy plant with its small, pretty coloured flowers grows wild and abundantly across the moors and heaths of Europe, and increasingly in the southern hemisphere too. Also known by the folk name ling, heather has a sweet scent, and is a favourite flower of the bees. Heather honey is delicious, rare and much sought after, and perfect for faery cooking.

Traditionally heather was used to treat arthritis, rheumatism and gout, heal eye infections, stomach aches and ulcers, prevent and dissolve kidney stones and help nursing mothers produce more milk. A sacred druid herb, it also promotes peace and wellbeing in the home – it can be hung in bunches inside or woven into decorations like Brigid/Bride crosses to maintain a happy household. In the bedroom it can help you sleep better, and in a magical room or near your altar it will increase the effectiveness of other herbs.

Magically, it's used for protection and healing, while purple heather specifically enhances psychic awareness, white heather is worn or carried as a talisman to attract luck and prevent harm, and red heather is good in spells to add passion. People used to make an offering of heather to the faery folk on Beltane Eve, to encourage and invite their presence, and a field of heather is said to be a portal to Faeryland, so a heather bush is perfect for your fae garden.

Marigold

The pretty golden flowers of this hardy, easy to grow perennial are also believed to attract faeries to your garden. Long blooming and vibrant in a range of yellow-orange-reds, marigolds create a splash of vivid colour and lift the spirits with their magical properties. Also known as calendula, it is a visionary herb, used especially in divination for a soulmate, and is an ingredient in love spells and a potion to help you see faeries. It is used to consecrate ritual tools, and the flowers are placed on altars or strewn around a ritual room to purify and cleanse, and to prepare for Beltane rites.

Marigolds were planted on graves and at burial sites to bless the dead as they journeyed to the next world. They have long been used in cooking, with the flowers added to salads or healing soups, while medicinally the deep orange varieties have been used to treat skin disorders such as eczema and psoriasis, as well as wounds, insect bites, measles, fever, epilepsy, headaches and jaundice. Just the sight of the bright flowers, which open as the sun rises and close as it sets, can increase happiness, comfort the heart and improve eyesight.

Mint

Mint, also known as monk's herb, is an important ingredient in faery drinks and faery food, and its heavenly scent and pretty flowers make it a beautiful addition to a magical garden. It's a perennial, meaning it will thrive for several years, and it can be grown in a pot inside or in an outdoor garden. There are several varieties, including peppermint and spearmint, and they all grow quickly and well – and can even take over the garden if you don't trim it regularly, so there's no reason not to use lots of it (mint flower ice-cream anyone?).

Medicinally this herb has long been used to aid digestion and stomach disorders, and treat sore throats, cold and flu, asthma, colic, earache and ear infections. It eases depression, sunburn and headaches, and is a stimulant, aiding long study sessions and any mental activity. It was a sacred herb to the druids, and is protective both physically and emotionally, warding off illness and negativity. It is commonly used in money spells to attract wealth, prosperity and luck, and can be placed on an altar during spellworking to assist the magic and boost the healing properties of rituals. It also has restorative powers – eating the leaves or drinking an infusion during trance work can help ground you and restore your energy.

A Faery Infusion

An infusion, known in faerytales as a witch's potion or brew, releases the medicinal and magical properties of a herb into water, which can then be drunk in order to absorb the energy and vibration of the herb internally, or added to a bath, compress or poultice, or used to anoint your body or clean magical tools. They are simple to make – pour one cup of boiled spring water over 1 teaspoon of dried herbs or 2 teaspoons of finely chopped fresh herbs, using a teapot, lidded jar or cup (but if using the latter, cover it with a saucer so the essential oils don't escape in the steam, as they are part of the magic and healing power of the infusion). Infusions are usually left to brew for a few hours or overnight.

You can also make an infusion by using the heat and power of the sun to release the energy of the herb into the water – simply place the herb, covered with spring water, in a clear glass jar and leave outside in the sunshine. Some herbs, such as feverfew, angelica, calamus and mallow, are so fragile or have parts that are so highly volatile that cold water is recommended so the active properties are not destroyed by the heat. In this case, soak quarter of a cup of fresh herbs in a cup of cold spring water overnight. Strain and reserve this liquid, then pour a cup of boiling water over the herbs. Allow it to cool, then mix this infusion with the original brew, to maximise the active substances. Other herbs, especially when using the roots, seeds or bark, need to be simmered in hot water for some time to extract the magical or healing properties, which is known as a decoction. Once you've made your infusion, strew the used herbs around the plants in your garden for extra nourishment.

Roses

These beautiful flowers and their sweet scent should attract lots of faeries to your garden, and there are miniature varieties that can be grown in a pot if you don't have a yard, as well as a rainbow of colours to choose from. Roses represent love, and are sacred to the love goddesses, so they can be used in love spells and to attract romance as well as self-love into your life. Specific colours also have different meanings, such as red for passionate love, yellow for joy and friendship, pink for sweetness, dark pink for gratitude and white for innocent love, so you can choose the one you need most. Sprinkle fresh rose petals on the floor and dance, releasing their fragrance as they're gently crushed under foot, and ask the faeries to grant you your heart's desire. You can also make rose oil and anoint your heart chakra as you meditate on love and compassion.

Medicinally, rose petal tea has been used since the time of the Romans to ease indigestion and hangovers, while rosehips are taken to prevent colds and as an anti-inflammatory to treat osteoarthritis, rose oil soothes skin disorders, depression, anxiety and PMS, and rose water is used in many cultures as a beauty treatment and general tonic and to calm eye irritation. You can also add fresh or dried rose petals to your bath, which will centre you, improve skin tone and prepare you for a faery ritual.

Milkweed

These plants are considered weeds, and even pests, by some, but they have their own beauty, and are very attractive to the fae, with their presence in a garden thought to invite the Little People to come and play. Milkweed is also a butterfly magnet, with monarchs in particular laying their eggs in the flowers, and insects, bees, moths and other herbivores loving the milky nectar it produces.

Medicinally milkweed has been used to treat skin irritations, and research is now being done into its efficacy as a skin cancer remedy. It can help in treating asthma, bronchitis, fever, kidney stones, parasitic worms and abdominal conditions too, and has long been used as an antidote to poison ivy stings and to increase and improve blood circulation.

Milkweed pods can be used by faeries as little beds, and the fine down released from them, exposed when the fruit releases its seeds, can be collected to make soft mattresses and pillows. These silky tassels can also be added to human dream pillows to encourage your dreams of the fae, and when the fluffy seeds fly through the autumn air, you can make a wish for each one you catch. Magically milkweed is used in blessing rituals, and in spells to bring inspiration and creativity. It is also a herb of the autumn equinox and a part of Mabon festivities, and is believed to help you see faeries.

Chamomile

This pretty herb, with its sweetly apple-scented flowers, makes a perfect ground cover for your faery garden, which will also prevent weeds and soil erosion. The Ancient Egyptians dedicated chamomile to their sun god Re in recognition of its immense healing benefits, and other cultures also held it in high regard, and still do today.

Chamomile is one of the most mainstream of all the herbs. The tea is available in supermarkets and restaurants around the world, and is consumed by even those uninterested in the healing power of herbs in order to soothe the nerves and promote restful sleep. Medicinally chamomile is taken internally, in the form of an infusion, to ease stress, anxiety, insomnia, stomach problems and headaches, and it can be used as a mouth or eye wash as well as a hair rinse. A compress or ointment made from it can also speed the healing of wounds, burns, rashes and inflammation.

Magically chamomile is considered a herb of purification and protection. It's used in a bath to prepare for a ritual, in incenses and oil burners to encourage relaxation and peace, is burned or sewn into a charm bag to draw love to you, and is one of the ingredients in a faery dream pillow.

Faery Dream Pillow

To entice the faeries into your dreams, make a dream pillow to place under your normal pillow at night. You can sew together two pieces of soft fabric, such as velvet or satin, or use a drawstring organza bag to hold your herbal blend. Mix together 1 part dried chamomile flowers, 1 part dried rose petals, 2 parts silky tassels of milkweed, 1 part dried lavender, 1 part dried primroses, 1 bay leaf and a sprinkle of dried thyme. Replace the flowers every six months. You can also experiment to create your own recipes with the faery flowers you like best, or you can make a dream pillow from fresh poppy flowers, or have an afternoon sleep in a field of poppies, to welcome the faeries into your dreams.

Vervain

Vervain, a small perennial plant with lilac flowers, is used in love potions and healing spells, and has long been considered sacred. It was revered by the druids, who used it in initiation rites, to crown priestesses, as a protection while working magic and invoking spirits, and in the water they sprinkled on people and objects as a blessing. It was also used by Roman priests on their altars, to sweep the area clean and energetically cleanse the atmosphere.

Today it's used in many recipes and rituals by magical herbalists, including protection spells, purification bath sachets and exorcism incenses, and it's either worn or scattered through the house to calm emotions and induce peace. It boosts the Sight and other divinatory methods, prevents bad dreams, attracts money and good fortune, and is placed in a baby's cradle to instil happiness in the child.

Medicinally vervain has been used to treat nervous disorders, insomnia, fevers, ulcers, wounds, infected gums and tooth decay, liver disorders, fatigue, asthma and postnatal depression, as well as to enhance contractions during childbirth (so it should be avoided during pregnancy) and increase milk flow. A poultice of the herb can ease headache, rheumatism, neuralgia, sprains and bruises.

Vervain is also known as the herb of enchantment, herb of grace and herb of the cross (as it was believed to have been used to staunch

Jesus's wounds when he was crucified). It is a feminine plant associated with the planet Venus and the goddesses Venus, Isis, Ceridwen and Juno, as well as the gods Mars, Jupiter and Thor.

Elecampagne

Also known as elfswort, this herb with its sunny yellow flowers that look like dandelions is closely associated with elven magic, and will connect you with the old, deep and grounded earthly powers of the elves. It's used in love potions and rituals of deep magic, and in rites of initiation. The root can be scattered around the home to welcome faeries, and the flowers can be worn to attract love and increase divination powers, faery communication and the Sight. Medicinally it has been used to treat lung conditions such as asthma and bronchitis, as well as colds, skin disorders and upset stomachs. It soothes nerves, and can be used as a cleansing tonic to prepare for magical rites.

Jasmine

This beautiful, delicate white star-shaped flower is beloved of the faeries, so if you're performing a faery ritual you can wear the flowers in your hair or place some in a vase on your altar, drink jasmine tea, make a sachet of dried jasmine flowers or anoint your body with jasmine oil. It is also associated with psychic protection, spiritual health and love. In the Philippines, the name of the jasmine flower, sampaguita, comes from the words for "I promise you", and represents a pledge of mutual love – thus a young couple traditionally exchanged jasmine necklaces instead of wedding rings.

In India jasmine flowers represent divine as well as romantic love – the flower is called "moonshine in the garden", and ancient paintings depict moonlit lovers near jasmine plants. For thousands of years the Chinese, Arabians and Indians used the oil in love spells and as an aphrodisiac, claiming that it penetrated the deepest layers of the soul and opened emotions. It was introduced to Egypt in the time of the pharaohs, and Cleopatra seduced Mark Antony with it.

As well as being used in love magic and to enhance spirituality, peace and psychic awareness, the scent of the flowers is relaxing and can lift depression, boost confidence and revitalise energy, while medicinally jasmine oil tones the skin and improves elasticity, helps reduce stretch marks and scars, soothes the respiratory system, easing coughs and laryngitis, and reduces muscle pain.

Faery Flower Oil

Jasmine, like most flowers, doesn't bloom all year, so you can make a magical faery oil to use when the flowers are out of season. Magical oils concentrate the power of the plant into a versatile and easy to use form – the oil retains the full scent of the herb, as well as its magical vibration, which means you can store them for a long time. Even dried flowers and herbs lose their scent, whereas magical oils retain theirs. Scent is a very powerful, potent sense, creating an intense reaction in the body both physically, emotionally, mentally and spiritually. Certain scents activate and stimulate different areas of the brain, and trigger different emotions that will aid the magical outcome you are after.

One of the oldest methods of fragrance extraction is enfleurage, which is a simple way to make scented oils. Fill a jar with the flowers or herbs you want to make the oil from – you can use either fresh or dried ones – then cover the flowers with a carrier oil such as pure virgin olive oil, safflower, sunflower, jojoba or almond oil, filling the jar completely. Tightly cap the jar, then leave it in a warm dark place for three days. The mix should be shaken each day to ensure all the flowers are covered and the fragrance is dispersed into the oil. The process should be repeated every three days, straining the spent flowers and discarding them, and refilling the jar with fresh ones, until the oil is heavily saturated with fragrance. The scented oil should then be stored in an amber bottle. You can add a few drops of benzoin tincture (or vodka or apple cider vinegar) as a preservative if you wish. You can try this with any flower you like, including jasmine, rose, gardenia and lavender.

Morning glory

There are a thousand species of morning glory flower, most of them flowering early in the morning (hence their name) and withering by the late afternoon, while other varieties, such as moonflower, open in the early evening, bloom all night and die by the morning. New flowers begin the cycle again each day, so a plant will appear to bloom for some time. In Australia they grow so quickly that they can take over an area and squeeze other plants out, but they are great for covering walls and back fences, and providing shade.

Morning glories come in a variety of colours, from vivid purples and pinks to whites and blues, and their petals form a five-pointed star shape within each flower, adding to their magic. Aztec priests and shamans from ancient cultures took advantage of the plant's hallucinogenic properties, and the Chinese used it for its medicinal qualities, although it can be toxic so it should not be ingested. Morning glory flower essence is used to encourage speaking your truth, overcoming shyness and uncovering your creativity, and is said to awaken you to your purpose.

Daisies

These pretty little flowers, which are easy to grow, represent love and sunshine, and can be planted to attract faeries, and particularly dryads, to your garden. Sitting in a field of daisies, or by a plant, is said to help you communicate with the spirit or deva of all your plants. Daisies are also strung into garlands to wear in your hair, especially at Midsummer, or around your wrist or ankle, and love divination has long been performed by counting the petals of a daisy ("He loves me, he loves me not...").

Feverfew

Also known as Midsummer daisy, which links it to the faeries, this pretty herb is carried to ward against sickness and protect you from accidents while travelling. Magically it is a herb of protection, purification, defence and cleansing. Medicinally it has been used to reduce and guard against fevers – hence its name – and in the treatment of migraines, to improve digestion and kidney function, ease arthritis and rheumatism and soothe coughs. It should not be ingested during pregnancy or while breastfeeding. Renowned 17th century herbalist Nicholas Culpeper said it was commanded by Venus, and thus helpful for women's conditions.

Clover

The rare and pretty four-leaf clover is associated with luck, because it represents a perfect balance of the four elements. Finding one is also reputed to protect you from mischievous faeries and their naughty spells. Traditionally people would place one under their pillow at night so they would dream of their beloved, and they were used in divination of a romantic kind. Clover is also used in rituals of love and fidelity, and to consecrate magical tools. It is a sacred faery plant, and will attract them to your garden. Faery lore states that if you lay seven grains of wheat on a four-leaf clover you will be able to see the Good Folk.

Rosemary

Traditionally known as the elf plant, this hardy woody shrub with pale blue flowers and evergreen leaves will entice magical beings to your garden, as rosemary bushes are thought to provide a place for faeries and elves to hide. It represents love and fidelity, so it has long been woven into wedding garlands and bouquets, while three sprigs tied together with red ribbon and hung on the door will invite love in. Medicinally rosemary has been used to stimulate the liver and gall bladder, improve digestion, ease spasms and soothe headaches. It also aids memory and learning and strengthens brain function, and can be used as a general tonic.

Magically it represents purification and protection – wreaths were hung on doors to ward off evil spirits, and it can be burned to dispel negative energy. You can sprinkle the leaves in a bath to purify yourself energetically and prepare for a ritual, and put it in a dream pillow to protect from nightmares. It also symbolises remembrance, so it has been planted on graves to honour the deceased's memory and as a sign of immortality, while the Ancient Romans burned it during sacrifices.

Pansies

The gorgeous flowers of this plant look like faery faces bobbing in the sunshine. There is a legend that pansies were created by the faeries from the colours of nature – blue for the sky, red for the sunset, yellow for the sun and brown for the earth. They have long been used in love potions and rituals to see and attract the faeries.

Honeysuckle

This pretty flower is carried to forget a past love. It is also used to boost psychic powers and assist with divination, clairvoyance and psychic awareness, by simply crushing the flowers and rubbing them on your forehead or using a magical oil to anoint your forehead and body, and in spells to increase abundance. Growing honeysuckle in your garden will attract money and luck as well as the fae, or you can simply keep a vase of fresh flowers in the home, which will achieve the same magic. This plant also has protective powers.

Faery Ring

A circle of mushrooms, toadstools or flowers, or even a circle of flattened grass, is said to mark out the boundaries of a faery ring, the magical space where the faeries have danced, and which they use as portals in to and out of the faery realm. You can plant your own circle of flowers or mushrooms to encourage faery visitors.

Some mushrooms associated with the faeries include fly agaric, yellow faery club, slender elf cap, dune pixie-hood and dryad's saddle, but some have hallucinogenic properties and are poisonous if ingested, so leave them for the fae to use as they will.

Trees

Trees are also sacred to the fae, and the older and wilder a forest, the more likely it is to be inhabited by magical beings, who dance amongst the trees, create faery rings in stands of pines, make homes in the hollow of oak trees and gather fallen autumn leaves, acorns and pine cones for garments and furniture. Faery lore states that when ash, oak and hawthorn, known as the tree faery triad in Britain, grow together, it creates a powerful place where the portal to Faeryland opens up, and it's easier to see the faeries. Three thorn trees growing together also creates deep faery magic.

Trees have been vital to humanity also, honoured as a gift from the goddess that both sustained physical life and symbolised the eternity of existence. Ancient peoples worshipped within groves of sacred trees, rather than indoors, so they could be connected to nature and nurtured by the strength of these majestic plants.

Grow a sacred tree for the faeries to play within and make their home, create a wand from a fallen branch, use the leaves in herbal preparations, sit beneath a tree and connect with the dryads that live within it, or get involved in tree planting and reforestation projects to show your love for the earth. All trees and plants have healing power, magic and something to teach – here are just a few of those that are associated with magic and the fae.

Ash

Faeries flock to the leafy ash, considered by many cultures one of the most sacred of all the trees, symbolising beauty, ambition and magic. The wood of the ash was used to make druid wands specific to healing and solar magic, while the leaves were placed under the pillow at night to stimulate visions and prophetic dreams. The tree itself represented the element of air, but it was also associated with fire, and was thus connected to resurrection and renewal, while its deep roots symbolise grounding and protection.

Oak

Considered the king of the forest, the oak is sacred in all cultures. Druids revered it for its size and great age, and it represents courage, strength, stability and endurance, an attraction for humans as well as fae. The wood has long been used for divination and to make wands, the roots to create magical tools, and the acorns to provide a nutritious food. The faeries also make use of the acorns, for hats, decoration and food, and the leaves for shelter and clothing.

Acorns also have their own magic for us. They can be used in spells for protection and fertility, both literally, for the conception of a child, and metaphorically, when you seek creativity and the birth of new ideas and the fruition of your new projects and dreams. According to legend: "Faery folks are in the oaks," and these ancient trees provide a safe haven for magical beings.

Hawthorn

Sacred to the faeries, and renowned as a home for dryads and other fae, the hawthorn is a Beltane plant, and has long been linked to fertility and magic. A contradictory tree, with beautiful white blossoms sitting right next to large thorns, hawthorn represents duality and balance, a melding of masculine and feminine as well as life and death. The wood is popular for wands, and the flowers and branches are used for love spells and in marriage rituals, as well as for protection and healing. Hawthorn trees are often used as wishing trees, where people tie ribbons and scraps of material to the branches to request luck, protection and a connection with the faery folk, and the berries are known as pixie pears.

Shhh! Faery Secret

Don't sit under a hawthorn tree unless you have plenty of time to spare. They often harbour secret faery portals and you may find yourself off with the faeries for a very long, and rather unscheduled, visit to Faeryland!

Elder

In faery lore, these trees protect the fae from negativity and bad spirits. The queen of the forest, elder holds the wisdom of the crone and has powerful feminine energy. It represents renewal and regeneration, aids emotional transformation and deepens visions and visualisation rituals. The wood was traditionally used for protective wands, and was associated with the summer solstice and the sun. It was used for magic involving nature and the spirits of the earth, and has powerful healing properties. Elderberry wine is considered the nectar of the faeries, and drinking it can reputedly help people see them. Adding dried elderberries to an incense can also help attract faeries to you.

Apple

Loved by faeries for their fragrant blossoms and abundant fruits, the bark or apples themselves can be used in faery magic and love spells, which are especially potent on Midsummer Night. The apple tree represents innocence, youth, peace and joy, and the wood is used to make wands. The apple was also the mystical fruit of the Otherworld, associated with the goddess and used in fertility rituals and love spells as well as to increase abundance. It symbolised wisdom and hidden knowledge, which was revealed in the five-pointed star found when an apple is cut crossways.

Ivy

This beautiful twining vine is used by faeries as decoration for their celebrations, associated with ancient gods and their revelry, and wound into garlands for human faery festivals and handfastings. It symbolises endurance and survival through all situations and conditions, as it clings on through the harshness of winter. The five-pointed leaves have long been used as an amulet of protection, it was woven into headpieces to symbolise clarity and knowledge, and was a powerful healing tool. Because it grows in a spiral pattern it also holds the qualities of rebirth and interconnection.

Mistletoe

Associated with the winter solstice, this evergreen bush is considered a gift of the gods, representing the sacred marriage of heaven and earth. The berries were used in love spells and incenses – a connotation they retain today in the ritual of kissing under the mistletoe – and the leaves were hung around the home to protect against negativity. It often grows around oaks, a magical combination. Mistletoe is also a magical activator, and adding some to a faery ritual or spell at Midsummer will empower it and help you to see the fae.

Holly

Another sacred herb of the druids, this was once brought inside homes during winter so the faeries and nature spirits had somewhere to stay, protected from the icy cold and snow. It was given as a gift at Midwinter to symbolise friendship, and made into wreaths at priestess initiation rituals. It is a protective herb, planted in gardens and around the house to guard against mischievous spirits, and made into an infusion to sprinkle on newborns to protect them from harm. It represents endurance and foresight, and brings luck and love.

Blackthorn

These trees are especially sacred to the lunantisidhe, shy Irish nature faeries who live within blackthorn bushes and protect them. Magic wands – and the shillelagh of the leprechauns – are made from blackthorn branches, and are said to grant wishes and offer protection to the user. However you must ask permission of the lunantisidhe to use it, or find a fallen branch for it to work. These wands are also effective as divining rods.

Pine

Faeries love the stability of pine trees, as well as the cleansing power and fresh scent. A tree of purification, pine is known as the sweetest of woods, and can be burned to cleanse an area physically and psychically, while a branch can be used to sweep a place of old energy. Pine represents friendship, stability and reliability, and the wood nymphs said to live within these trees can be called on for strength and courage. Pine cones can be used in fertility spells and carried as charms, and a pine needle ritual bath will help stimulate and cleanse emotionally before a great faery magic working.

Hazel

This tree represents knowledge and inspiration, as well as forgiveness. The wood has long been used to make wands for healing and ceremonial work, and forked twigs of hazel were used to divine the location of water and energy leys. It's associated with the sun, so it can be used in solar magic, it helps people understand the traits of humans and animals, and is also effective when working with faeries. Hazel buds were part of an old potion that helped people see the fae, along with wild thyme and marigolds.

Natural Magic

Once you have created your magical faery garden, you definitely won't want to scare off your fae visitors with chemicals and pesticides, so look for natural options for pest control and fertiliser. Creating your own compost heap is a good place to start, as this will help your plants as well as being good for its recycling aspect. It's also beneficial to strew the herbs from a pot of herb tea around the garden once you've made it, to add nutrients to the soil and feed your plants, or to add them to your compost. Nettle tea is not only rich in iron for human consumption, it's also especially good for adding vitamins and nutrients to the soil, while chamomile tea, and its flowers and leaves, will soothe and nurture you as well as giving your plants a lift.

To keep caterpillars off young plants, make a triple strength elder leaf tea, leaving it to stand for 24 hours, then straining and diluting the tea liquid with water before spraying it on the seedlings. Add the stewed leaves to the soil for an extra boost.

For a herbal spray to discourage slugs and snails, do the same with wormwood.

To create a general garden insecticide, chop up one unpeeled onion and one unpeeled head of garlic, add one tablespoon of cayenne pepper and simmer in a pot with two litres of water for 20 minutes. Allow to cool then store in the fridge for up to a month. To use, add one tablespoon of brew to half a litre of water and spray on your plants.

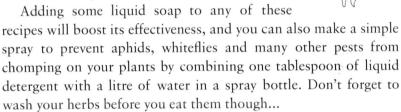

Adding some liquid soap to any of these recipes will boost its effectiveness, and you can also make a simple spray to prevent aphids, whiteflies and many other pests from chomping on your plants by combining one tablespoon of liquid detergent with a litre of water in a spray bottle. Don't forget to wash your herbs before you eat them though...

Placing fresh grass clippings around seedlings will protect them from snails and also guard them from the elements until they're strong enough to survive on their own. You can also use straw, seaweed, rocks or old newspapers as mulch, laying it around your plants to conserve the moisture in the soil, protect the roots, deter unwanted plants from growing and prevent soil erosion.

To repel insects such as aphids, grow basil, hyssop, calendula, nasturtiums, coriander or tansy in your garden, and to strengthen your plants and protect them from disease, plant lemon balm. To attract more butterflies and bees, which is essential for pollination as well as adding to your garden's faery appeal, plant lavender, mint, rosemary, bergamot, catnip, dandelions, mallow, sage, thyme, marjoram, anise, basil, borage, lemon balm and/or yarrow.

Also, learn as much as you can about the plants you want to grow and their needs for optimum health. Some, like lavender and sage, don't require much water, and will die if they get too much. Mint and angelica on the other hand needs lots of water to survive. Growing plants with different requirements too close together will make it much harder for your garden to flourish.

Most of all, have fun! Creating a faery garden is the perfect way to connect more deeply with nature, the faeries and your self, and to bring some natural magic indoors.

Lucy's Backyard Garden

One book I adore is Patricia A McKillip's *Solstice Wood*. It is a beautiful novel about the various and disastrous misunderstandings between faeries and humans, and its poetic pages right the wrongs of so much horrid propaganda. Fearful of faery power and strength, their natural abilities and their shapeshifting magics, humans are too quick to label what they do not understand as evil and other. How to overcome this? Plant a faery garden of course!

Thanks to creating a beautiful, very small faery garden, my connection with the faery realm has become more and more true and tangible. My home is a very odd, very old cottage in Sydney, built in 1882. It was first lived in by Elsie and Ethel, two women described in the building papers simply as spinsters.

Their father built the row of houses on my street, and my first order of business after moving in so very many years ago was to make their acquaintance. After chatting with Elsie and Ethel over the years, we've developed a lovely relationship, and they've helped me stay in their house – although for a long time I thought they wanted me to be the third spinster!

But we've all come to a lovely, peaceable working agreement, and one of the things I spoke to them about recently was the idea of a faery garden down the side passage of the house and in the tiny patch of dirt in the very small backyard courtyard, which has been sadly neglected for years. Elsie and Ethel are whimsical sisters, often "seen" with tea and liberty-print clothing, and hats with flowers. They loved the prospect of more faeries about the house, and offered up their ideas. It seems these gorgeous elderly-lady spirits just love faeries.

So, plans for a faery garden were unfolded and hatched between the faeries, Elsie, Ethel, me, my daughter and our animals and existing plants. Everyone was included. And as plans for creating small altars in a twisting, winding mini stepping-stone-strewn light well were acted upon, we transformed what was once an oasis for mildew and dog poo into a sanctuary for the faery folk.

I think our faery kin know us by our energy – we can say and sometimes do whatsoever we may like, but until our energy has some kind of harmony and accord with theirs, it can be nigh on impossible to see and feel the faery world. So, intent and action via the garden were my aims. I spent time picking up rubbish, not only at home, but all about my home in the neighbourhood.

Recently a lovely new friend told me that at times the faeries seem overwhelming to her – she can't keep up with what feel like demands. But the fae have told me that they do not wish for us to feel troubled or burdened. They are about fun and delight. So while we can tend a garden, and clean up litter, do not become a martyr to it all. Simply do what you can when it comes up. It is easy to carry a plastic bag with you when you go out, and pick up some rubbish. I do, and I am rewarded in my own backyard far more than the threefold law seems to account for!

So often, while humans are roaring about, so unseeing and unfeeling, often complaining about this or that great nothingness, the faeries are tucked behind a wide green tree, creating wonder and magic with tiny toadstools, feathers and twigs. Look closely around you, and you'll be able to discover tiny structures, and sleeping faeries resting for a while in material form.

If they are spied or seen accidently by a clumsy one they vanish, quick as a flash! But if we choose to see them, we can. Look around you. Fuchsia petals wrap around the sleeping fae. Honeysuckle blossoms are their chalices. Walnut boats take them out on puddles for lazy days on the lake of Avalon.

I have created my garden with what they have shared with me. There is a small house for them to shelter within, a spirit house from Thailand made of dark, glowing wood, beautifully carved. So that they know it's for them – which I'm sure they do – I have placed some tiny statues of faeries inside the house. It looks beautiful.

I have placed a magical mushroom family within the garden, encouraging mushrooms and toadstools to grow in their rings, so the Seelie and Unseelie Courts can hold their great meetings at Lughnasadh within my garden, if they so honour me. And I have "planted" brightly painted red and white toadstools

of various sizes, for more shelter as winter comes. Small pathways made of rose quartz lead from one faery section to the next, and exquisite figurines of faeries created by faery artists like Jessica Galbreth and Jasmine Becket-Griffith are studded between the star jasmine and honeysuckle vines. Large, ornate keys hang from trees. There are bells in the branches. It is beautiful.

Above it all, a grand old avocado tree watches over things. Inspired by the principles of the founders of Findhorn, who invited the faeries in to work with their gardens, I have asked the fae to work with the avocado. On her trunk is a clay-fired Green Man, watching over and protecting the faery garden, and within her high branches hangs the most plump, bright green and very nearly ripe harvest of avocados. They are very high up, so I am asking the faeries to please help me bring them down softly onto the ivy that grows along the small garden floor to cushion their fall. And plenty will be left in the trees for the birds and the fae.

In late summer and early autumn, I saw great black butterflies in my garden each day, spending their time moving from one tiny section to another, lazily lounging in the sun, flying so sensuously with their full, heavy black wings. Small wanderer butterflies have recently made a golden appearance too, so I know the time is coming for change, and migration, and movement. My faery garden has become a faery oracle, as well as a delight to the senses!

My enchanted fae garden is so very small, but within it I have herbs to welcome them – lush and fragrant thyme, rosemary, parsley and oregano. The neighbour's lemon tree leans further and further over the fence in close conversation with the avocado, and the lemons, once bitter and small, are now rounded, full and juicy. Their sweet smell drifts through the garden, and their blossoms during the last springtime were a delight for weeks on end.

So while my faery garden is a humble place, it is also an oasis of enchantment in a city of four million people. I know what the human population is. And I feel sure that there will be faery babies birthed in this garden when springtime comes again, and so, in this city of glass towers and lost souls, a few more faeries will now be found.

Faery Gardening Tips

☆ Invite the faeries in. Speak with them. Make stone circles for them to dance and play in. Offer them shelter (wide-leafed ground plants, mushrooms) and homes for them over the colder months.

☆ Place images of faeries within the garden so that they – and you – are clearly reminded that they are welcome there.

☆ Leave one section of the garden completely untended.

☆ Hang beautiful images of insects. I have many iron dragonflies and butterflies, which drew even more of these faery friends this year.

☆ Grow food, which is an act of healing and self-empowerment. Leave some for the fae too, and for any animals and insects that consider your garden a safe haven.

☆ Let the faeries know if you're going to change something. See how they feel about it – it is, after all, their garden. If you plan to mow the lawn or remove a tree, let them know in advance so they can energetically arrange what needs to be done so that no faeries or energy lines are disrupted.

☆ Don't use pesticides. Chat with the faeries, who often ride the backs of snails and fly with the ladybirds – they can help keep the insects at bay. Otherwise, there are natural alternatives.

There's a whimsy to the fae, and a deep shamanic tradition, that will reveal itself over time, in layers. Their nectar, their sweetness, their blossoms and their blessings create a happy and playful environment, where humour abounds and blends with a gentle spirit.

Faeries love festivities, get-togethers and gentle lunacy. They are sometimes so subtle that they can't be seen by some humans, so shy that they hide. But give them a place to dwell and you will find they come forward more often to play – and more importantly to work their gentle healing magics with you. Give them a place to have fun with you, the plants and the animals, and they'll bless you seven-fold!

And of course, gardening with the fae will introduce you to the local faeries – be sure to grow plants that produce nectar and fruits, and offer shelter. The rest is up to you! May your faery garden bloom and grow, in sweetness and love, and bring you and the faeries into an ever deepening and very happy relationship.

Guardians of the Earth

"You must be the change you want to see in the world."
Mahatma Gandhi, Indian political and spiritual leader

"I would feel more optimistic about a bright future for man if he
spent less time proving that he can outwit Nature and more time
tasting her sweetness and respecting her seniority."
EB White, American writer

Becoming an Eco Faery

As faeries are the spirit or embodiment of nature, connecting
with this magical energy will increase your love for the earth and
activate your environmental consciousness. In turn, doing your
bit for the planet and reducing your environmental footprint will
help align you with the energy and inspiration of the fae.

Faeries fill us with joy, laughter and lightness, whether you
believe these magical beings are literal or simply a beautiful figment
of the imagination. They remind us to have fun, to enjoy every
moment, to recognise the small triumphs in a difficult process, and
to take pleasure in simple things – the warmth of the sunshine, the
sweet scent of jasmine, the kiss of a loved one, the taste of
strawberries in summer, the sound of bird song or a favourite tune...

As the spirit of nature, faeries also remind us to care for the
earth. They are powerfully connected to and intrinsically linked
with the natural world, and inspire us to forge our own unique
relationship with it. They are the protectors of the wild places, the

beautifiers of stark cityscapes, the conscience and heartbeat of the planet. They call to that part of us that longs for and connects with the beauty of nature – our appreciation of a beautiful sunset, our awe at a sudden thunderstorm, the peace that comes from sitting in the shade of an ancient tree, the joy of splashing through the waves, dancing in the rain or watching a butterfly drift on a gentle breeze, and the healing that comes from tending our own little garden and connecting deeply and tangibly with the earth.

Communing with nature provides a sense of peace. It lowers stress, eases depression and puts you back in touch with yourself. Diving into the ocean, walking around the harbour, sitting in the sunshine or playing a CD of forest sounds can transport you to another state of being and transform your mood. Even just looking at pictures of nature or imagining yourself there has been proven to lower stress levels and induce a feeling of tranquillity. The natural world lifts the spirits, calms the mind, soothes the soul and gives perspective on anything that is worrying you.

Feeling that you're a part of nature also leads to a greater sense of environmental consciousness, because you stop seeing yourself as separate from the earth and its creatures, and instead become part of a greater whole. You realise we are all connected, dependent on each other, and that we all have a responsibility to halt the destruction of the planet and its flora and fauna.

One of the simplest ways to attune yourself with the energy of the fae is to become an eco warrior and embrace and care for the environment. There are many ways you can get involved, from simple things like donating to a cause or lobbying politicians, to more committed and complex methods such as taking part in the physical labour of healing the land or starting your own group to work on an issue close to your heart. There are many organisations that conserve the world's precious natural resources, and so many inspiring and committed people who are doing amazing work that you can support regardless of the amount of time you have.

There are lots of ways to be an eco faery and make a difference in the world, so let your imagination run wild and find something that resonates deeply with you and can become a meaningful part of your life. Reduce your ecological footprint, take action to help the earth, spend time outside in nature and open your heart to the world, embracing its wildness and caring for its plants and animals.

☆ **Spend more time outside.** Start to pay attention to the places of nature in your area, be it a lone tree or a huge park, and notice the birds, bats, squirrels and other creatures that visit, and the plants and flowers that grow there. Become more aware of the turning of the seasons, and when different foods are in season in your area. Out of season foods, like tropical fruits in the middle of winter, require more fuel and create extra emissions and greenhouse gases as they have to be flown in from around the world. Eating seasonal, organic foods also has health benefits, and results in a renewed connection to and awareness of the land and this beautiful earth. Attune yourself to the cycles of the moon too, feeling your energy ebbing and flowing as it does, making a wish on the new moon and dancing under the full moon, just as the faeries do.

☆ **Plant a tree.** Nurturing a plant and seeing it grow and flourish brings a sense of happiness and achievement, as well as helping the world by increasing the amount of oxygen in the atmosphere. You can plant a tree in your backyard, ask your council for permission to plant some in a park or reserve, on a nature strip or at a local school, or be part of your area's Tree Day, which aims to inspire people to plant, nurture, protect and celebrate trees. National Tree Day is Australia's biggest community tree-planting event. Held at the end of winter, in late July/early August, more than a million native trees and shrubs are planted around the country each year, while in Northern Australia, people plant native trees on Tropical Tree Day, which takes place in early summer. There are many international counterparts – the US celebrates Arbor Day on the last Friday in April, the UK on the last Sunday in May (when they also celebrate Be Nice to Nettles Week!) and New Zealand on June 5.

☆ **Save endangered rainforest** (and faery habitat) from your desk by clicking on www.therainforestsite.com or www.ecologyfund.com every day. Advertisers pay each time someone clicks on the sites, and the funds raised are used by conservation groups to buy and preserve land in Peru, Ecuador and other locations worldwide. It costs you nothing – just a moment of your time every day – and is an easy way to combat deforestation and promote awareness. You can also buy beautiful clothes, jewellery and artwork through the sites, with a percentage of sales going to purchase more land.

The loss of old growth trees and their ecosystems has serious ramifications for the whole planet in terms of protecting against ozone depletion and the effect of greenhouse gases, as well as the extinction of native tribes and animal species, and the loss of unique plants that could form the basis of cures for a number of illnesses. Sign up with a group such as Nature Conservancy (www.nature.org), Greenpeace (www.greenpeace.org) or Care2 (www.care2.com) to lobby the governments who control these wilderness tracts.

☆ **Take part in nature regeneration projects** through Conservation Volunteers, which organises activities throughout Australia, from Sydney Harbour to the Red Centre and countless beaches, national parks and small towns across the continent. You can protect endangered animals such as sea turtles, work alongside scientists and rangers to monitor sites for pests that are decimating the local wildlife, plant native flora to stabilise sand dunes, collect seeds and record growth rates in national parks, or construct pathways and fencing. Some projects take just a few hours, while others involve a week or two at the site and include camping or staying nearby (www.conservationvolunteers.com.au). There are international equivalents too; do an online search for "conservation volunteers" to find a local centre, or visit www.i-to-i.com for exotic inspiration – you could do conservation work on the Galapagos Islands, hands-on work with endangered wildlife in South Africa, sea turtle conservation in Costa Rica or Panama, Amazon rainforest preservation in Ecuador and so much more.

☆ **Recycle everything you can.** Check with your local council if you're not sure what you can leave in the recycling bins – things like greasy pizza boxes for example can't be recycled. Find out if there's somewhere nearby to deposit aluminium cans, and pick them up off the street or go door-to-door to ensure they're recycled, which can be a fun project to do with a child or friend. Recycling just one aluminium can will save enough energy to run a TV for three hours, and sometimes you'll even get money in exchange, which can be put to good environmental use. Australians now recycle the equivalent of 1 billion newspapers each year, which are transformed into newsprint and other paper materials such as boxes, egg cartons and even kitty litter.

☆ **Clean up your local area.** Adopt an area in your neighbourhood, be it a street, a small part of your local park or a stream, and take responsibility for it. Pick up litter, let the council know if plants are dying or water pipes have burst, and any other issues. Take a bag with you when you go to the beach or for a walk and pick up litter, and make sure you leave nothing but your footprints when you spend time in nature. And take part in Clean Up Australia Day or one of its overseas equivalents, which aim to clean up, fix up and conserve the environment, and take place at beaches, parks and along highways, amongst other places. Australia's event is held on the first weekend in March (www.cleanupaustraliaday.org.au), and is the nation's largest community-based environmental event. You can volunteer at an existing site, choose your own and register it, or be sent a resources pack to organise your own project at any time of year.

☆ **Make your phone more mobile.** More than 90 per cent of the materials in mobile phones, batteries, chargers and accessories can be recycled and used as raw materials for new products. But in Australia only nine per cent of people recycled their previous phone, and there are 16 million old mobiles sitting in cupboards and drawers, taking up space. Yet one tonne of mobile phone circuits can yield the same amount of precious metals as 110 tonnes of gold ore, 123 tonnes of silver bearing ore and 11 tonnes of copper sulphide ore. If you get a new phone, put the old one to good use by handing it in for recycling. Mobile phone retailers and Australia Post make it super easy. Check out www.mobilemuster.com.au for details.

☆ **Trash equals treasure.** Reconsider all your rubbish to prevent unnecessary landfill, because taking things to the tip or throwing it in your bin allows toxins to leach into the soil and waterways, uses up precious arable land and wastes energy to transport it, bury it or burn it. Have a market stall instead of throwing things out, because your trash could be another person's treasure. Take unwanted books to your local library or a literacy foundation such as The Australian Literacy & Numeracy Foundation (www.alnf.org), America's Got Books (www.gotbooks.com), the UK's Book Aid International (www.bookaid.org), New Zealand's Adult Reading Assistance Scheme (www.aras.org.nz), or to a second-hand bookstore to get some money back. Offer magazines and toys to hospitals, schools or preschools. If you have old furniture, appliances, musical instruments, windows, tents or other things you no longer need, place a free ad on the OzRecycle Community website (www.ozrecycle.com) and have someone who needs it come and pick it up from you. And if you need something, check the site in case someone near you has one they'd love to gift you with.

☆ **Consider your transport options.** While cars certainly have their place, you'll be doing a lot of good for the environment (and your wallet) if you can avoid having one, choose a more environmentally friendly one next time you buy one, or even just leave it at home sometimes and use alternative methods for getting around. Ride your bike, get the bus, car pool to work or walk there – it might be the prettiest and most peaceful hour of your day, and not only will it help the planet, it's great exercise and a good stress buster.

☆ **Take a faery shopping bag.** Buy a fabric bag with a faery on it or make your own, so you're more likely to remember to take it shopping with you. Plastic bags are terrible for the environment, requiring a lot of resources to be made, taking years to break down, and harming wildlife that gets trapped in or suffocated by them. Any kind of reusable shopping bag, from the green supermarket ones to a pretty fabric one, is a good thing.

☆ **Give your old clothes a new life.** Many charities rely on donated clothes to help those in need, and sell the surplus in their stores to raise funds. So if you have clothing you no longer wear, drop it off in a charity bin or at a store. Many animal welfare agencies also rely on donations of old clothes, towels and sheets to use for animal bedding. Or have a clothes swap party with your friends – you all get new outfits for nothing, have fun doing it, and avoid the emissions and energy necessary to produce new clothes. Some states have clothing exchange nights (www.clothingexchange.com.au), or you can offer items on eBay or have a market stall to offload old clothes and raise money, or cut them up and use them for dusting around the house or for craft projects or dress-ups.

☆ **Choose "green" coffee.** Takeaway paper or styrofoam coffee cups add to your environmental footprint, especially if you have several a day. There are now many reusable ceramic or plastic cups available from a range of companies, such as the Hunger Site's Lux Life Ceramic Travel Mug, which also provides 50 cups of rice to the starving with each one purchased (www.thehungersite.com), the I Am Not a Paper Cup, a thermal ceramic mug with a re-sealable silicone lid (www.nigelsecostore.com), and the closer to home, and thus less air miles involved, Keep Cup, which comes in three sizes to suit what's on offer in cafes (www.keepcup.com.au). Some coffee chains, such as Gloria Jean's, have reusable mugs available, with free refill offers to make it worth your while. Ordering takeaway food can also be an environmental nightmare, so be conscious of your usage – only take as many napkins, containers, bags and plastic cutlery as you actually need, and reuse as much as you can.

☆ **Conserve water.** People in the west take water for granted, but it's a finite resource that must be protected. More than 1 billion people around the world don't have access to clean, safe water for drinking, cooking and bathing, and 3.4 million people, mostly children, die every year from water-related diseases such as hepatitis A and typhoid fever. Even in Australia and other western nations it's a precious commodity that needs conserving. Be water wise, and turn off the tap when you're brushing your teeth, fill the sink when washing dishes, keep a bucket in the shower to collect the water that's wasted as you adjust the temperature, and use it on your garden, and keep your showers short – play or sing your favourite song while you're in there, and make sure you're done by the time it finishes. You can also emulate actor Alyssa Milano, who raised $100,000 for Charity:Water (www.charitywater.org) by using her birthday to ask friends and fans for donations instead of gifts, helping provide safe drinking water for those who don't have it, or support Water For Water (www.waterforwater.com.au), which provides clean water in areas such as the Philippines, where few people have access to it.

☆ **Cut down on paper usage** to slow rainforest destruction. Swap paper napkins for cloth. Refuse the handful of serviettes at takeaway places (and ask them to offer less in future). If you must print documents, buy recycled paper and print on both sides, or make notepads out of paper that's been printed on on one side, or the back of used envelopes. Get a chalk or white board to leave messages for your family, rather than using paper. Support authors who use the most environmentally friendly options available. And recycle your Christmas cards through Planet Ark. Free reply paid envelopes are available from Australia Post until the end of January. Last year Planet Ark received 12 million cards, which were turned into new packaging and recycled paper products, saving a huge amount of energy, water and trees (www.planetark.com/cards).

Create your own cards, or try making your own handmade paper for letters. Instead of buying metres of wrapping paper, use magazine pages, the comics section from the newspaper or your children's school paintings to wrap presents. Save scraps of fabric from your sewing projects to wrap small gifts, buy cheap colourful material to wrap all your presents, which is much prettier, and recipients can re-use it for birthdays throughout the year, or use a tea towel for two gifts in one. Reduce your junk mail too – be selective with what you sign up for, and if you're getting postal mail you don't want, call the company and ask them to stop sending it. Only print emails you absolutely need, and ensure you only print the relevant page(s), rather than the whole back and forth conversation.

☆ **Lower your electricity use** to save money and the environment. Turn off lights when they're not in use and shut down your computer – and encourage office co-workers to do the same (or turn theirs off when they leave for the weekend). Switch appliances off at the wall, as keeping the clock running on a microwave or DVD player eats up power, and unplug them if you don't use them often, especially if you go away for a week or more. And sign up for Earth Hour (www.earthhour.org) and turn everything off on the last Saturday in March. This annual global event, which began in Sydney in 2007, involves people and corporations turning off the power for an hour, saving an immense amount of electricity and raising awareness about climate change, in the hope that people will make power reduction and resource conservation a regular part of their life.

☆ **Use natural not chemical cleaners.** To remove stains in the bathtub, start by rubbing with a fresh cut lemon – this will work for lighter stains. ☆ For more serious stains, wipe around the tub with a wet cloth covered in baking soda, or one dipped in vinegar. Or make a simple paste with 1 cup of vinegar and 1 teaspoon of baking soda – rub onto the tub, then scrub with a nail brush before rinsing off. ☆ For glass shower stalls and mirrors, a sponge dipped in white vinegar will remove soap scum and build up. For shower curtains, wash with hot soapy water, then rub some lemon juice on it and leave it in the sun to dry. ☆ A cleaning spray made with distilled water and lemon essential oil will disinfect surfaces and faucets as it cleans; use 10 drops of oil per 100ml of water. ☆ Another good spray is 1 part water and 1 part vinegar; this can also be used to mop floors and as a fabric softener. ☆ To clean your children's bath toys, soak overnight in a solution of water and vinegar, or add a few drops of tea tree essential oil to a bucket of water and soak them in that. ☆ Put a few drops of tea tree oil in a small dish, then fill it with water and pour it in the last rinse of your washing machine for a fresh, clean wash. ☆ Lavender essential oil has a great fragrance and is an antiseptic – add a few drops to your mop water for floors, or make a spray of 10 drops in a bottle of water to use on bench tops, sinks and cutting boards. ☆ To remove the gummy residue from price stickers, use orange essential oil, which also removes pine resin from Christmas trees and is a good natural insecticide. Keep it in the fridge though – it has a shorter shelf life than most essential oils. ☆ When you're done cleaning, burn some lemon or pine essential oil in an aromatherapy vaporiser – they're antiseptic, smell fresh and clean and lift the mood.

☆ **Give kids cash instead of gifts.** If you have children to get Christmas and birthday presents for, start a bank account for them rather than buying small disposable gifts that will quickly be outgrown, discarded or forgotten, and ask friends and family members to contribute too. You'll be helping the environment by lowering consumption and air miles and thus emissions, and will also save on giftwrapping, packaging and, if they live interstate or overseas, postage and more travel. And of course what kid wouldn't be overjoyed to be presented with a bank account with a substantial amount of money in it when they finish school!

☆ **Keep your cool.** When the temperature rises, open all your windows to take advantage of any breeze, and turn off lights when you don't need them, as they generate heat. Keep the bathroom door closed, especially after showers, and do your washing at night to help lower humidity. Choose energy efficient appliances of all kinds, as they give off less heat. And if you do have an airconditioner, make it more effective and ensure it uses less power by keeping windows and doors closed while it's on, turning it off when you go out, and not going for the big chill – even a one degree difference will save emissions (and power bills). Maintain it well, cleaning the filter monthly to avoid dust reducing the air flow, and keep the outside part of the unit shaded. If you're buying a new airconditioner, make sure you get the right one for your space, as studies have found that 50 per cent of airconditioners are too big and use too much power for the area they're cooling.

☆ **Dispose of your computer thoughtfully.** In Australia each year around 2.5 million new computers are bought, while 1.6 million broken or outdated ones are dumped in landfill, and the same again are left in storage. (So imagine how many there are in the UK or the US!) Only 500,000 are recycled, yet computers and their components are extremely toxic in landfill, leaching lead, cadmium, mercury and other nasty metals into the soil. There are a number of companies that either recycle, refurbish or reuse computers – visit www.recyclingnearyou.com.au to find the closest one to you. Some will pick up from your home, either free or for a small fee, while others allow you to drop your old computer equipment off to them. In the US, the Computer Recycling Center (www.crc.org) promotes the re-use of computer and electronic equipment, and recycles unusable items to keep them out of landfill. There are many computer recycling options in the UK too, and Apple also provides a recycling service for its customers.

Shhh! Faery Secret

Faeries love to wash in water that is left out especially for them, particularly in areas that have low rainfall. Leave a teacup filled with fresh or rain water out near your back door so the faeries can have a lovely bath!

☆ **Educate yourself.** Becoming better informed is the first step in helping the planet. Find out about issues like climate change, deforestation and animals that are threatened or endangered. Read up on harmful chemicals and food additives. Learn about permaculture, composting and companion planting. Be aware of who you vote for, what they stand for and where their preferences go. Eat organic. Discover which plants grow best in your area, those that are native, and look into their medicinal properties. Study herbalism. Find inspiration from other eco warriors, and from within, to start making this world an even better place.

☆ **Let your voice be heard.** Write letters to your politicians about local issues and emphasise your concern for the environment. Sign up with groups such as Sea Shepherd (www.seashepherd.org), Avaaz (avaaz.org), the World Wildlife Fund (www.wwf.org) and Greenpeace (www.greenpeace.org) and join their email campaigns to lobby for change. Choose a cause that means a lot to you – if you're a surfer, find an ocean protection charity, if you love trees sign up for a rainforest cause – and raise money and awareness for it. Write a story for your local paper about your pet issue, volunteer to help a group associated with it, tell your friends about it or hold a fundraiser to help finance their environmental work.

☆ **Make your own beauty treats.** Creating your own products from natural kitchen ingredients avoids the excess packaging that comes with the store bought kind and cuts down on waste. There are many wonderful books and courses that will teach you how to make different kinds of beauty products. For now, you could whip up a jar of bath salts by mixing 2 cups of Epsom salts with 1 cup of coarse sea salt. Add several drops of essential oils (try lavender, vanilla or chamomile for relaxation, or rosemary, ginger or citrus to invigorate) and mix well. Leave them out to dry for a few hours then pour into glass jars to store. If it's a gift you can add a few drops of food colouring with the oils to make it look pretty, or dried flower petals. ☆ You can also mix together 1 cup of Epsom salts and 1 cup of baking soda with a few drops of essential oils for a bath-time treat. ☆ Make a relaxing bath milk by blending together 2 teaspoons of powdered dried lavender flowers, 1 cup of milk and half a cup of honey, or simply add a cup of rose or other flower petals and half a cup of coconut milk to the bath. ☆ To cleanse skin, puree together 1 kiwi fruit, 2 tablespoons of plain yoghurt, 1 tablespoon of apricot oil, 1 tablespoon of honey, 1 teaspoon of almond meal and 2 drops of orange essential oil. Massage into your skin then gently rinse off. ☆ To exfoliate, mix the juice and pulp of half an orange with 4 tablespoons of cornmeal. Rub over skin then wash off. ☆ To improve skin tone, combine 1 mashed avocado, 1 cooked and mashed carrot, 1 beaten egg, 3 tablespoons of honey and half a cup of cream. Spread over your face and neck, and leave for 10-15 minutes before rinsing off. Or simply mix one part honey and one part natural yoghurt and apply to the face for a soothing mask. ☆ To add colour and shine to brunette hair, make up a pot of strong rosemary, sage or raspberry leaf tea. Allow it to cool, then use it as a rinse after washing your locks. ☆ To add richness to red hair, use black coffee or an infusion of hibiscus or rosehip tea as a final rinse. ☆ And to give blonde tresses a boost, steep a pot of chamomile or marigold tea, allow to cool, then pour over your hair after washing.

☆ **Create a new generation of eco faeries.** Kids and teens are joyfully idealistic and will be happy to do their bit to protect the earth, so educate them about issues and channel their enthusiasm to create change. Encourage them to become environmentally aware. Teach them how to reduce their impact at home, help them clean up their local park, talk to their teacher about growing vegies at the school or having a bake sale to help a local eco charity, and buy or make them a faery outfit and help them plant their very own faery garden and leave notes there for the fae. Let them plant trees, visit national parks and play outside, fostering a love of nature within them.

Of course it's not just the environment that the faeries care about – they inspire people to become more caring of each other as well as the earth. There are countless ways to make a difference in somebody's life. Visit kids in hospital and spread some faery cheer, or become a volunteer for the Starlight Children's Foundation. Offer to read books at your local school – faerytales of course – sponsor a child, do the 40 Hour Famine, help the homeless, run (or walk) for a cancer charity, and do what you can to help the people you encounter every day. It will lift your spirits as well as making the world a happier place to live in.

Environmental Calendar

January: Recycle your Christmas cards, either using them as part of a craft project or to make gift tags for the coming year, or by sending them to an organisation that will recycle for you. In the US, contact St Jude's Ranch for Children (www.stjudesranch.org), in the UK, the Woodland Trust Recycling Scheme (www.woodlandtrust.org.uk), and in Australia the wonderful Planet Ark (www.planetark.org).

February 2: Celebrate World Wetlands Day, which raises public awareness and promotes the conservation and wise use of wetlands.

February 27: Polar Bear Day is a celebration of these majestic creatures native to the North Pole, who are threatened by pollution, poaching, global warming, industrial accidents and loss of habitat.

Early March: It's Seaweek, which educates about marine and coastal environments and works to conserve such areas (www.mesa.edu.au).

First weekend in March: Pick up rubbish as part of Clean Up Australia Day – or just do it anyway, on any day. In the US there's an Adopt-a-Highway program, and most towns have clean up days.

March 22: It's World Water Day, so be water smart, and support a water charity or donate to World Vision so they can build wells.

Last Saturday in March: Turn off your lights – and as many appliances as possible – for Earth Hour (www.earthhour.org).

April 7: It's World Health Day. The UN's World Health Organization created this day to raise awareness of global health issues.

April 18: Celebrate World Heritage Day, which raises awareness of the wonderful monuments and sacred sites that need protection.

April 22: It's Earth Day! Horrified by oil spills and the degradation of nature, a US senator called for an international day to inspire awareness of and appreciation for the earth. In 1970 Earth Day was launched, marking the beginning of the environmental movement.

April 25: World Penguin Day honours these creatures native to the southern hemisphere – they're found in Antarctica, Australia, New Zealand and South Africa – as they begin their annual migration.

Last Friday in April: In the US, National Arbor Day encourages people and groups to plant and care for trees (www.arborday.org).

May 4: It's Faery Day! Faeries are synonymous with Beltane, and have long been honoured on this day, with offerings left out so they won't do any harm. In modern times the World Fairy Festival runs on the Saturday closest to this date (www.worldfairyfestival.org).

Mid-May: Plan an event for World Migratory Bird Day, which highlights the need for protection of birds and their habitats.

May 23: Today is World Turtle Day. Turtles are emerging from winter hibernation and searching for mates and nesting areas at this time, but they are endangered. You can help (www.tortoise.com).

May 29: Oak Apple Day commemorates the restoration of the English monarchy in 1660, and was later transformed into Arbour Day, when trees are planted. It had its roots in paganism though – a Garland King would ride through the streets completely disguised in greenery, and oak sprigs were worn and displayed.

June 5: It's World Environment Day. A UN-declared holiday, it aims to improve the state of the environment around the world, stimulate worldwide awareness of the issues and encourage political action.

June 8: World Oceans Day celebrates all the organisations committed to ocean conservation and marine life.

June 15: Global Wind Day was set up to spread the positive message about wind power and this wonderful sustainable energy source.

June 17: It's World Day to Combat Desertification and Drought.

June 22: On this day in 1633, the Pope forced Italian physicist, mathematician and astronomer Galileo Galilei, now known as the Father of Science, to recant his view that the earth rotates around the sun, rather than vice versa, on pain of torture. Despite being correct, he spent the last years of his life under house arrest, accused of heresy, banned from teaching and forbidden to publish his works.

June 24: It's Fairy Day, a special annual celebration for faery believers, collectors, artists and the young at heart, which was founded by beautiful faery artist Jessica Galbreth (www.fairyday.com).

July 20: It's Friendship Day in South America, so celebrate the wonderful friendships in your life – and be a friend to the planet.

1st Sunday in August: It's National Tree Day in Australia, the country's biggest community tree-planting event, so plant a native tree or shrub. Arbour Day's been observed in Australia since 1889.

August 6: Hiroshima Day is a day of peace marches and vigils to commemorate the dropping of the first atomic bomb, which landed on the Japanese city of Hiroshima in 1945. It helped end World War II, but killed 70,000 people instantly, and that many again through exposure to the deadly radiation. In the Shinto religion it's Hiroshima Peace Ceremony Day, and in the US it is Atomic Bomb Day.

August 9: It's the Day of the World's Indigenous People, honouring the achievements of indigenous peoples, and aiming to find solutions to some of the problems faced in areas such as culture, education, health, human rights, the environment and economic development.

Late August: Take part in Keep Australia Beautiful Week. Plastic lasts thousands of years (if plastic bottles had been around when dinosaurs roamed the earth we'd still be finding them today!), and some materials never break down. Pick up litter and reduce waste.

September 4: In the US it's National Wildlife Day, set up to honour eco warrior Steve Irwin's work, and raise awareness of endangered animals and how we can help them (www.nationalwildlifeday.com).

September 7: It's National Threatened Species Day, commemorating the death of the last Tasmanian tiger at Hobart Zoo in 1936. It's also Biodiversity Month, which raises awareness about the impacts of land development, introduced plants and animals, grazing, salinity, changed fire regimes, pollution and a changing climate on the world's threatened species and their shrinking habitats.

Mid September: National Bilby Day was set up by conservationists to help halt the steady decline of this delightful marsupial.

Mid September: In New Zealand it's Conservation Week, celebrating the country's unique wildlife and natural areas (www.doc.govt.nz).

September 16: International Day for Preservation of the Ozone Layer.

September 21: The International Day of Peace highlights efforts to end conflict, encourage ceasefires and promote peace. It's also World Gratitude Day, so express your love and appreciation to others.

September 22: World Car-Free Day helps take the heat off the planet, and put it instead on city planners and politicians to give priority to cycling, walking and public transport all year.

Late September: In the US, National Public Lands Day is the largest hands-on volunteer effort – people pick up rubbish, build trails, plant trees and restore water resources (www.publiclandsday.org).

Early October: Walk to Work Day promotes regular walking and physical activity. The whole month is International Walk to School Month, and there are other events too (www.walk.com.au).

First Monday in October: World Animal Day celebrates the animal kingdom, and highlights endangered and threatened species and how we can help save them. It's also the UN's World Habitat Day, which concentrates on the state of our towns and cities and the basic right of all people to adequate shelter.

During October: National Water Week encourages the protection and rehabilitation of water environments such as streams, wetlands, beaches, waterways and estuaries (www.nationalwaterweek.org.au).

Second Monday in October: Canada's Thanksgiving Day, Jour d'action de Grace, is a festival of gratitude for the harvest and the blessings of the prior year, and a time of family gatherings.

November 6: It's International Day for Preventing the Exploitation of the Environment in War and Armed Conflict.

During November: National Recycling Week focuses on recycling, minimising waste and managing resources (www.planetark.org).

Fourth Thursday in November: It's Thanksgiving Day in the US.

December 5: International Volunteers Day, established by the UN in 1985, honours all the people who volunteer for a good cause, and highlights the role they play in their community and environment.

Early December: It's Coastcare Week (www.coastcare.com.au).

Cara's Faery Magic

Cara Walker is a faery entertainer at schools, events and shopping centres in Western Australia, where she shares her passion for environmental awareness and the fae as Faerie Cara. She films the TV segment *Talking Green* for Foxtel, is the author of the book *The Return to Faerie: A Guide to Faerie Conscious Living*, and founded the group Eco Faeries, which performs around the world. Visit her and learn more at www.FaerieCara.com.

I first discovered faeries when I was 13, when I started working as a faery entertainer. Growing up I'd been more of a scallywag than a faery princess, but that made me a good faery performer. Despite being dressed in a pink tulle costume, I was loud and mischievous, unlike all the other people I worked with.

When I was 19 I went to Ireland for two years, and discovered the true essence of the fae. I listened to Celtic stories told by firesides in thatched cottages and pubs, found out my great grandfather was a famous sgealaidhthe, an Irish storyteller, and went to the forests, hills and wild, damp and freezing places of this beautiful country, where my entire perception of faeries was ripped wide open.

Before discovering the true light of the fae I'd been pursuing a destructive pathway. I was lost. But when I stopped running from myself and instead listened to the voices in nature, I found my true self waiting patiently for me. I no longer needed distractions from life – suddenly all I wanted to do was sit in a forest and simply listen. My eyes glowed, my dreams were filled with visions of ancient beings, and my bloodline was ignited. I felt a part of something much bigger than me, a great web of tradition, honour and presence.

This sense of awareness still lives within me, and faeries come to me with messages. They come and go as they please, but if I ask them for help they always answer – just not always in the way I had planned!

When I begin connecting with a new faery I notice things missing or moved, noises in my home at night, shadows shifting or lights dancing past my vision. I also hear a ringing in my ears so I know it's time to tune in. I ask them to come through and show themselves while I'm meditating or before I go to sleep. And some places have thinner veils between the worlds and I don't need to meditate or seek them in dreams there. But either way, I live my life completely open, aware and grateful for their constant connection.

I think faeries are important to us today because of the way the world is. When we step away from the chaos of human existence and instead listen to nature, to the stories of our ancestors or even to our own heart's yearning, then we find the faeries waiting to share the magic of the earth with us. They guide us, laugh at us, humble us and support our wildest pursuits. And they cherish adventure. Whether it is to discover the hidden caverns of your true self or the wild places of the world, there will always be a faery willing to journey with you.

I believe in faeries as the spirits of nature. I believe the tales of our ancestors are spoken from events that occurred "once upon a time" and are then echoed throughout the generations in folklore. I believe we can still hear those voices in nature, and the stories of our foreparents, if we choose to listen.

I've worked as a faery for more than half my life. Now I embody the tradition of faeries, I speak through folklore and teach communities to work with nature. My dreams and meditation journeys are valuable resources for me as I take steps further into the unknown. I follow my visions, even if they don't make sense at the time, and I simply trust, knowing that the faeries are leading the way.

Fun With the Faeries

" 'Come dance with us sweet nature's child,'
She heard their voices sing.
For lost was she to mortal man,
Within the faerie ring."
Steve Fox, The Faerie Ring

Throw A Magical Faery Party

Faeries can be serious and wise, and inspire us to make the world a better place, but they can also be light-hearted, joyful and filled with mischievous fun! In all the legends of the faeries and their enchanted realm, the music, dancing, revelry, feasts and celebrations are paramount. Haunting ballads and lively jigs. Slow, airy waltzes and dancing until you fall down exhausted. Unrestrained merrymaking and boisterous festivity. Tables heaped with every delicacy imaginable, washed down with crystal goblets of elderberry wine and honey mead. Rituals to welcome the sun, moon and stars and honour the passing of the seasons. Elegant silk and satin gowns threaded with gold and glittering with diamonds – or cobwebs and flower petals sparkling with dew, depending on the depth of the glamour.

There are tales told of people who visit this magical world and are gifted with marvellous talents to share with humanity, and those who enchant a faery king or queen and remain there with their beloved. There are those who stumble into Faeryland and are made to dance until they collapse, exhausted, and die, and those who join in the feasting and are unable to return home. But overwhelmingly the stories are of laughter chiming like silver bells, romantic liaisons and courtly revels, candlelit meetings and light-hearted joy.

A faery party is a thing of wonder and endless fun, and holding your own, whether in honour of the fae or for your human friends, is a magical thing to do – and preparing for it is half the fun. Whether you're planning a lunchtime soiree, an afternoon high tea, a garden picnic, a faery dress-up party, a midnight feast or anything else, make it as memorable and magical as possible.

☆ Make invitations by cutting out faery wing shapes from cardboard and decorating them with glitter, gold stars, stickers and bright colours, or design a pretty flyer with your favourite faery artwork.
☆ Create an enchanted location. String faery lights up, light candles to add to the mysterious atmosphere, burn incense or have vases of strongly scented flowers, and twine ivy in wreaths around the room.
☆ Set a place for the fae, be it a tiny plate, a thimble or a shell. To aid you in seeing them, have a vase of foxgloves as the centrepiece.
☆ Plan some activities. Organise some music for when you feel moved to dance – faeries love to dance – and prepare games with prizes if it's that kind of party. Paint each other's faces, have a wing making workshop or decorate cupcakes. Faery energy is all about getting in touch with your inner child and having fun, losing yourself in the moment and sharing your joy with loved ones.
☆ Whip up a feast fit for the fae, with sweet treats, tasty savoury morsels and delicious drinks that capture the magic of the occasion.

The following recipes can be made for yourself, served to your guests or left out as offerings to the faeries. They're easy enough to make that kids can join in (and fun enough to delight them into helping), and were whipped up with a fork and a wooden spoon instead of an electric mixer or beaters, with a favourite coffee mug as a rolling pin, so you don't need to buy anything specially.

They were all tested at our own faery party, to much applause, but feel free to change and adapt them to your own tastes. It's fun to create recipes, connecting with your inner faery as you play around with the ingredients and re-imagine them. Trust yourself and your instincts, experiment to get the flavours you love best, and have fun! Cooking times will vary a little depending on your oven and your adaptations, so keep an eye on your treats and take them out when they're lovely and golden and smell divine…

Faery Bread

Who can resist this magical treat, a staple from childhood parties, and strangely enough, an Australian invention! No one else in the world seems to know what it is, but we can share this faery secret...

Ingredients:
☆ Butter
☆ Thinly sliced fresh bread (white is traditional, but just like the healthy faeries, we prefer wholemeal)
☆ Hundreds and thousands

What to do:
★ Butter the bread then sprinkle the hundreds and thousands on top, making a sweet and colourful treat.
★ Slice into triangles or use a cookie cutter to cut them into hearts, stars or faery wing shapes.

Faery Wand Cookies

You don't have to be a kid to find these adorable bikkies cute. Serve them standing up in a cup or vase, so each guest can choose their own wand, or on a platter. You can also shape them into more traditional cookie shapes if you prefer, and ice them or add choc chips.

Ingredients:
☆ 125g butter
☆ ½ cup raw sugar
☆ 1 egg
☆ 1 tsp vanilla essence
☆ 2 cups plain flour
☆ Hundreds and thousands
☆ Wooden skewers

What to do:
★ Lightly beat the butter, sugar, egg and vanilla together. (It takes a bit longer to do this with a fork and a spoon, but it does work!)
★ Add the sifted flour and mix well. Knead the dough on a floured surface then refrigerate for at least half an hour, which will help

the cookies better hold their size and shape as they cook.

★ Roll out the dough until it's about half a centimetre thick. Use a star-shaped cookie cutter to make your cookies.

★ Place the stars on greased, baking-paper lined trays with a skewer placed under each one. Sprinkle with hundreds and thousands.

★ Bake in a preheated 180C oven for around 15 minutes, or until crisp and golden.

☆ To make your faery wands even prettier, soak the wooden skewers with food colouring for 15 minutes, allowing them to dry before use, or tie some gold curling ribbon around each skewer or cover it in glitter glue after baking. You can also ice the cookies with magical patterns to make each wand unique.

Faery Fruit Wands

For another kind of wand, try these healthy fruit sticks, which are brightly coloured and of the earth, just how the fae like things... Thread any kind of fruit you like onto the skewers, chopped up so the sizes are all similar. You can also add marshmallows...

Ingredients:
☆ 2 punnets strawberries
☆ ½ rockmelon
☆ 1 green apple
☆ Any other fruit you like
☆ Desiccated coconut
☆ Hundreds and thousands
☆ Your favourite chocolate
☆ Wooden skewers

What to do:
★ Hull the strawberries and cut the rockmelon and apple into diamond or star shapes. Thread either a single fruit piece onto each wooden skewer to make wands, or several pieces for a kebab.

★ Put the coconut and the hundreds and thousands on separate saucers and melt the chocolate in a small bowl sitting in a saucepan of boiling water. Dip the wands in the melted chocolate then roll them in coconut and/or hundreds and thousands to add glitz.

Faery Wing Cupcakes

You can play around with the flavours of these yummy cupcakes – add cinnamon or nutmeg for a spicier taste, lemon or orange rind for added zest, or half a grated apple for a summery, Avalonian flavour. And while these faery wing cakes are super cute, you can also make plain cupcakes and decorate them in your own unique faery style. There are gorgeous edible icing faeries available in supermarkets, or you could trace out ladybirds, butterflies, hearts or stars with icing, or cover the cupcakes with red icing and add dots of white icing or white chocolate chips so they become faery mushrooms. The only limit is your imagination... You could also make some tiny cupcakes, with the miniature patty pans which are now available, perfectly sized for a faery!

Ingredients:
☆ 125g softened butter
☆ ¼ cup honey
☆ 1 tsp pure vanilla essence
☆ 2 eggs, lightly beaten
☆ 1 cup self-raising flour
☆ ¼ cup milk
☆ Jam
☆ Hundreds and thousands

Icing:
☆ 3 tablespoons honey
☆ 125g cream cheese, softened
☆ 1 tsp pure vanilla essence
☆ Food colouring

What to do:
★ Cream the butter, honey and vanilla, then stir in the beaten eggs.
★ Add the sifted flour and mix well, then add the milk. The mixture should be quite wet and runny, nothing like the cookie dough.
★ Spoon into patty pans sitting in a cupcake or muffin tray – make sure they are no more than two thirds full or they might overflow.
★ Bake in a preheated 180C oven for 20 minutes, or until they are golden on top and a skewer inserted into the middle comes out clean.

★ Allow to cool as you make the icing. To do this, cream the honey, cream cheese and vanilla, then put a quarter of it in a small bowl and add some food colouring – this icing is for the faery wings, so choose a colour that screams magic to you. Leave the rest plain or colour it a contrasting hue.

★ When the cupcakes are cool, cut a circle, which takes up about two thirds of the surface and is a centimetre deep, out of the top of each one. Cut this piece in half – these are the faery wings.

★ Put half a teaspoon of jam in the cupcake hole, then fill it with a dollop of plain icing. Ice the faery wing pieces with the coloured icing and add hundreds and thousands to them, then position two wings on top of each cupcake, holding them in place with the plain icing. Or simply slice the rounded top off each cupcake and cut it in half for wings, ice the flat surface of each cake and place the wings on top, dusting them with icing sugar or hundreds and thousands.

Choc Chip Cupcakes

These are so delicious fresh out of the oven, as the chocolate chips inside are all melty and warm. But they're equally tasty eaten later, topped with icing and more chocolate chips.

Ingredients:
☆ ⅓ cup raw sugar
☆ 2 eggs
☆ 1 tsp pure vanilla essence
☆ ⅓ cup vegetable oil
☆ ¼ cup milk
☆ 1 cup self-raising flour
☆ 3 tblsps powdered cocoa
☆ ½ cup chocolate chips

Icing:
☆ 125g butter, softened
☆ 1 tsp pure vanilla essence
☆ 1 cup icing sugar
☆ 2 tblsps cocoa powder
☆ 3 tblsps milk
☆ Chocolate chips to garnish

What to do:

★ To make the cupcakes, lightly beat the sugar, eggs and vanilla, then slowly pour in the oil and the milk. Add the sifted flour and cocoa powder and mix well. The mixture should be quite wet and runny, nothing like the cookie dough. Stir in the chocolate chips.

★ Spoon into patty pans sitting in a cupcake or muffin tray – make sure they are no more than two thirds full or they might overflow.

★ Bake in a preheated 180C oven for around 20 minutes, or until they are golden on top and a skewer inserted into the middle comes out clean (well, except for the melted chocolate inside!).

★ Eat them warm, fresh from the oven, or allow to cool and top with icing and extra chocolate chips. To make the icing, cream the butter and vanilla, then slowly add the icing sugar and cocoa powder, mixing well before adding enough milk to reach the desired consistency.

Honey Cakes

These delightful little treats are light and fluffy, and perfect to leave as an offering to the fae, or to keep and enjoy yourself. And they'll make the whole house smell deliciously of sunshine and honey.

Ingredients:
☆ ½ cup milk
☆ 1 tblsp honey (or more to taste)
☆ 1 egg
☆ ½ cup self-raising flour
☆ 1 tsp cinnamon (optional)
☆ 1 handful elderflowers (optional)
☆ Oil or butter for cooking

What to do:

★ Whisk the milk, honey and egg with a fork.

★ Add the sifted flour and mix lightly (don't over-beat as they'll become tough). If you want to, add cinnamon and/or elderflowers.

★ Heat a frying pan and lightly grease with butter or vegetable oil.

★ Drop small spoonfuls of the batter into the pan, and lightly cook each side. Don't be alarmed if, when you flip them, your honey cakes turn up at the edges and look like upside down mushroom tops!

Cinnamon Scones

Scones are an English countryside staple, especially served with homemade strawberry jam and fresh cream, which makes them a faery favourite too! You can use flavoured yoghurt if you prefer (peach and mango is yummy, or strawberry), in which case you may not want to add the honey. You can also add chopped dried fruit – apricots, sultanas, apple – or glaced cherries or ginger, or make savoury scones by replacing the honey, vanilla and cinnamon with ¼ cup of grated cheese and some mixed herbs.

Ingredients:
☆ 50g butter
☆ 2 cups self-raising flour
☆ 250g plain yoghurt
☆ 1 tblsp honey (or more to taste)
☆ 1 tsp pure vanilla essence
☆ 1 tsp cinnamon

What to do:
★ Rub the butter through the flour, then add the other ingredients and mix well. The mixture should be quite wet.
★ Knead well, then shape into balls and flatten a little. Place on a greased baking tray and glaze the top of each scone with a little milk mixed with yoghurt.
★ Cook them in a preheated 220C oven for around 15 minutes, or until golden brown and firm, and cooked right through. (The size of each scone will obviously influence cooking time – the larger they are, the more time they will need.)
★ Serve the scones warm and fresh from the oven with butter, or with jam and cream as a special treat.

Shhh! Faery Secret
Faeries love a cosy eggshell bed, so after cooking, put the shells out in the garden for the fae to nestle into. Rinse out the egg, dry it, and place a small, soft piece of fabric inside, so they can snuggle up comfortably at night.

Strawberry Jam

This is a very simple recipe, but it works well enough. Most jam recipes suggest that you use white sugar, caster sugar or even high-pectin jam sugar, and that will probably make it much thicker and bought-from-a-store looking, but this one was yummy and certainly did the job spread on warm scones.

Ingredients:
☆ 2 punnets (500g) strawberries
☆ 500g raw sugar
☆ 1 tsp lemon juice

What to do:
★ Hull and slice the strawberries, put them in a small saucepan and mash them with a potato masher. Add the sugar and lemon juice and leave for half an hour so the sugar can soften the fruit.
★ Stir over a low heat to dissolve the sugar, then bring to the boil and stir often, keeping it as hot as possible without boiling over while the liquid thickens.
★ Pour into a jar sterilised with boiling water and allow to cool a little before storing in the fridge. Eat within two weeks.

Faery Thumbprint Biscuits

These cute little biscuits, also known as Jam Drops, can be filled with your favourite jam (fill some with apricot jam, some with strawberry and some with blueberry for a pretty, colourful effect), or anything else that takes your fancy, from chocolate chips or hazelnut spread to nuts, seeds or custard.

Ingredients:
☆ 125g butter
☆ ½ cup sugar
☆ 1 tsp pure vanilla essence
☆ 1 egg, lightly beaten
☆ 1 cup plain flour
☆ 4 tblsps self-raising flour
☆ Jam

What to do:

★ Cream the butter, sugar and vanilla, then add the lightly beaten egg and mix well.

★ Sift in the flours, combine well, then turn out onto a floured surface and knead. Refrigerate the dough for half an hour to better maintain the shape of the drops while they cook.

★ Shape into teaspoon-sized balls and place on a greased baking tray. Using your thumb, press a hole in the centre of each bikkie and fill them with jam or any other filling.

★ Bake in a preheated 180C oven for 15-20 minutes, or until the biscuits are firm and golden. Be careful when you take them out of the oven as the jam will be very hot.

☆ If you'd prefer to make savoury treats, leave out the sugar and vanilla and fill the depressions with cheese and tomato, or beaten egg, crumbled feta and shallots, or anything else you can dream up.

Faery Shortbreads

Ingredients:

☆ 2 cups plain flour
☆ ½ cup icing sugar
☆ 250g butter
☆ 1 tsp pure vanilla
☆ ½ cup choc chips (optional)

What to do:

★ Sift the flour and the icing sugar into a bowl, and rub the butter into it.

★ Add the vanilla and mix well. If you want to make Choc Chip Shortbread, add them now and stir through, then turn the dough out onto a floured surface and knead lightly.

★ Refrigerate the dough for half an hour before rolling out and cutting into the desired shape – hearts and stars are cute, or you can press the dough firmly into a baking tray, covering the whole surface, and score into rectangles with a knife, creating lines where you want it to break once cooked. Sprinkle with raw sugar if you'd like.

★ Bake in a preheated 180C oven for 15 minutes, or until firm and golden brown.

Faery Sandwiches

Balance out all the sugar of the faery cakes and cookies by making a selection of savoury sandwiches. Grab a loaf of fresh bread and whip up a variety of fillings. Those served at a ritzy hotel's high tea are perfect for your faery party – cream cheese and salmon; egg and lettuce; cheese and tomato; ham and pickles; avocado and rocket; cucumber – or whatever you like best. Use a cookie cutter to cut them into star shapes, or toast them golden brown.

Irish Pancakes

Known as boxty, these pancakes are an Irish tradition, often served for breakfast to use up leftover mashed potatoes, or as a snack or side dish. Add garlic or other herbs, finely diced ham, crumbled feta or other favourite ingredients to spice them up, or leave them plain and serve with sour cream and sweet chilli sauce.

Ingredients:
☆ 1 cup grated raw potato
☆ 1 cup mashed potato
☆ Shallots, finely chopped
☆ Parsley, finely chopped, or other herbs
☆ 1 cup plain flour
☆ 1 egg, lightly beaten
☆ ½ cup milk
☆ Salt and pepper to taste
☆ Oil or butter for cooking

What to do:
★ Combine the grated and mashed potato in a large bowl and stir in the shallots and herbs.
★ Add the sifted flour and the lightly beaten egg, and mix well. Add the milk, and salt and pepper to taste.
★ Spoon tablespoons of mixture into a heated frying pan and cook well, about four minutes each side, until golden brown and warm.

Mini Quiches

These delicious, easy to make treats will be popular at any party. Experiment with flavours – try fried mushrooms, zucchini and capsicum; spinach and feta; sweet potato and shallots; corn kernels, asparagus and fresh parsley, coriander or oregano; ham and tomato; salmon and dill; a blend of various cheeses with rocket and vegies...

Ingredients:
☆ Filling
☆ 4 eggs
☆ ½ cup milk
☆ Herbs, salt and pepper
☆ 12 slices wholemeal bread
☆ Butter
☆ ¼ cup grated cheese

What to do:
★ Prepare the filling. Beat the eggs with milk, herbs, salt and pepper.
★ Cut the crusts off the bread and roll each slice out as thin as you can. Cut each slice into a circle with a round cookie cutter or a large jar, around 12cm in diameter. Butter the circles and push each slice, buttered side down, into the hole of a muffin tray.
★ Spoon a little filling into each case. Sprinkle with grated cheese and pour some of the egg mixture over the top.
★ Place in a preheated 200C oven for around 25 minutes, or until the quiches are puffed and golden, and firm to touch.

☆ Using bread for the cases is easy – and you can feed the offcuts to the birds or ducks in your backyard or local park. You can also make your own pastry, use store-bought pastry cases or sheets of puff or filo pastry, or turn them into mini frittatas with no pastry shell.
☆ To make pastry, combine 2 cups plain flour, 250g butter, 1 cup water and a pinch of salt. Add mixed herbs if you'd like. Mix well until a firm dough forms – add a bit more water if it's too dry. Turn onto a floured surface and knead. Refrigerate for half an hour or more before rolling out and cutting into rounds. Place them in the holes of a muffin tray and cook for 10-12 minutes, then allow to cool before filling with your ingredients and baking.

Corn Fritters

Ingredients:
☆ ½ cup milk or buttermilk
☆ 2 eggs
☆ 1 cup plain flour
☆ 420g can corn kernels or creamed corn
☆ Finely sliced shallots, chives or other fresh herbs
☆ Oil or butter for cooking
☆ Sour cream, avocado dip, guacamole to serve

What to do:
★ Whisk the milk and eggs, then stir in the flour.
★ Add the corn, shallots and herbs and mix them in, but don't over-beat or the fritters will become tough.
★ Spoon tablespoons of mixture into a heated, oiled, frying pan and cook for two minutes on each side, or until golden brown.

Pumpkin Fritters

Ingredients:
☆ 2 cups cooked, mashed pumpkin
☆ ½ cup self-raising flour
☆ 2 eggs, lightly beaten
☆ Pinch of salt
☆ Pepper, curry powder, chilli flakes or any herb or spice you like
☆ Oil or butter for cooking

What to do:
★ Combine all ingredients thoroughly, and shape into small round balls, around a tablespoon full in size.
★ Spoon the mixture into a heated, oiled, frying pan and cook for two minutes on each side, or until golden brown.

☆ These are delicious as either sweet or savoury fritters. For sweet, swap the pepper and herbs for a teaspoon of cinnamon and a tablespoon of sugar or honey, and dust with cinnamon sugar. You can also add other vegies for savoury fritters. And they can be deep fried if you prefer, which will make them a little more doughnuty...

Faery Flower Tea

Herbs and flowers are the perfect ingredients for faery beverages. This one looks beautiful served in a large glass teapot, but use whichever herbs you like best. Add honey if desired.

Ingredients:
☆ A handful of chamomile flowers
☆ A handful of jasmine flowers
☆ A handful of rose petals
☆ Mint leaves and lemon slices to garnish

What to do:
★ Pour boiling water over the flowers, steep for five minutes and serve hot, or allow to cool and serve in glasses over ice, garnished with mint leaves or lemon slices.

Iced Peach Tea

You can use any tea for this – black, green or herb, Earl Grey, English Breakfast or plain Liptons, cinnamon or vanilla flavoured...

Ingredients:
☆ 4 tsps your favourite tea or 4 teabags
☆ 4 cups boiling water
☆ 1 tsp cinnamon
☆ 1 can peaches or 1 cup peach nectar
☆ Lemon slices and mint leaves to garnish

What to do:
★ Place the tea (or teabags) in a large pot or jug and pour the water over the top. Steep for 10 minutes, or longer to taste. Strain the tea leaves out, or remove the teabags, and stir in the cinnamon.
★ Pour in the peach nectar, or lightly blend the peaches and their syrup and add that to the tea.
★ Refrigerate until cold and serve over ice, garnished with lemon slices and mint leaves.
★ You can also serve this tea hot – simply add your peach liquid to the hot tea and reheat, being careful not to bring to the boil.

Iced Mint Tea

Ingredients:
☆ 1 bunch fresh mint
☆ 4 cups boiling water
☆ 1 tblsp honey

What to do:
★ Slightly bruise the mint leaves and place them in a large jug.
★ Pour boiling water over them, stir in the honey then leave to cool.
★ Serve over ice, garnished with fresh mint leaves.

Faery Sight Tea

Ingredients:
☆ 1 tsp fresh thyme leaves
☆ 1 cup boiling water

What to do:
★ Pour the boiling water over the herbs, steep for five minutes and drink it hot, sweetened with honey if desired.
NB. Thyme is a powerful herb with many healing benefits and powers, and should not be taken during pregnancy.

Faery Punch

Ingredients:
☆ 1 bottle natural mineral water
☆ 1 bottle sparkling apple juice
☆ 1 bottle pineapple juice
☆ 1 bottle ginger beer
☆ 1 punnet strawberries, sliced
☆ 1 apple, diced
☆ 1 bunch mint

What to do:
★ Combine ingredients and serve over ice.
★ Use your imagination to create the perfect drink for you, adding different fruits, juices or soft drinks, or cinnamon and other spices.

Faery Nectar

Ingredients:
☆ 1 honeydew melon
☆ 1 lime
☆ 1 sprig mint
☆ Piece of fresh ginger
☆ 1 tblsp honey
☆ Strawberries

What to do:
★ Juice or blend all the ingredients (if juicing, peel the lime, if blending, squeeze the lime and use the juice). Serve over ice, garnished with fresh mint leaves and sliced strawberries.

Elderflower Cordial

Ingredients:
☆ 20 elderflower heads
☆ 2 lemons, sliced
☆ 1kg sugar
☆ 1 litre boiling water

What to do:
★ Place elderflowers, lemons and sugar in a large bowl.
★ Pour the boiling water over it, cover the bowl with a tea towel, and leave in a dark cupboard for 24 hours.
★ Strain and bottle, and store in the fridge. To serve, pour over ice and top up the glass with mineral water or soda water – about one fifth cordial, the rest water. Garnish with fresh lemon slices.

☆ If you can't find fresh elderflowers, you can make tea from the dried flowers. Use 1 tsp of dried flowers per cup of boiling water, and steep for 5-8 minutes. Serve hot, or cool then pour over ice. Always use a teapot (or cover the cup with a saucer) when making herb tea, to retain the essential oils, which contain many of the herb's therapeutic properties.

Wendy's Faery Magic

Wild, passionate and empowering, internationally renowned Australian chanteuse Wendy Rule is a witch who weaves together ritual, music and magic to take her listeners on Otherworld journeys through her performances and her recordings. She has released six beautiful albums, as well as creating numerous side projects, which all draw on her deep love of nature and mythology, and range from jazz to lush gothic in style. Some people use her CDs as hour-long meditations, as the soundtrack for yoga, massage or reiki, or as a guide for deep ritual. Wendy is a wandering gypsy who performs all over the world, but her home camp is in Melbourne, Australia. Her amazing work can be discovered at www.WendyRule.com.

For as long as I can remember, I have always had a very close relationship with the faeries. I was quite obsessed with them as a small girl, and was able to communicate with them easily. In fact, the line was so blurred between the everyday world and the Otherworld that I would often confuse them, and be very perplexed when I was physically unable to fly! I spent a lot of time seemingly alone in nature, quite happy to sit up a tree for hours surrounded by what my parents called my "imaginary" friends.

Now, as an adult, even though my relationship with the faeries is less tangible, I still feel their presence around me. I must remind myself to slow down and consciously create the space and time to connect with them, or else their trickster side will do something naughty to demand my attention!

For me the connection is very much on an emotional level. I feel their presence everywhere, but especially when I am in nature. I feel that the faery world is very real, in a literal sense, and coexists with our own. Sometimes these lines become blurred and we are given access to their world. I often find myself there in dream and ritual. And I trust that as I get older

and have more time in quiet reflection, my relationship with the fae will deepen even further. I will be quite happy to be "off with the faeries" as an old woman!

My music is very much inspired by nature, and because I regard faeries as the spirits of nature, they colour everything that I do. They are the essence of magic, shapeshifting and changing to reflect their environment, and they teach me to retain a sense of wonder at the world.

Faeries come and find me,
Sleeping, waiting, deep within the forest dreaming.
Weave your music through the air transparent,
Shimmering in sound above me.
I will hear then what can never be heard,
I will hear then what can never be heard...

Faeries come and find me,
Sleeping, dreaming visions of an image splendid.
Sail in waves of colour,
Unknown secret iridescent waves of rainbow.
I will see then what can never be seen,
I will see then what can never be seen...

Faeries come and find me,
When the moon is risen I will waken gently.
Feed me flowers, berries,
Fruit of forest, delicate to send me dreaming.
Then I'll stay here, dancing endlessly with you.

From the CD Deep Within A Faerie Forest.

Getting Crafty With the Fae

"Oberon, king of the realms of delight,
May your domain over us never fail.
Mab, as a rainbow-hued butterfly bright,
Yours is the glory that age cannot stale."
Joyce Kilmer, American poet

How to Make Faery Wings

Faery wings are more than decoration – they are a symbol of your own wings, the part of yourself that is coming to life as you become more entwined with the love of the fae, and the understanding of their ways. Perhaps you've discovered faery blood thrumming in your own, or you may have experienced visions where you fly. Maybe you can even feel your wings etherically, see them psychically, and flex them, stretch them and even fly with them during visions!

The first step to creating authentically magical faery wings is to spend some time very quietly, very sweetly, "seeing" your wings. You may want to do this, or you may simply wish to create your wings spontaneously, which is, after all, very faery! However, it can be a wonderful idea to allow yourself some quiet time to fully envisage your wings, so then you can recreate them in the physical world.

How to Feel and See Your Faery Wings

Find a quiet place outside. A perfect place would be by the ocean, in a garden or a forest, on a mountain, in a beautiful field or with a tree or plant that is special to you. If this is not easily available, simply create this landscape within your mind, and journey there. Run through your chakras, up and down, quite quickly, just to touch base and see what is happening with them. Where are you feeling whole and well? Just acknowledge any feelings that may come up but do not get distracted. Send love and healing faery energy to all your chakras, then move on.

Now that you feel well, and tuned up again, take your focus to between your shoulder blades. See if you can feel any tickling, and prickling, and delicate strange little feelings there. Imagine something coiling out of your DNA, and nudging just beneath the skin there. Begin to see in your mind's eye the wings gently pushing through your skin, without breaking or harming it, just as your fingernails grow, just as your hair grows – this is perfectly natural, without pain. There may be sensations, a kind of uncoiling feeling, a release, and energy may feel like it is pouring into this area.

Begin to see your wings growing, and as they do, notice how they are forming. Are they light, transparent, celled and gossamer? Are they long and tapered, or large and full-bloomed? Do they feel heavy? Do they feel light? Are they ragged and long? Do they have sparkles, and are they shining in the light? Do they camouflage you? Can they stretch out now? Let them dry in the sunlight, and feel your blood pumping through your wings. Sense them becoming integrated, a part of you. See them. Stretch them. Now give them a flap a few times. Are you ready to fly?

Moving your wings, feel the air gather and pocket under them, lifting you up gently. Raise them higher, and bring them down faster, once, twice, three times, and feel yourself lift off the ground. Stand up, and now flap your wings again and again, and take off. Point your head in the direction you wish to go, and feel the way your wings catch the breeze, and how just a turn of the head, or a slight shift of your weight, can help you change direction. Notice how high you can go – some wings are designed to fly high, for a vantage point far above, others are for being with the flowers and plants, for quick and easy tending of your garden and your soul. Your wings are yours alone, and may change each time you connect with them...

Now come back. Draw a picture of yourself with your wings. Let your imagination roam free, and draw yourself as you appeared in your faery wing vision journey.

Create Your Own Beautiful Faery Wings

Now, let's get busy making some enchanted faery wings that will perfectly capture the essence of your magical self!

You Will Need:

☆ **Wire.** Two metres of sturdy wire – 12, 14 or 16-gauge are recommended. The wire needs to be flexible, thin enough to twist and work with your hands, but strong and durable too. Two metres should be enough, although if you want to make large double wings you may need a bit more. Alternatively, old-fashioned wire coat hangers work a treat as a ready-made wing frame!

☆ **Fabric.** Transparent and lightweight fabrics such as organzas work very well. Remember, your wings will be attached to your back, and you want them to feel light, not burdensome. A wonderful substitute for fabric is pantyhose, which comes in such beautiful faery colours, or simply black, which is stunning and strong too.

☆ **Decorations.** You may wish to use fabric paint, or fabric pens and textas. Feathers, shells, beads and sparkles can be added too. An incense stick can be used to very gently and safely create holes in your wings, to give that raggle-taggle faery feel, if you wish it. Gather any ribbons, fabric scraps, pretty cords and tassels or felt flutteries that take your fancy. Lightweight crystals and gemstones also look beautiful and can be attached quickly with a glue gun. You may also want flowers (fresh or fake), twigs, leaves or feathers.

☆ **A hot glue gun.** This can be purchased for as little as $12, and will no doubt be used over and over again as you discover the wonder and bliss of making your own magical creations.

☆ **Needle and thread, and some pins.** Just in case.

☆ **Elastic or ribbons.** To hold your wings on with.

Taking Flight

Step one: Take your wire, and cut four pieces for the four wings. You may wish to cut one or two wire "bendies" at this point too. For people who want a simpler method, remember that good old-fashioned wire coat hangers are wonderful, and almost perfectly sized. Simply bend them – gently, so they do not snap, until you get a shape you feel is right. Wings aren't perfect, so please don't fret about making yours match, or being totally even and so forth. That's not how nature works, and we're creating a connection to your wild free nature with these wings, not a reason to beat yourself up.

Step two: Shape your wire. Perhaps the upper wings will be larger, and the lower wings smaller. You may not wish to have two wings on either side, and simply go for one large wing on each side of your back. Play with and mould the wire until you get the feel and the look that is right for you. Remember, all the time you are doing this, you are feeding your own faery energy into the wings. And you may want to ask for a faery companion to help inspire you along the way, gifting you with ideas and whimsy!

Stay in the energy you wish your wings to have – make the process flow, light and easy. When you're done shaping, lay the frames down on a single colour background, like some delicious green grass, to see how they're working together. Twist the ends of each wing together, leaving yourself at least a few centimetres extra so you can bind the wings together at the end of this process.

Step three: It's wing pretties time! If you have pantyhose for the substance of your wings, snip off the legs – one leg for each wing! Simply stretch these over the wire, quite tightly, then tie the ends off neatly. You may wish to use one colour for the top wings, and another shade of the same colour for the bottom wings, or contrasting shades, like a blue and a green for example. If you are using fabric, cut it to fit your wire frame, then slowly and carefully glue it onto the wire with your hot glue gun. Make it as neat as you can, but do not become too worried. Focus on attaching it, and not burning yourself, as hot glue is painful to get on your skin! Keep some cold water on hand should you accidentally "glue" yourself (I have done this with my fingertips – ouch! But it healed quickly.) You can always camouflage the untidy bits with some pretty decorations later. This process is about feeling and vibe, rather than perfectionism!

★ Here's another method where you don't even have to use fabric to make the wings. Instead you can use beautiful satin ribbons in a rainbow of colours, or pretty cords, to criss-cross between the frames of the wings, making a kind of tapestry pattern that's all your own. After you have completed weaving your wings, decorate them by gluing crystals, twiggy bits and other decorations onto the ribbons, and tucking in fresh flowers. Bind the wire with the same coloured ribbons as well, and you will have the most gorgeous, unique creation!

Step four: Now your fabric is on you may wish to paint some swirls, spots or spider webs, or butterfly camouflage cells, on your wings with fabric paint. Another method is to trace patterns using glue, then sprinkle beautiful sparkles along those lines, which gives an ethereal, delicate feel. Or you can use glitter glue if you have some to trace pretty patterns on your wings. Once this is done, it's a very good time to have a cup of tea and let your wings dry.

Step five: Now, let's join these faery wings up. Of course, you may have opted for a simple design with two wings made out of one piece of wire, like a figure eight... clever you! You can have another cup of tea. But if you've got four beautiful wings to join together, let's get started on this engineering feat!

Remember how you have some wire left over where you joined the ends of each wing frame together? Excellent. Now, twine together the top left and the top right wings, carefully and slowly, joining the two frames into one lovely bi-winged faery creation. Now, with the other two lower wings, take these winglets with their extra wire, and wrap them together also. This will form a kind of funny little bar in the centre, that will sit comfortably, we hope, on your back, and look perfectly at home there.

Now, fiddle a little... The heavier your wings, the droopier they will be! You may love the look of wings drifting softly downwards, or you may wish for uplifting, high, fully spread wings. Do try to keep them lightweight so they become a true part of you, and an expression of you, rather than a troublesome or awkward costume at worst, and a pretty decoration at best.

Now take a small piece of extra wire, and bind over the place where the two uppermost wings meet, wrapping around where you joined the extra bits. Done. Take another piece of wire, and bind together the join of the two bottom winglets. Done. Next, take another piece of wire, and bind both sets of wings together. You can even pop in a couple of liquid nails if you wish it to be really sturdy. Or, if you have masking tape handy, bind them all up together with this around the wires – it will provide some nice padding for your back so it is protected from any pokey-out wire bits.

Step six: To cover up all the wire, and/or your masking tape, let's wrap a scrap of fabric over them and around. There, better already! When that's done, let's take some beautiful ribbons. You may wish to dangle these from the cross bar. And doesn't that sparkle pattern work beautifully! And look, someone over there has popped little holes in their wings, making them all tattered and faery beautiful! And over there, someone has put pearly tips on wires! (These are the bendy bits you may have cut for this purpose earlier – small pieces of wire, proportionate to your wings, that you can turn into butterfly-like antennae, long and straight, with a lovely spiral or a pearl at the end.) And look, yet another faery has made hers out of the most delightful spider web stockings, and placed curly-whirly wire bits extending from the centre. Lovely!

Step seven: How do you attach your wings to your body, I hear you ask? Well, there are two methods. You can cut two lengths of elastic that are long enough for your arms to pass through, and stitch the ends to the support bar, forming two loops. Then put your arms through the elastic loops – and ohmigosh, you have wings! Alternatively you can take two lengths of coloured ribbon, about 50cm each in length, and stitch one end of each of them to the centre of the back bar. Then you can loop a ribbon around each arm, and tie them together to keep your wings on!

Now, don a pretty, colourful, layered dress or a pair of tattered leggings. It's not about expensive clothes here, it's about expression. What is your fae flavour? Ask your faery companion, and she may even deliver to you a vision of your faery self. Clean up the pins and needles, and put everything away so you can find it all again later. Thank the faeries for their inspiration and help, then pop on some wonderful fae music and prepare to fly!

How to Make A Faery Crown

This is a lovely way to dress up and enter the faery realm. A faery crown will frame your face and eyes, and give you a beautiful feeling of being at one with nature and all her spirits.

When making a magical faery crown, it's important to let go of our traditional and quite biased ideas about what a crown is. Many people, for example, believe crowns indicate royal or elite status. But in Faeryland, crowns connect us with the entire world and all of creation, above and below, and help us integrate those more airy and galactic energies into our whole selves.

They also help us pay attention to the messages we are always receiving through our crown chakra. Crowns are magical objects, and even when worn by royalty, or people wanting to display their wealth and status, they are still very powerful in an enchanted sense. All around it you can see the energy of the crown, which of course has been created over time by the various beings who have worn it. Some, made with magical intent and purpose and imbued with this energy by their creators, are very potent. Many of the English royal family's crown jewels have this build-up of energy around them. Usually they are made of gold and precious stones, and great symbolism has been woven into them.

The Saint Edward's Crown worn by the current Queen of England at her coronation, for example, has such magic. This very ornate and rather heavy crown is studded with 444 precious stones – a number said to be sacred to the angels, and thus providing the wearer with heavenly protection! It also includes many symbols, such as the cross and the fleur-de-lys. All of these give it a very heavy and ceremonial energy, suitably so when you consider what duties a head of state must undertake.

So, a crown shows people who you are, and what you represent. A monarch is the head of state and has many responsibilities and privileges, and their crown shows all of that. Similarly, your faery crown is your opportunity to show other faery people and the fae themselves who you are, and what your intentions are magically.

Now, before you do a thing, connect with that magical aspect of your self, and how you relate to the world, so you can capture that essence in the crown you are going to make. What sort of energy do you wish to be a part of, and project?

Spend some quiet time in meditation, visualisation or creative day-dreamery before making your crown. How do you see it? Is it bright, golden and shining like the sun? Is it silvery, moonlit and sparkling? Or is it made of flowers, ferns and the jewels of the growing world, like berries and seeds?

If you would like some ideas for inspiration, you could choose one of the seasons, or make one of each to wear at festivals, rituals (and normal days at work!) throughout the year. An autumnal crown could feature beautiful falling leaves and flowers in colours of red and gold, and be about transitions and change. A summer crown could include delicate fruit blossoms and sunny flowers, and represent fruition and abundance. A spring crown could be made of jasmine and daffodils, and symbolise the fertility of your dreams. And a winter crown could be made from bare pieces of woods and twigs, silver glitter and white frosty patches, to symbolise the introspection of nature and your own self-reflection.

Or you could create a butterfly crown, a dragonfly crown or even a moss or fern faery crown! Imagine, and wonder, and the faeries will gift you with bright ideas and wonders to create.

When you have seen your crown, and felt its energy, come back and get ready to be creative. You may wish to make a little sketch, or jot down some notes, to help guide you and remind you of colours and details. Please don't get caught up in a literal representation of what you may have seen in your vision – it is the energy you are bringing through that is of most importance. And remember to invite the faeries in – they will crown you queen of your world!

You Will Need:

☆ **One of the following,** or a combination of all three, to make the circlet, which is the basis of your crown.

> ★ A one-metre-long section of a lovely plant that has vines or tendrils, such as ivy or jasmine.
>
> ★ Pipe cleaners, in colours that work with your theme.
>
> ★ 12 or 14-gauge wire. This has plenty of strength, and lots of bend for twirly bits!

☆ **Decorations.** Bells, ribbons, symbols, charms, pretty stones and crystals (lightweight, and of suitable energy, so you don't get a headache!). Also perhaps paint, glitter, fabric flowers and sparkles.

☆ **Natural growing things.** You might choose fern fronds and flowers, some short, stemmed sections of leafy green plants, seeds and berries, and even some flowering herbs for a lovely aroma.

☆ **An offering.** This is to exchange with the faeries for the magic that will be imbued in your crown, and any pieces of plants you may take for your creation.

☆ **A hot glue gun,** or liquid nails if you wish to use glue. The faeries will help you with this decision. Let them know if you are using crystals, for example, as liquid nails are very helpful in keeping them bonded for a year and a day, at least!

☆ **A fun and positive energy.** Please put away any thoughts that making a crown is difficult – it is very simple and easy, and lots of fun when you decide not to worry about it. Also be aware that your hands carry lots of magical energy – and will channel that energy into the crown itself. So, clear your mind of thoughts such as: "Oooh, this is hard" and the like (or just ask them to wait until you're finished), and think thoughts and feel the flowing energy of: "Oh, it is so easy," and "I didn't know how beautifully perfect it would be." Let nature and the faeries be your guides and you can't go wrong.

Putting It All Together

Step one: Take your section of vine or curling tendril from any plant with natural rope-like sections. Alternatively, the green wood of a strong wooded herb, like rosemary, is perfect too. The new-growth stems have strength and flexibility – perfect for crown making! Rosemary also has the magical influence of helping us to remember, and will bring a sweet smell to your headpiece.

If you wish to have a wholly natural crown, create a circlet out of your vine or climbing or trailing plant, by winding it into a circle-shape. If you wish, you could divide your strands of plants into three sections and weave them by plaiting the sections together before winding them into a circle. This may become a little more complicated than you wish, although it is a wonderful way to pour magic into your crown. Each thread or section carries energy, so it can be well worth the extra time to create this style of crown. It simply requires more time, patience and magical intent.

An alternative is to create a circlet out of a pipe cleaner, or a few of them, depending on how tight or loose you wish your crown to be.

Another option is to create the circlet out of wire, which can then be wrapped with ribbon, or painted and coated with sparkles.

Step two: Once you've made your circlet, it is now time to decorate. Sometimes I achieve height in my crown by working with naturally strong spiky plants. The slender fronds of ferns are also wonderful for this purpose, and give height without drooping – which can lend a rather forlorn air to your headpiece. Small pieces of plants, such as gum leaves with a little stem and some buds, can then be added. Attaching them is easy – simply wind them on with some wire, or a small section of pipe cleaner. Some people like to use glue to attach the odds and ends, but it isn't always necessary, and can be a little fragile and take time to dry. If you do use glue, check in with the faeries, and then be sure to use a good strong hot glue gun or the very tough and strong liquid nails.

If you wish to have some higher sections, take a section of wire and build some arches or pointy sections at the front of your crown. You can twist and twirl the wire, until it pleases the eye. Then simply tuck in your flowers, or use a hot glue gun to add semi-precious stones or shells. And don't forget to add some ribbons, and perhaps tie some bells to their ends for a very pretty and musical note.

Step three: When you are done, let your crown "settle" for a little while, especially if you've worked with glue. If you're creating a crown using live foliage though, it's important to keep it fresh by wetting it down, or creating it as close to its time of wearing as possible. When I make a crown I often spend very little time on it, with wonderful results. I allow the faeries and the plants to guide me in choosing what to add, and always make an offering in energy exchange for anything I might take from nature.

The most important aspect of crown making is that it expresses a previously hidden part of who you truly are, and shows off your magical nature!

And remember, anyone can wear a crown, but to radiate true magical energy, you have to remember that you are the sovereign in your world, and know that you will use your power wisely and well!

How to Make A Magical Faery Wand

Wands are beautiful magical tools that not only carry their own intrinsic energy, but can also hold, direct and amplify energy from another source – like you, nature and the fae.

Wands are associated with both the element of fire, for creativity, purpose, motivation and drive, and with the element of air, for inspiration and ideas, intellect and soaring energy. In truth though, you can create a water wand, an earth wand, a pixie wand or a house blessing wand – any magical faery wand with its own unique theme, purpose and power – so do not become too attached to simply one quality. When making a faery wand you have a wide variety of inspiring sources to choose from, as the faeries work with, and in some ways transcend, all elements.

Before you begin, ask the faeries to guide you and help you "see" the energy of your wand. Visualise the colours, energies and stones that are being drawn to you and your wand-in-making. This will give you a kind of energetic blueprint and some true guidance so that when you go shopping you don't become overwhelmed by all the pretties available. It's a little like deciding what to cook and buying the ingredients, but leaving enough room for the faeries to offer spontaneous guidance. It's best not to have too firm an idea in your mind of how your wand *must* look and be – it's best to blend a mixture of both planning and pleasurable surprises!

You Will Need:

☆ **A length of wandwood.**

☆ **Binding cord,** such as leather strips or natural fibre cords, some thick and some thin. Embroidery cottons are also particularly wonderful to add an array of colour.

☆ **Ribbons.** In any colours, widths and sheens that suit the particular wand you are making and its purpose.

☆ **A crystal point.** Consider the shape you want, and the type of crystal that suits you and your magic-making. In consultation with your wandwood, choose a piece that speaks deeply to you.

☆ **Hot glue gun or liquid nails.**

☆ **Sandpaper.**

☆ **A feather.** Or two. In a colour you like, or from a bird that resonates with you and speaks to you from the fae.

☆ **Some beads, bells or charms.** Dragonflies, stars or symbols you love, for example a seven-pointed star would be perfect.

☆ **Some paint,** or a tool like a wood burner. Please only use this under guidance, or by very very carefully following the instructions. It is quite an investment, so it can be wonderful if you feel you are drawn to make lots of magical wands and staffs, but it is not necessary if you just want to make one, or a few.

Putting It All Together

Step one: Take a walk to find the perfect piece of wood for your wand. Some magical wands are made of metal, but while faeries can withstand the impact of various iron and mineral compounds (as they are of the earth), it is the disruption to the electromagnetic fields that metals can have that makes working with them difficult when working with the faeries. So, for a faery wand, use wood.

This walk will mean going to a natural place to find your wandwood. Wandwood is magical. It already knows you, and is calling out to you. Wandwood will send you on a quest to find it, and all that takes place during this quest will be meaningful and purposeful and have a message for you.

Where to find wandwood: I find my most magical wandwoods at the beach. I am a bit of a sea witch, and so for me it is perfect. Lakes too, and waterfalls and rivers, may have this kind of wandwood. Most wandwood that has been smoothed by the sea has a fascinating energy – cleansed again and again by salt water, worn smooth to the touch by the waves and the grit of the sand, and hard and strong. The wood that remains is very much the raw "bone" of the wood. I love driftwood, and am so fortunate to have found so many beautiful pieces.

However, we do not all live near beaches or lakes, so alternatives can be found in forests and parklands, or even your own backyard. Always look for fallen wood, rather than having to break branches off a tree or bush. Fallen wood will call out to you.

When you find a piece of wood that feels right for you, check it for:

◇ Strength. Check to ensure that it's not hollowed through – although sometimes you can find lengths of wood perfectly hollowed through, which make beautiful musical instruments and whistles.
◇ Length. This needs to feel right for you. Some magical traditions have very strict guidelines, for example, one criteria is said to be that the wand reaches from your elbow to the top of your middle finger. If this happens naturally, wonderful, but this is not vitally important for your magical faery wand.

Step two: Now look closely at your wood. Note what kind it is, if it is eucalyptus, oak, ash, bamboo or something else – all will have a different energy. Gaze at the wand with your faery sight, slightly blurred and off centre, not looking "hard" at it. See if any shapes emerge from the wand, perhaps an eye or a head, and swirl together. You might be "seeing" the lines and eddies of power that your wand holds within its energy field.

Spend some time now with your length of wood. See yourself using it as a wand. Let it speak with you, whisper to you, of its purpose and its magic and the ways in which it can be used. Have a dialogue with your wood – make suggestions to it, and listen and feel for the answers. Discover whether it would prefer amethyst as a point, for magical energy and psychic focus, or citrine, for bringing in golden power and abundance, and leading you and creating a circle of sunlit solar energy, or another one. There are so many different kinds of crystals, all with different powers and purposes, so decide, with your wood and with the fae, which one will be best for the wand you are making now.

Shhh! Faery Secret

Faeries don't like people who try to save them, or improve their manners! They don't feel guilt or shame as we do, and trying to make them feel they should or ought to do things will only cause them to hide from you.

Once you have spoken to your faery wandwood, and know its purpose and what it wishes to be, it is now your job to help this come through to the physical realm.

Step three: If you have collected magically water-smoothed driftwood, you can skip the next bit. However, if you have forest-gathered your wandwood, pay attention! Gently remove any loose or lifting bark to reveal the beautiful colour, markings and flesh of the wood beneath. Now, if some bark wishes to remain on your wand, so be it. It may be creating a shape or a symbol for you to work with. I have wands that have moss and even shells on them, and I love the interplay of the elements and their organic quality. They will continue to change as the elemental forces interact, which makes these wands even more magical and fae-like!

Once you have removed the loose and coarse bark from around the piece of wood, you may wish to smooth down your wand with some sandpaper. Some woods do not need this at all – they are perfectly smooth to the touch, but others may be rougher and less comfortable to hold in your hands. Your hands and your wand need to love each other, and to enjoy the feel and touch of each other, so be sure to ask your wand what it prefers.

Remember that every touch of your hand, every thought that you have while co-creating your wand, will imbue it with your own energy. Be mindful and work with clear, aware intention – not faking it, as the faeries will know you're not sincere, but with truth, and a kind of direction. Your wand will direct and expand this energy, so be sure it is an energy you personally and on a planetary level would like to see more of in this world.

Step four: Setting your crystal point is a most important moment, so ask the faeries to help you with this. If there is not already a kind of hollow at the end of your wand suitable for your crystal point to snuggle into and settle in for life, ask the wood's permission to hollow out a small section. Then you may wish to use some liquid nails to set a kind of base for your point. And don't worry, the energy will be able to run through the glue if you ask the faeries to help bless the energy and keep it clear.

Step five: Once you have set your point, you now have the true structure of the wand. Gaze at it again, and refer to any notes you may have made in your meditation on your wand. What colours will work best with it? What symbols does it seem to want? Is it a fire wand, with brilliant golds and reds, helping you align to your faery gift of power? Or is it a heart-space wand, pouring love and luminous green energy into the world?

Are there any shapes within the form of your wand that you wish to bring out, through using paint, or carving the wood slightly to accentuate what your fae-sight can see? If so, do this now.

Step six: Once this is done, take an embroidery thread that corresponds with your energy and wind it around your wand. You may wish to criss-cross the threads, or simply spiral them about the wandwood. If you do this, use a little glue to secure the thread at pertinent points. You may also wish to leave your wand bare.

However, at the place where the crystal point meets the wood, this is a wonderful site to bind the energy together, with a secure piece of cord, strip of leather or suede (my favourite in some ways), ribbon or thread. Again, work with some glue to secure the binding in place. You may wish to first lay down a beautiful scrap of fabric, like suede, and then tie the bindings over this for a more layered effect. This can create an organic feel, with the crystal appearing as the flower emerging from the leaves and bud of the fabric.

When winding the thread, remember that you are weaving magic in – so observe your thoughts, and treat every one of them, and your every touch, like an ingredient in a magical potion.

Step seven: You may now wish to add some powerful finishing touches. A feather, found on a sacred walk, or gifted to you by the birds, or by a friend, is a wonderful addition to many wands. Over time I have collected lots of beautiful parrot and parakeet feathers, and some owl, eagle, kookaburra, hawk and kite feathers, gifted to me by nature, or from very special people.

If these are not readily available, remember it is not legal in many places to buy bird feathers like eagle, owl and so on. You may wish to wait until you are gifted one, or you may visit an aviary or even a zoo, where you may be gifted a feather of power. Please do not feel you must wait until you are gifted a "powerful" feather, for they are all powerful. If you have the gift of the feather in your mind and one arrives at your feet the next time you exit your home, well, that is your feather. It has come to you with a purpose. Attach the feather to some thread or ribbon, and then string beads along the thread to give it an anchor in the world, so it will not float away. The energy of the bird whose feather has been gifted to you will now become an important part of your wand. Long tail feathers can be dramatic features of your wand, just as shorter, fluffier feathers can be.

With some wands, I have studded their "spine" with small crystal points. And I have one that was created by the magical wand and staff maker Natasha Heard, and this wand is an auric clearing tool, which literally combs out energies, and removes tangles and knots from my own energetic field, with its amethyst crystal spine. Use your trusty hot glue gun for this purpose, and perhaps smooth some sparkles over any areas of glue that smudge your wandwood.

When you have finished creating your own unique and magical wand, you may wish to sit with it for a wee while, just feeling it, loving it, thanking it. Once you have truly fallen in love, it is time to dedicate it to your faery workings with a small ceremony.

This can be as simple or as elaborate as you wish, and can be done beneath sunlight, sunrise, sunset, moonrise or moonset, or performed on an auspicious day, like an equinox, a solstice, or a celebration such as Beltane. During this ritual you may wish to attach one last symbol to your wand. I would do this by painting or burning into the wood a seven-pointed star – that way, the portal to the faery realm is always within your wand!

Every wand will have a different energy – some will feel like dragonflies, others more like butterflies, some will have a gentle lunar power, and others will feel they can draw an etheric portal through which you can enter the Seelie Court, or be transported beneath the Hollow Hills of Gwyn ap Nudd himself. Whatever the magic of your faery wand, treat her with love and respect, just as you do the faeries themselves, and you will have a long and lovely relationship full of enchantment – and more than a few surprises!

Amelia's Faery Magic

Inspired by the creations of nature, Amelia Sayers has grown her own fantastical range of jewellery and accessories, from ornate crowns and tiaras to faery wings and masks. She also delves into the mystical eastern art of mehndi, deftly painting undulating vines, creatures or mandalas on any willing subject, and is exploring pregnant belly art, props for costumes and fantasy photo shoots. Visit Amelia at www.WhereTheWildThingsGrow.com.

I first discovered faeries when I started on the path of paganism nine years ago. Faeries and their stories are a wonderful, light way for people, and especially children, to make a connection to the earth. We need them to inspire and educate us about the natural world and her needs. To be able to see past ourselves to what the earth really needs back from us.

As much as I create faery-like pieces, I feel my connection is more to nature herself. Being outside in nature invites a deep connection, but even just going through nature on a train with a notebook handy can bring all sorts of new ideas to mind. I'm always scribbling or sketching something new, some whimsical collar, crown or wing design. Bushwalking, diving and even exploring nurseries can also provide rich ground in which to find new ideas and colour combinations. Nature has the most fascinating palette after all, and I love to collect samples of her work and take them home to experiment with their colour and energy with dyes, fabrics, fibres and beads.

My work is my way of taking nature's amazing creations and expanding and stretching that essence to as many fanciful places as I can – making my own versions in celebration of her, which are wearable and will last forever. Something that a person can take away with them that has been inspired by nature. It's my way of giving them a connection to her.

Sometimes I feel the faeries have gifted me with faery sight, as I can find ethereal possibilities in unlikely materials, like Christmas decorations, hardware supplies and recycled objects. They also bring me ideas for utterly whimsical, impractical creations, not always fitting for mundane life, but I'm hoping that one day we'll be freed of conservatism and wear our wings and finery out and proud all the time!

Communication with the fae happens when I open myself to their messages and wisdom. Lying on the grass under a willow tree works wonders, as does daydreaming on the edges of napping. I just let it flow in, quickly write it down or sketch it out, and always say thank you. In the middle of creating I'll often stop and ask the piece what it wants to be, give it time to breathe and evolve on its own. And when it's time to stop, I get the message because I keep dropping things, or run out of something – I can only throw up my hands and say: "Okay, I get the message!"

I often see faeries as a flash of light from the corner of my eye, perhaps a slight movement as I open a door, or look away. They used to hide my tools, but I think we've come to a better arrangement these days. I see them also in the many faces made in tree bark, leaves growing together, branches – always there, keeping a glinting eye on us.

We need the faeries to teach us the values of truth and playfulness, which we tend to lose our grip on from time to time. Faeries show us the need to be in our personal truth always, and to own and accept all parts of ourselves. Allowing ourselves to play, and to shine, is important too, so we can achieve balance between work, rest and play. This creates a beacon for others to follow, giving them permission to be their truth, to shine their light. All of this is so important to the health of us and of the earth.

Speaking With the Faeries

"Weave the words with me,
The words that will entwine.
To the place between the worlds,
Betwixt the kiss of night and day."
Alicen Geddes-Ward, The Kiss of Two Worlds

How to Hear Their Messages

The more you communicate with the faeries, the more you may notice that there are some very odd words that slip from betwixt their whimsical lips. Not only that, but much of their speech is delivered in riddles and rhymes, and can have a tumbledown, higgledy-piggledy quality that makes translation challenging, and keeping up almost impossible!

But we can easily, with just a little practise and the willingness to play, learn these words, and learn the ways in which to use them and other faery communication skills, like poetry, sound and rhythm. This form of language can unlock and open wide the doors between worlds, thin the veils, and help make our faery meetings strong, enjoyable and very clear indeed.

Sometimes the words that come easiest, the faery language you are most able to "get", comes from a connection with your bloodline and faery relatives through the ages. I have Welsh and Irish ancestry, with a lot of other bits and pieces thrown in for good measure. As I don't actively use those languages (though my blood recognises them), it took me ever so long to work out that one faery was attempting to give me a blessing when I encountered her – she kept making a sound like someone clearing their throat, which I eventually discovered was a Gaelic word, "beannacht", or blessing.

Thankfully, while I may not have recognised her words, her energy was not difficult to read at all, so I said yes to what she appeared to be offering. I met her at Bride's Mound in Glastonbury, where I had asked for true love to enter my life. (Now, several years later, I know that I have indeed been given the blessing of true love.)

This understanding of some faery language is a great help when "translating" their messages, as Janelle, a fantasy writer and singer from Victoria, discovered during the Wild Woman Weekend retreat, where we were exploring communicating with the faeries.

"I was told my faery name during the meditation when I was growing my wings," she remembers. "I thought it was an odd name for me because it started with Lynn. I couldn't see myself as a Lynn, which I think is why I promptly forgot the name – until I walked the labyrinth and was re-gifted the name again. *Lynndragana*.

"At first it was just a name, but I thought I'd research the part I didn't feel connected to. It turns out that in Gaelic 'llyn' or 'lynn' means 'lake' or 'waterfall'. Waterfall dragon! And where did we receive a message from our faery selves? Serpentine Falls. And what did I take so many photos of? The dragon head in the rocks and a pale blue dragonfly. Now I've really connected with the fae."

Learning just one Gaelic word – that "lynn" meant waterfall – helped Janelle understand the message the faeries were sending to her. You can see why learning some of their words, or having a reference guide handy, can be so helpful.

Another possibility is to begin to use language the way the faeries do – whimsically, tumbled, and in a far more blended and imaginative way than our textbooks teach. Faeries use words like "tripsied" for fallen over, "tricksy" for someone who plays tricks, or as a substitute for "difficult" or "hard to understand", and they definitely use lots of onomatopoeia, making their words sound like the thing they are describing. *Smash*, *crash*, *flash* and *kaboom* are all examples of the onomatopoeic words the faeries love.

To attune your ear to faery language, read some Dr Seuss, a man who played with the puns and possibilities of language, or some old Irish riddles, to get used to the structure. Lewis Carroll's *Alice in Wonderland* also contains passages similar to faery speak!

One of the great ways to speak with the faeries is to use poetry or song. Most poetry and song that is English in heritage has a kind of rhythm that was popularised by Shakespeare. It has the effect of sounding very sing-song, and sometimes this means that as we sing or say the lines, we begin to chant, and then we begin to slip into a kind of trance, which in turn helps us communicate even more effectively with the fae.

Here's a faery poem I wrote that you may wish to use, or you can write your own.

> *Faeries sweet and faeries wild,*
> *Come to visit me, your child.*
> *Let me know when you're about,*
> *Tell me stories to banish doubt.*
> *All about me circle round,*
> *Treasured memories once more found.*
> *Faeries sweet and faeries wild,*
> *Come play with me, your faery child.*

Some faeries use the structure of triads to deliver and share their messages. Triads are three observations which together deliver wisdom. There are hundreds of triads in existence, as Irish and Welsh monks wrote this form of ancient knowledge down in the 11th century. Although it can seem archaic to us, many faeries I have encountered love to speak in triads. Here are some examples:

☆ Three demonstrations of wisdom – holding to reason, holding to imagination, holding to improvement.

☆ Three things on which every person should reflect – whence they come, where they are, and whither they shall go.

☆ The three most beautiful sights – a potato garden in bloom, a ship in sail, a woman after the birth of her child.

☆ Three manifestations of humanity – affectionate bounty, loving manner, and praiseworthy knowledge.

There are some neat serendipities in languages too. For example, in Welsh the word "Ywerddon" means a Faeryland over the seas, while the Welsh word for Ireland is "Iwerddon". It's much too cosy for this to be a coincidence!

A Small Glossary of Important Faery Words

These are from the Gaelic language of the Celts. Play with them, and let them be musical, and you won't go far wrong with these words! Faeries from the Celtic lands often use this language to speak. Here are some words they have used with me, which took me a while to get used to! Pronunciations are in brackets.

Aisling: Dream state induced by faeries. (Ash-ling)

Anam Cara: Soul-friend. Faeries can help you find your soul-friends, the three special friends we are gifted with in life. (Ann-um kar-ah)

Annwn: A Faeryland realm. (Ann-oon)

Aonach: A formal faery gathering. (Eee-noch)

Ardrian: Faery high queen. (Ard-ree-ahn)

Asrai: Water faery who appears to forewarn of rainstorms. (Az-ray)

Awen: The gift of divine, flowing inspiration.

Ban: White.

Ban-Charach: Dear woman, loved woman. Beloved. The beat of one's heart. Some faery men love to address human females by this term. This is why we melt when we hear these words! (Ban-cararc)

Ban-Draoi: Head female druid – faeries often work with them, so if you attract a faery who wants to alert you to them, perhaps they are telling you that you too are a female druid. (Ban-droy)

Beag: Little. (Beck)

Beathe: Birch. (Beth)

Bo: Cow.

Bragr: Magical rhymes, from the Icelandic. (Brag-ir)

Breac: Speckled. (Bree-arc)

Bricht: Bright magic, literally to bring some light, like a magical torch, or metaphorically to illuminate. (Brite)

Calleach: Old woman, wise woman, crone. (Cal-ee-arc)

Cairn: Rocky area, stones. (Care-n)

Caiseal: A stone fortress. (Cash-el)

Coille: Wood or forest. (Keel)

Coinneach: Moss. (Conn-ee-arc)

Cremave: A magical faery healing stone.

Crochan: A healing pool, well or body of water that is inhabited by healing faeries.

Cu-sith: Faery hounds. (Coo-sith)

Cwn Annwn: The red-eared, white-coated hounds of the Wild Hunt, who chase down destructive, evil souls. (Cwinn ann-oon)

Damh: Stag. (Daav)

Dan: One's path, the events you are creating and attracting due to past and present-time actions, or even the actions of ancestors.

Darach/duir: Both meaning oak. (Durr-ach/doo-weir)

Dolmen: Sacred stones, two upright forming the "walls", a third atop the two to create a "roof". They were once covered with earth and grass, but this has been eroded away to leave the bare stones.

Druidheachd: Druid-magic, sorcery. (Druid-hark-ed)

Dubhachas: Gloom, depression brought on by believing in the illusory world of humans. (Doov-acars)

Dun: A mound, faery fortress. They are worlds between worlds, and many faeries make their home within one.

Eas: Waterfall, as in Saint Nectan's Glen in Cornwall. (Eee-ars)

Eilean: Island.

Eolas: Magic; magical power.

Eun: Bird.

Fada: Long.

Fionn: White, as in holy, pure.

Fior: Truth. Faery truth is binding, and while faeries may riddle, they do not, and never will, nor can, lie.

Fuarun: Well or spring.

Gal-Grian: A burst of energy from the faery goddess Grian, shooting forth new light into someone who has been hurt or wounded, healing golden light that can help us overcome even the most bloody and awful of wounds, be it energetic, physical, emotional or mental. The greatest manifestation of this energy takes place at Newgrange each year at the winter solstice. (Gull-gree-arn)

Glas: Grey-green.

Glen: A glen, a narrow valley.

Gorm: Greeny-blue.

Inis: An island within the landmass, like Avalon. (Inn-ish)

Iolair: Eagle. (Eee-oh-lar)

Lynn: Large waterfall.

Mor: Round, great. (Author Caiseal Mor's name means "great stone fort" in Irish Gaelic.)

Nevis: Stormy, venomous, troublesome. Faeries have tried to warn me about people, places or situations using this word, but until I understood its meaning I did not get the message!

Oenghus: The fae often work with this Celtic deity of air, breeze, change, music, journeys and romantic love. (Ang-gus)

Righ: King. (Reeg)

Ros: A wood.

Ruadh: Reddish-brown. (Roo-arrd)

Tulach: A hill. (Too-lark)

Finding Your Faery Name

Finding your own true faery name is lots of fun, and a wonderful way to connect with the enchanted realm. Most of all, finding your own faery name is a chance to reclaim and return home a lost part of your magical self. Sometimes we search a little too hard for this part of ourselves, and the name eludes us. Sometimes we ask, and it comes to us in the most unexpected of ways – while dancing, cooking, tending the garden or staring at a candle. And at other times we have a nickname, or have been called Flower, Little One, Blossom, Willy Wagtail, Billy Butterbottom or the like for such a long time, and simply have not recognised it as our faery name.

Shhh! Faery Secret

Faeries cannot tell a lie – but they sometimes don't understand just what it is we are asking. This has led to some people suggesting that they are tricksy, but it is really that we humans are awfully confusing at times!

It can be very healing and empowering to find your faery name, as it can help you express a part of yourself that you may have trouble bringing forth under "ordinary" circumstances. Having a faery name and a faery alter-ego allows you to explore that free and wild part of yourself, safely and beautifully, and can help bring it into balance and friendship with your more everyday self.

It also allows you to be free to be who you wish to be, other than a rigid expression of a name someone else gave you. That name is a beautiful part of you, but it often does not express all of you, especially those magical, hidden parts that you are now bringing into the light for healing, play and laughter.

Often once you find your faery name, working with that name will help you find solutions to problems and come up with creative ideas and adventures you feel your "normal" self isn't always capable of, or ready for.

Linda, who also attended the Wild Wisdom of the Faeries' Wild Woman Weekend (www.WildWomanWeekend.com) in WA this year, discovered that her faery name had those qualities.

"My faery name was spoken to me. As soon as Lucy asked us to think of our name, 'Miss Eliza' came straight in very clearly. Being a Virgo, I told myself to sit with it for a while, as I hadn't done what I was asked, and let it simmer," she says.

"Later I went into the labyrinth and asked for my name, and as I started walking, the word 'Justice' came in. I kept repeating it in my head, and then I heard 'Menza', and then 'Justice of Menza'. I kept walking to be sure, and after making an offering in the centre, of wine on earth, the voice said very clearly: 'Miss Eliza, Justice of Menza,' and I was sure. I came out and spoke it for the first time, and I am still sure now," Linda explains.

"It means so much to me. Since that time a lot has happened in my life, things that have needed shifting have come to the surface and are being dealt with, and a project I'd struggled to get off the ground early this year has started falling into place. It's as if Miss Eliza can do all the 'faery' things better than Linda ever could. Drawing on her energy quietens my inner critic and frees me up to express myself!"

Walking a labyrinth truly seems to work to allow you to get in touch with other forms of knowing. Jane also found her faery name after travelling through the labyrinth at the faery weekend.

"My faery name is Bee-belle. I was told my name when I went into the labyrinth. It was the first word that came to me when I asked the faeries what my name was. I asked them how I can see them, and a faery told me: 'Bee free and you will see.' I feel it suits me. I also had my little bell ringing, as it was attached to my hair, and that's where the belle part came in," she says.

You can see that being in a quiet, still, in-between place like a labyrinth is a wonderful way to still the chattering mind, and allow the faery voice to enter. So too can you find your name in meditation, or by taking yourself to a favourite place in nature. This is how Di, a beautiful pagan from Queensland, came to her own faery name.

"I had a guided meditation dealing with the fae loaded onto my iPod. I went out into the forest to my sacred place, to my favourite tree, and listened and waited, and it came to me," she explains.

It didn't all come at once though – there were other messages, pointing her in the direction of her faery name.

"I just kept hearing the System of a Down song *Ariel*, then I looked up and saw the branches of a brigalow tree, lit up by the moonlight, and I actually heard a little giggle so I knew they were near. I kept asking for my name, but the only answer I got was: 'Look, we've already told you!' I found I had 'lost' about two hours – a sure sign of having slipped into the faery realm! I went out at dusk, and by the time I got back to the car it was eight at night. What is my fae name? Ariel Brigalow Moondust."

Inspiration From the Trees

You may also wish to incorporate the name of a tree into your faery name. Rowan is a protector of magical beings, and is a beautiful tree to invoke or include in your name, as it will provide you with magical protection. Oak will make you strong. Hawthorn will inspire creativity. And willow is wonderful for faeries who adore fresh water, or who are overcoming headaches or sadness.

You may wish to include the Celtic name of one of the trees too, or use gum, eucalyptus or other tree and herb names from your own local area. Their botanical names and their traditional folk names often have a wonderfully magical sound to them too.

Here is a list of Celtic names used in the magical Ogham or Irish alphabet of trees, which apply to your birthdate too, adding an extra dimension of protection to your new faery name. The modern name is first, followed by the ancient name in brackets. Whichever one resonates with you is the one to use in your magical name.

☆ **Birch (Beith):** December 24 to January 20. This is a wonderful name for faery people who wish to reveal their inner strength.

☆ **Rowan (Luis):** January 21 to February 17. This tree is a protector of magical ones, including witches and faeries.

☆ **Ash (Nuinn):** February 18 to March 17. Empathetic, speedy and light, the energy and wisdom of this sacred tree can help you relax if you push yourself too hard.

☆ **Alder (Fearn):** March 18 to April 17. Strong faery people love working with this tree, and this name!

☆ **Willow (Saille):** April 18 to May 12. This beautiful, soft-natured tree provides help for faeries thirsty for knowledge, as well as those who suffer from headaches.

☆ **Hawthorn (Huathe):** May 13 to June 9. Creative faeries, and ones who need help with boundaries, are drawn to this tree.

☆ **Oak (Duir):** June 10 to July 7. This tree has a very strong, wise, long-lived and protective energy.

☆ **Holly (Tinne):** July 8 to August 4. The energy of this magical plant can generate charisma, admiration and even fame.

☆ **Hazel (Coll):** August 5 to September 1. Faery people who wish to find hidden treasure should work with this beautiful tree.

☆ **Vine (Muinn):** September 2 to September 29. Charming faery people full of laughter love the vine (and sometimes the wine too!).

☆ **Ivy (Gort):** September 30 to October 27. A travelling faery being, an explorer and adventurer, will feel aligned with ivy.

☆ **Reed (Ngetal):** October 28 to November 24. A wise faery person who loves ancient ways and places will work well with this plant.

☆ **Elder (Ruis):** November 25 to December 23. This wonderful tree is perfect for a free-spirited faery being who welcomes change.

Other Forms of Faery Inspiration

The faeries can also share your name with you via a dream, as happened to Tamara at the faery weekend. She had been a little worried because nothing had come to her at first, but with the fae you must be patient, and trust.

"My faery name is Aurora, but it took me a while to receive it. On the Saturday night there was a lot of discussion about our faery names, as many people had received theirs that day, but nothing was resonating with me. Then that night I had two faeries come to me in a dream," Tamara reveals.

"One was quite insect-like in his qualities. He was shy and green, and was hiding behind me – he came up to just below my shoulder. The other one was tiny, a crazy little faery who appeared to be free-falling down a portal – and he was having a ball doing it, with lots of excitement and energy.

"When I opened my eyes the next morning, the name Aurora was the first thing that popped into my head. When I got home I googled Aurora, as I wasn't sure of its meaning, and the images were awesome and inspiring – like a faery rave!"

Are you still searching for your faery name? Relax, and let your mind wander. Anything in nature can provide the catalyst for you to discover it. Stars, planets and celestial bodies... Gemstones, crystals and minerals... Clouds, thunderstorms and rainbows... Liminal times of the day or night, and the in-between places within the world. Even the names of birds, animals and insects like dragonflies may inspire you.

One thing is for sure, when you ask for your faery name, do listen carefully, because the faeries will answer you, but you must have the eyes to see and the ears to hear them. Sometimes the answer will come to you in an instant, in a flash of inspiration, and at other times it can take a little while. But be patient. They will answer you, and the answer will be a blessing. If you'd like some inspiration to start you on your way, to follow are some faery names to help the awen flow bright and strong and pure!

Don't forget to ask the trees, the forest, the flowers, the streams, the rocks, the creatures, the bees, the butterflies and the dragonflies. And a wonderful faery secret is that all ladybirds can carry your messages and requests straight to the faeries, who will send your name back to you via a dream within the next three nights.

A Magical List of Faery Names

Aeval: A faery name for women who have great sexual desire.

Aine: Beautiful faery goddess of the moon (pronounced awn-ya).

Annwn: For faeries who love playing in underwater castles.

Aoife: Beautiful, radiant, joyful (pronounced ee-fa).

Ariel: A faery of wit, learning and light.

Arwen/Awen: A name fit for a faery or elven princess, meaning one who brings divine inspiration.

Blathnaid: Flower, blossom (pronounced blaw-nid).

Branna: Beauty with hair as dark as a raven.

Brianna: Noble, virtuous.

Cliodna: For faery people who wish to walk in, and be, beauty (pronounced clee-ona).

Daimhin: Little deer (pronounced daw-veen).

Daireann: Means fruitful, bountiful (pronounced dar-rawn).

Ealga: Brave, noble, strong (pronounced ale-ga).

Eibhleann: Pleasant, beautiful, radiant (pronounced ave-linn).

Elrond: An elven prince. (JRR Tolkien uses many elven names beginning with "el". He was an expert in ancient Anglo-Saxon languages, and derived the names for his elves from actual words. They are full of magic! You may wish to try some of his names, like Elwe, Elladen, Elmoth, Elvena. Play with the "El" until a sound that feels right to you comes out. This could be your elven name.)

Enda: Freedom of spirit.

Eowyn: Courageous faery.

Este: Healer faeries are sometimes drawn to this name.

Estelliane: A starry-hopeful faery person name.

Felicity: A faery name for one who brings harmony and congeniality.

Fiona: Fair, bright, beautiful.

Galadriel: Elven royalty, and the giver of magical gifts.

Glorfindel: A name for clever faeries who can create abundance.

Ide: Thirst for goodness or knowledge (pronounced ee-da).

Keela/Kyla: Means beautiful, a beauty that only poetry can capture.

Leanan, Leanne: A faery name for inspiring sweethearts, although its usage, as in the leanana sidhe, a faery muse who exhausts those who call her, can be slightly sinister.

Lorien: One who dwells in Faeryland.

Maedbh: Cause of great joy and intoxication (pronounced may-v).

Mara/Meara: The sea.

Melissa: A wonderful name for a faery who loves the bees, it is also used by the helpers in goddess temples around the world.

Morgen: Priestess-faery of the sea.

Morwen: Sea-elf, oceanic traveller faery name.

Nessa: A sister-friend faery name.

Niamh: Brightness, a youthful, innocent heart (pronounced neeve).

Nissa: An elven one.

Nolana: One who hears the bells.

Nyxia: Faery of night, a wonderful name for faeries who come out to play under stars and moonlight.

Oona/Oonagh: Faery queen, the one, unity.

Orlagh: Golden princess.

Ossa: A faery lady of the seas.

Rionach: Queenly (pronounced ree-in-ock).

Roisin: A name meaning little rose (pronounced (ro-sheen).

Saoirse: Meaning freedom and liberty (pronounced sear-sha).

Shea: Rich and lovely, a palace.

Sheelagh: A name that means pure and musical.

Sorcha: Dark faery, royalty (pronounced sor-ra).

Teagan: Irish form of the Welsh Tegwin, which means beautiful.

Trixy/Trixie: One who brings joy through kind-hearted jokes.

Vaire: Weaver.

Vana: Ever-young.

Varda: Of the stars.

Xylia: Faery of the forest.

Yseult/Isolt: A name associated with love (pronounced ee-solt).

The Seven Gifts of Faery

"Faeries, come take me out of this dull world,
For I would ride with you upon the wind,
Run on the top of the dishevelled tide,
And dance upon the mountains like a flame."
WB Yeats, *The Land of Heart's Desire*

Seven Magical Faery Workings

This is a deep meditational and practical journey through the Seven Gifts of Faery. After completing the acceptance rite for each gift in the meditation, you may wish to embody the energy by creating the magical working listed for each gift. This will ground the energy in a very solid and real way. Or you may prefer to go through each gift, accepting each one, and then make your way through the magical workings, one by one, at a later stage. It is recommended that you do both the practical and the etheric workings outlined here, as together they interweave the celestial and terrestrial aspects of these gifts, and thus you will be balanced and in tune with the faery world, and your own inner faery nature.

In each magical working you will be asked to create a protective circle of blue fire. This is the colour of the fire the faery elementals burn when they need protection from any harsh or undesirable energies. It is simple to create this by visualising this blue circle of flame around you. If you are in the southern hemisphere, you may wish to draw it in an anti-clockwise, widdershins direction, as this is the natural way energy flows in this hemisphere. To close the circle of blue fire, ask the faeries to snuff it out in a clockwise direction. This works in the opposite way for people in the northern hemisphere – clockwise, or deosil, to open, anti-clockwise, or widdershins, to close. If you have any doubts, watch the way the water gurgles down a sink in your home, and you will see the natural flow of energy demonstrated very simply. Or if this all seems too complicated, ask the faeries to ignite the circle, and extinguish it, in the way the energy needs to flow. Let's begin with the first deep meditational journey...

Approaching the Faery Realm

Welcome to the world between the worlds. Welcome to the enchanted, blessed realm of the fae, a faraway land of legend, of myth, of stone circles, forests and castles in ancient lands. Yet the faery world is as close to you as the nearest plant, stone, tree or field of flowers, for the fae are with every living creature, and are of each of the elements. They have been here since before time began, and are of both the celestial and terrestrial spheres.

They are known by many names – the Tylwyth Teg, the Tuatha de Danaan, the menahune, the devas, the djinn, the Seelie and Unseelie Courts, the Good Folk, the sidhe – and many rumours and lies have been told of their powers and their intentions by those who envied them their ability to make the green world spring to life, to cleanse the waterways, to nurture and heal the animals, to love, dance with and inspire humans. And so we have distanced ourselves from them, feeling they are creatures of storybooks and fancy.

But they are as real as the natural world, beings of natural harmony, creativity, protection, growth, magic, love and laughter. The realm of the fae has seven bright gifts to offer every living being. And when you activate these seven gifts you will be grounded, sensual, powerful, compassionate, clear, psychic and in communion and harmony with all creation!

Do you wish to discover more? To fully enter the world of the fae? To be offered their blessings and their magical gifts?

Then come now. Take a deep breath, and release. *Ahhh...*

See now before you a deep green forest. It's filled with thick emerald greens, brightest flowers, singing birds, dancing butterflies and dragonflies, and many magical creatures. There are rainbows, and light, and a mist of rain falling gently in the warm air.

See now at the edge of the forest that there is a shining path twinkling out from the darkness of the trees. Walk towards this path, and as your feet connect with the soft fallen leaves, you begin to feel lighter. Feel the softness of the air, sense the sweet scents of the plants, listen to the music of the forest. As you approach this powerful faery path, you must enter with a heart that is free, a heart that is open. Fae are very wild, and very shy, and will not come to those who are hiding who they truly are.

So, with every step, allow who you truly are to begin to shine out, honest, authentic, clear. There is no judgement, only being. And as you acknowledge who you are freely, the fae will see your shining soul in all its beauty. And the path will take you through the heart of this ancient emerald forest. You walk... And you walk...

Just as you start to feel that the deep green forest seems endlessly made of tangled, ancient dark, a clearing opens up before you. Sunlight streams in, lighting up this place of openness, butterflies of all shapes, sizes and colours fly about you, as do dragonflies and tiny birds, and they gather around you, forming a path which you follow into the meadow, into the grove.

Surrounding this bright opening is a ring of trees, guardians of the grove, faery trees. Each of them has a sound, a tune, a quality of energy that is utterly unique. And taking just a moment, you draw in a very deep, very cleansing breath, and still surrounded by your butterfly companions – the messengers of the fae – you move to greet one of these trees. As you move towards it, you sense its energy radiating out to you. Strong, healthy, warm and welcoming. And this tree, you now notice, has a door at its base. A small door with a seven-pointed star on it – the door to the faery realm...

The door gently opens, and within the darkness beyond the door you see sparkling lights glowing in the dark. These lights slowly reveal themselves to be small beings, winged, with diaphanous clothing made of the air itself. They beckon you forward, and the door opens wide, and you step within this enormous tree, and somehow you have stepped through this tiny door. And you begin to move with these lights. At first, you feel only wonder, but before long, you are laughing and dancing and moving with them.

You are led down a winding hall, lined with roots and leaves, with the smells of the deep earth, rich and loamy, all about you, and these beings light your way in the darkness, leading you onwards...

Soon you reach a room within, a cave, which is glowing with crystals, and sound, and energy. And within this space is a bed of gold, shining brightly. The faery beings with you explain that this is the bed of transformation, and that if you wish, you may now be gifted with the seven bright gifts of the fae.

You nod, and gently you are lifted off the ground by these tiny beings, and effortlessly they float you through the air, and lay you down so gently on this glowing golden bed of transformation.

You sigh as you lay down, feeling its comfort, its deep healing, its beauty, its acceptance of all that you are, its understanding and support of all your potential. As you lie there, soaking in its deep peace, a faery comes towards you. She is your own faery godmother, your own protective faery, who has been with you throughout the ages, throughout all time, throughout all your lifetimes. She holds a bright wand, shining at its tip.

Telepathically she explains to you that she will share with you the faery gift of your ancestry... if you wish.

The First Gift of Faery : Ancestry

Your faery godmother explains that faeries are deeply connected to the history, to the true story, of this beautiful blue and green planet, and that they know and understand your own story, which has been unfolding for millennia. As faeries are extremely long-lived, she says, they have seen a great deal, and they are willing to reveal to us the patterns we may be repeating on a personal and planetary level. Many fae, like the Tuatha de Danaan of Ireland, shapeshifted into the sacred land itself, and thus they house and hold the bones of our ancestors, and their wisdoms too.

This also means that, because all food grows from the earth, and the earth itself is faery, all food grows directly from the realm of the fae. On the surface of the planet, each plant has its own faery who weaves the sunlight into nutrients, who offers food and drink, who collects dew, and who cradles the tender buds of the newborn flowers. All crops grow and all fruit ripens with their help, thus all we eat is faery food! And when we chemically interfere with this process, the faery energy, the nwyfre or life force within the plant, is diminished, and we lose our Sight, our way, our own energy, our own nwyfre.

Know now that your own faery godmother is protecting you, and guiding you to fully awaken this gift of the truth of your ancestry. The truth that you too are a faery, that you too are of this earth, that you too belong here, and are beloved. She asks if you wish to have this gift awakened within you, and if you agree, she shines her wand of love and light on your base chakra, activating a deep understanding of who you are, where you are from, the lives you have led, the places you have dwelled, and what you need to flourish in this world, in this lifetime...

Faery Magic to Connect With Your Ancestry

The perfect time of the year to connect with your ancestry is of course at Samhain, which is a seasonal festival that celebrates and acknowledges the leaving of the light from the world. This falls on October 31/November 1 (sunset to sunset) in the northern hemisphere, and on April 30/May 1 in the southern hemisphere.

This is a perfect time to set up an altar to your faery forebears, to your own faery blood. On your altar, place images of ancestors of your own bloodline (parents, grandparents, great grandparents), or of regions where you know you have come from. After drawing a protective blue flame all around you, set up your faery altar. Then, seated before it, allow the thoughts and feelings and messages from your faery kith and kin to come through for you.

As they do, you may wish to note them down, sketch the images, and discuss any issues you may have been experiencing in your life. Ask them for their advice and assistance in making the song of your fae blood become clearer and stronger, if this is what you wish to experience. When complete, thank your ancestors, and close your circle of blue fire.

Regarding timing: Although Samhain is the perfect time to connect with fae ancestry, there are many alternatives. For connection on any day, sundown is a wonderful time. Each week, Saturday offers this open and clear connection. On a monthly cycle, the dark moon is perfect, and yearly, Samhain is best.

Do keep images and mementos of your loved ancestors around you whenever you feel it is fitting. Having these energetic reminders of their connection and their relationship to you will assist you in hearing their wisdom, and feeling their protection, and connecting clearly with their messages and guidance.

The Second Gift of Faery : Sensuality

Your faery godmother now explains that she wishes to reveal to you the second gift of faery, the gift of sensuality. She whispers to you that faeries do not experience guilt when it comes to love and the pleasure of existing as a physical being. Too many humans, she says, have absorbed this guilt, and with it an unhealthy denial of their physical form – which can lead to a profound disconnection from their physical self, which then leads to a deep disconnection from nature herself.

When we are disconnected in this way, we can see ourselves as separate. Faeries know that the physical form is an articulation of spirit in material form, and thus it is sacred. Your body is a sacred form that is your speaking spirit, and so it needs to be loved and cared for. Imagine if you were to experience less guilt about how and who you loved. More joy about being in your body. Better health, as your positive feelings and thoughts manifest as a healthier, more attractive body.

We would all have less anxiety over sensual relationships, which would lead us to fully enjoy our sexual and sensual potential and pleasure. And less fear and taboos would lead to a reduction of sexual guilt and that false sense of ownership that can poison love relationships. When you embrace this gift, your faery godmother explains to you, your sensuality becomes a precious gift that belongs to you alone.

If you agree, she now shines her wand on your sacral region. You feel a deep inner stirring, and a gentle release. You are now being released from any vows of chastity, as the faery energy and faery gift clear away any guilt you may have about your sensuality and sexuality. Your feminine self, which exists within men and within women, is now to be respected, revered and enjoyed. You now feel more attractive, and more beautiful as yourself.

The gift of sensuality also embraces your absolute right to your own freedom and selfhood. Do not yield it to anyone. Love who you will, says your faery godmother, and harm ye none.

Faery Magic to Awaken Your Sensuality

Sensuality is about how you feel within your body, and how bright and shining you allow this aspect of self – your attractiveness – to be. Many people have shut down their radiance, fearing it will draw to them undesirable attention. However, this can also result in a frozen energetic area belting the sacral region, almost like an etheric chastity belt. In truth, it is safe and beautiful to be shining, to be radiantly attractive, to be beautiful. Our sacred sensual and sexual nature is celebrated by the fae as an energy force, a form of nwyfre that is vital to the energy of your body, soul and mind.

To connect with and allow this gift to flow, have a ritual bath or shower. Surround your bathing area in a circle of blue faery flame for protection, and undress, gently, placing your garments down with respect. Step into the bath or the shower aware of your beauty and loveliness. Know that this is in truth who you are, even if you have conditioned your mind to observe and comment on your body critically.

Allow the water to flow, and see it falling on or swirling around not only your physical body, but also your light body, clearing from this field all beliefs about being unattractive, or less than beautiful. Allow these thoughts to be washed away. This process can be made even more effective by massaging your skin with sea salt. Let the salt crystals comb through your auric field and cleanse your skin.

Now this has been completed, take a pure oil, such as a capful of almond, peach, avocado or jojoba oil, and mix in with this some rose otto, geranium, orange or neroli – any essential oil which you find personally uplifting and which inspires you to feel light, free and beautiful. Please be sure to make this an essential oil, not a perfumed synthetic oil, as the faeries will keep their distance from the latter, even if your intent is good. They simply are not drawn to synthetic perfumes, or faery-repelling chemicals such as those found in many commercial body washes.

But to pure oils they will come, so as you smooth this blend over your sacral region, see yourself growing stronger and more attractive. So beautiful, so peaceful, and so very secure and safe. Allow the faeries to move through this region, clearing any debris that may have built up. Remember, cleansing and clearing is not something we can do just once. We need to do this on a regular basis, just as we would take out the debris and detritus that builds up in our home. Regular sacral cleansing keeps us feeling bright, beautiful, attractive and very safe.

As you continue, see yourself as beautiful, desirable, strong in body and mind, and very alluring. There is no guilt in this desirability. Women are beautiful. Men are beautiful. Loving your beauty is loving who you are.

Finally, give thanks to the faeries and to yourself for this clearing, and step gently out of the bath or shower, and dry yourself in luxurious, soft and fluffy towels. It can be wonderful to go straight to bed after this exercise, for a long, deep and restful sleep.

If this is not practical, light candles, speak softly, and keep the magic alive. Close down the circle of blue fire, thanking the elementals for your protection and safety, always.

The Third Gift of Faery : Power

We move now to the realm of the third gift of the fae. Faeries are very powerful – it is their nature to be so. Each of their expressions of power is unique. We humans often have a deep mistrust of our own power, because we have seen its misuse by others. We no longer trust ourselves. However, your faery godmother explains, with the help of the fae we can learn to work with our power in beautiful, responsible ways that bring creativity, joy and generosity into our lives, and into the lives of others.

True power is the activation of your life force in order to change the world and create within the world things of meaning and substance, beauty and goodness. True power lies in understanding the best ways in which to nurture your own talents and create the world in which you wish to live.

Your faery godmother asks now if you wish to have your true power activated, and if you agree, a light shines forth from the tip of her faery wand, illuminating your solar plexus chakra. You now feel the energy within this area clearing and brightening, becoming vital and strong, and any fears and doubts you may have about your right to live fully in your power seem to dissolve, as now you will work with strength, and honour, and be a gentle sovereign of your world. Guided by the energy of your gentle power, you will be lit from within, and radiate love. This faery gift of power will create and grow courage, strength and power. Feel the force within!

You know now that it is safe to be warm, to extend your energy, and you know that your truly radiant self will create great opportunities and abundance. When you connect with this gift of the fae, you will experience your own vitality in new and wonderful ways, feeling brighter and more luminous, and yet realistic and grounded, as you combine this gift of power with those of sensuality and of your ancestry. Know that all is supported, and you are shining brightly, when you embrace this gift.

Faery Magic to Safely Ignite Your Power

It may be time for you to take some significant action, which you have been procrastinating about for some time. You can now state that you are willing to do what must be done, and grow your own strength, asserting yourself, standing in your power and allowing it to flow through you.

On a Tuesday night, stand within your circle of blue flame. Light a simple beeswax candle – which is so sacred to the fae – and anoint it with an essential oil such as bergamot, which is very strong, healing and cleansing. Ask your shining self to step forward for you now, to come forward whenever there is need, and to take right action at the right time. Visualise your inner faery goddess, your own inner Grian, standing strong, your own inner sovereign alive, powerful and shining out from your solar plexus.

See all who you meet bathed in her strong, loving light, which blends the energy of the heart and the solar plexus. Allow Grian to be with you when you must do what must be done, and allow her to help you to do it with grace and ease, and see how simple and natural being powerful can be. In this way, you will restore your trust in the wisdom of your own power.

Thank Grian, and ask her to come to you when you call upon her, and help you to recreate this balance whenever you have need. Then thank her and farewell her.

Shhh! Faery Secret

If you wish for the faeries to help you, there's nothing they love more than some music and song, so climb a tree, or go into the forest, and sing them a little ditty you've composed. You'll feel their love immediately!

The Fourth Gift of Faery : Love

Fae beings love – they just do. They love us, despite humanity's reckless disregard for the natural world, our disregard even for our own good and happiness. They love, and they do not hold grudges. They heal their hurts swiftly, and they offer assistance in healing hurt hearts to animals, to plants wounded by pesticides and chemicals, to waterways bogged by rubbish, and to us.

They love us, and can help heal our wounded heart, if we allow them to activate this wonderful faery gift of unconditional love within us. They love us without a sense of attachment and ownership, and they love us without demanding anything from us. They love us because we are part of life, and they are here to protect, preserve and to watch over all living creatures.

Any lack of ease or impurity held within the heart can be lifted with a touch of the wand of your faery godmother, and if you agree now, she will activate this faery power. She shines her light upon your heart chakra, and this gentle light begins to dissolve, break up and clear any old hurts and disappointments, any anger and resentment, from the heart, replacing these with a pure, abundant flow of unconditional love.

You feel your heart returning to its innocent, wild state, ready to give and receive love, adoration, care and caresses. You are now ready to care for all life, and all others, and do so without self-sacrifice, as you now love yourself truly and deeply. Awakening this gift will allow you to receive love graciously and increase the level of peaceful, healthy love in your life.

Faery Magic to Heal Your Heart

Unconditional love is a kind of space that harmony can move through. Most relationships do have conditions – and in many, rightly so! It is important to have healthy boundaries and strong ethics in place, but in connecting to the deep source of love itself, there must be an open, harmonious energy. This will replenish you and fill you when you feel drained, tired and even totally exhausted.

When this well of unconditional love is tapped in to, any hurts will fade away, and you will start to hope, heal and feel again, without bitterness or suspicion, which so many people carry within their wounded hearts, without even realising or having an awareness of this hurt and its presence. "Anahata" is the Sanskrit word for the heart chakra, our auric centre of love and loving, which translates to "unhurt". A very fitting name...

Set your circle of blue fire by visualising it forming in a circle around you, protecting you from all outside influences. Seat yourself within it, and see the faeries coming towards you to assist you. Write on a piece of paper all the hurts and betrayals you feel you have borne, all the names of the people who have wounded you, or upset your peace. Then, one by one, go through the list and forgive them. If you cannot yet forgive them, forgive yourself for not being able to forgive them as yet. You will, in time, forgive. For through this process your heart can reconnect to the flow of the sacred well, and can be filled again with pure, shining love energy, which will then radiate outwards.

When you have forgiven what you can for now, thank the faeries, who will carry away your hurt and any unhealed energy, then clear it and recycle it in wonderful ways. And you will be left with the wisdom, and not be fated to walk the same path again. You will also have restored your wild, pure heart, which is the source of so much unconditional joy and love to you. Now close your circle of blue faery fire, and give thanks for this gift of love.

The Fifth Gift of Faery : Expression

Gift five from the faeries will now be offered to you, and it is a wondrous gift. Faeries have a song – they sing the energy of the world into being, your faery godmother says. You too have a song, and when it is stifled, your own being cannot flourish and be expressed clearly and beautifully, in harmony with the world.

The fae love to hear you sing, they love you to make sound, and to find your own signature tune or note. To help you do that, they wish for you to connect with your throat chakra – and to deepen its power, they suggest that you allow this gift to awaken with a touch from the wand of your own faery godmother.

If you agree, she shines this light on your throat, and you feel free now to sing out, to speak clearly, to say what needs to be said gently and without malice or ill intent. (Words are spells – they are very magical and very powerful, which is why silence is sometimes wise. Being always silent however is stifling.)

The awakening of this gift can give you the courage to speak up, even when others are trying to confuse you with their words, which are spoken most often in fear. Your faery godmother's healing wand will help you find your voice through this gentle activation of your throat chakra. When the light of the wand touches you through this centre, you will find easily the words of clarity and compassion, and the courage to speak them. You will be helped to know what to say, even when you feel lost for words. This gift is wonderful for all of us, and especially for those who say too little, or say what they wish they had not!

Faery Magic to Activate Clear, Easeful Communication

Singing and chanting are wonderful ways to activate this faery gift, and increase our sacred use of the throat chakra area. The more it is used in beauty, the more it will be activated intentionally and in flow. The spontaneous will no longer feel so scary, and timing will come naturally – with diplomacy when the matter is delicate, and the right energy sent outward with all your words.

When you awaken the gift of expression, you will be able to speak with a mixture of precision and poetry that is part of the fae's magic. So sing along to a favourite song, hum loudly, speak without fear, join a choir. Your words will give you the courage you desire, and inspire others who have trouble with expression too.

Open your circle of blue fire. Within it, it matters not whether you sit, or stand, or jump up and down. But within it, you are going to close your eyes, and gently drop and open your jaw. As you do so, take a deep, strong, long breath in, and a breath out.

Now, with no sense of self-consciousness – or if it does come up, gently ask it to move aside for a while – simply allow sound to come out. In time you will find yourself raising your head, and allowing the most gorgeous sound to flow out. No words, just beauty. Just a song you are offering to the faeries. And by doing this, any gunk or blockages in this beautiful throat chakra area will now flow free.

Alternatively, you may wish to sit within your circle of blue flame and say nothing. Simply breathe for a time. This is dependent upon whether you have been around many people who speak merely to fill up available space, in which case you may require silence. Even in silence though, you can allow your throat chakra to open and be expressed, with sighs, with breathing and releasing these breaths with a gentle sound to them. This way, the peace of silence so that the faeries can reach you and speak to you can be created, and the ability to allow sound, meaningful sound, to come out can be developed and nurtured.

The tone and quality of your voice carries as much meaning as any word, so be aware of how you are working with your own energy, and the energy of your throat chakra, and make it the most beautiful and healthful, supple and loving, energy you can!

After you have done this, close your circle of blue fire, and give thanks to the fae for the ability to express yourself so very gracefully, and with such dignity and purpose.

The Sixth Gift of Faery : the Sight

This very special gift is now available to be invited into your life. Are you ready to believe? For faeries can be seen! Faeries dwell between the seen and the unseen worlds, and they understand how to make visible what cannot always be seen with the eye, and what will not always be believed by the mind. The answer is to gently open and activate your spirit eye. This is often called your third eye, but the fae refer to it as the spirit eye. They can assist you in activating your Sight, or clairvoyance as it is also called.

Sight is the receiving of images and signs that are meaningful to you, and which you can interpret and translate into messages quickly and easily. The less effort required, the more active your Sight is, and the less headaches and "over-thinking" will occur.

The Sight is not to be confused with hallucinations or visions that can and often do disrupt our existence and even our safety. The Sight is clear, and sound, and we are able to work with it in disciplined and productive ways, at the appropriate time, for the good of all. Awakening and developing this gift means you will be able to see very clearly the wonderment all around you – lifting the veil that makes everything "real" seem drab and ordinary, and becoming able to see the exquisite beauty that is all around you, the poetry and music of life, in visual ways.

Even if your physical eyes are not "good", awakening your Sight will help you to truly "see", and thus understand, know and interact with the real world with wisdom and soul-intelligence. The faeries will also be more visible to you, very plainly and clearly.

Your faery godmother also explains that awakening the gift of the Sight means the fae will have permission to bring you many messages. They may begin to show you little mini-films with information that provides clear, step-by-step examples of action to take. They will not overload you with technical information – messages will be of most assistance when they are shown to you through a "film" screened in the spirit eye. This can be very inspiring, and can sidestep the apparent constraints of linear time, allowing you to "see" the future, or to clearly see how to create objects waiting for you to bring them to life. You can receive these messages from your own future self with a fully-awakened spirit eye.

If you agree, your faery godmother now shines this light from her wand into your spirit eye, and as the light shines down, you can see with your spirit eye the tiny faeries now busying themselves with tiny brooms, sweeping away any energetic debris from this area, clearing the blindness and the mistrust that can set in. After cleansing this beautiful spirit eye of yours, they anoint this area with their own nectar, allowing you to fully see them and experience them, even when your physical eyes are closed.

Faery Magic for Your Spirit Eye and Faery Sight

When working with the Sight, it can be very helpful to invoke psychic protection, and to practise keeping this newly refreshed area cleansed so that it continues to attract beautiful experiences, and so you remain strong, so that if you do see something that could be perceived as "unpleasant", you do not react with fear and sadness, rather with a kind of neutrality and choice.

When working with this energy, again encircle yourself with the protective blue flame of the fae. Within it, see a beautiful light emanating from your spirit eye, streaming out, pouring out... Check this light to see if there are any impurities within it. This is a little like running a tap after the water has been switched off for a while – it can sometimes choke, or spit, or stutter, before flowing clearly and cleanly once more.

This protected free flow will allow you to assess whether your spirit eye energy is running clean. You can then ask the faeries to assist you with a filter over the third eye, a crystalline filter that will ensure you see what is most beautiful and good. This does not mean ignoring that which seems dark or hard to bear, but just that you will not be picking up other people's sights and images. You may remove this filter at any time you wish – it is a kind of vision transmuter that will ensure you are clearly working from your own psychic space, and not straying into other people's areas.

Of course if you are doing psychic work in service to others, such as a reading, mediumship and particularly scrying, you may wish to temporarily remove the filter, and replace it with your strong and radiant chakra system's light body around you. Shielding, while it can be helpful at some times to have reflectors up, can result in isolation, and build up a dense layer of fear around people. It is so much better to focus on full faery-activated chakra health!

When this is done, allow the blue flame of the fae to dissipate and burn away, then go about your day or night as usual.

The Seventh Gift of Faery : Communion

This seventh gift will now be revealed, and it is a beautiful offering, for it is the gift of communion with all of creation.

The Celtic faeries the Tuatha de Danaan and the Tylwyth Teg, who are just some among many magical beings, know that the great "fire in the head" referred to in the Celtic legends – which is also known as the halo of saints, and the auras around the heads of the Hindu deities – is simply the energetic field radiated outwards by the fully-awakened crown chakra.

Having this bright and shining crown chakra means you are fully creative, and will be able to manifest and experience many natural states simultaneously, without confusion or stress. Thus, a fully-awakened crown chakra will mean that you glow with this faery fire all around your head. It is a kind of violet flame that surrounds the head, and it is the bridge between the celestial and terrestrial worlds.

Faeries are indeed of this earth, and are in many ways the actual earth, but there are also many celestial fae, and they too can communicate with you in meaningful ways, ways that are practical and joyful. Too many of us blow open the crown chakra before we are grounded and activated in our other chakras. The fae advise that it is best to do magical work from the ground up, so that when we do open this beautiful chakra to a fuller extent, we do so without running the risk of "blowing our minds".

When we activate and open the crown chakra safely and fully, we engage in a kind of beautiful communion with the galactic beings, the terrestrial ones, and with fellow humans, elements and elementals. The world becomes One, and we know we are simply energy, moving through form, but respecting the beautiful shape we have taken this time. A fully opened crown chakra can allow us to understand the true forms and names of the world – a stunning magical power that must be treated with great respect, and love.

To begin this process gently, you may wish to now have your faery godmother activate this gift. If you do agree, she shines her magical wand on the area of your crown chakra, and a warmth spreads gently around your head, and you feel light shining inwards and outwards from your crown.

She explains that tiny faeries are now clearing your crown chakra of any lingering heaviness and doubt, allowing you to connect clearly with all beings of love, light and magic. The world becomes an enchanted place when working with this gift, she says, allowing you to experience the wonder of all-that-is.

Gently allow yourself to shift your focus from the "thinking" head to the "communion" head. Your faery godmother's touch, and the activation of this gift, allow you to see your true self, as a celestial and terrestrial being, allowing sunrise and sunset to fall on your crown, removing any blocks to opening this gift.

Seeing the similarities and bringing awareness to the one-ness of all things will help you to see the truth beneath the dogmas that distort so many beautiful paths. You may now, with ease, tune in to the right side of your brain – the side that sees all as one, and is cosmic bliss itself, and which will also assist you in connecting with this special gift of the fae.

Let these enchanted beings tell you of how we are all one – and help you to know that there is a nirvana, and it lives within you, and can be brought to you by the blessings of the beautiful fae, who love you, and want you to know and accept and experience their gifts, so you can become all that you are...

Faery Magic for Fire in the Head

This is a very simple magical working to give you a complete way to thank the faeries for your gift of fire in the head – your awoken awen, your crown chakra inspiration, and the nwyfre, or vital life force, flowing through your entire being.

This simple, loving and fun activity will result in the faeries continually assisting you in activating a balanced sense of one-ness, allowing you to feel peace, and a connection to all that is. You will now be able to connect deeply, without "blowing your mind". Through it being a celebration, rather than an intense focus on the crown, you will achieve wonderful results in a fun and joyous way.

Any time, any day, prepare a miniature feast for you and the fae. Please do this outside. Instead of lighting the blue flames around you, this time draw a seven-pointed star around you in your mind's eye, or marked out with twigs, crystals and found things.

Light the feasting area with candles, or surround it with stones, crystals or any other natural marker. You will have more faery interaction if you have this feast at a liminal time, but any time will work. Scatter the area with some herbs to attract the fae, particularly thyme, and prepare a glass of faery nectar intoxicant of your own making to toast your new awareness with.

Here is a basic recipe which you can add to or adapt as you wish. Make it simple, delicious and pleasing to the eye!

☆ Sparkling mineral water.
☆ Your favourite fruit juice – apple and berries are wonderful.
☆ Fruits – strawberries, blueberries and raspberries are my particular favourites.
☆ Herbs such as mint.
☆ Some honey or sugar to taste (faeries do love sweet things).

Pour the sparkling mineral water into a bowl, add the juice, fruits and honey to taste. Add some mint, and keep it cool so its refreshing energy stays "alive" longer.

Keep your feast simple – some organic chocolate, fruits and sweets, nuts, seeds and little cakes could be all you need. Within the space, once you have laid everything out, thank the faeries for all they have already done, for you, for the planet, for each other, and ask them to come into your life even more. Let them know you will offer them their share of the feast.

If you do this with one or more of your faery loving friends, the energy expands, and this makes the fae so very happy.

Once you have completed your feast, leave a reasonable amount for the faeries, as well as something especially for them (not simply your leftovers, from which you have already taken the energy). Lift your arms to the sky and dance, have fun, and laugh! The faeries will return more and more frequently to this place – if you can, visit it often in person, and this will become a sacred faery place. If you cannot, visit it etherically from time to time, and they will continue their wonderful work.

Now close the seven-pointed star, if the faeries wish you to do so – consult with them first. They may wish to keep in place your gateway, which will make them feel more welcome.

It is now time, your faery godmother says gently, to depart this enchanted realm for now, and return to your own magical place, to your own beautiful world. You need do nothing, she explains, but lie back, and relax deeply, and breathe. The tiny faery beings will lift you up and return you to the place where you began your journey, and when you return to the world from whence you came, you will know that you have been gifted the seven bright jewels of the fae.

And you will now feel strong, and grounded where you stand on this planet. You will now love and be free in your sensuality, you will be powerful, and gentle and good in the use of that power. You will love, and be free to be loved in return, you will sing and speak your truth with ease, you will see and receive messages simply, easily, from the faery realm, and you will feel at one with all of creation. For you are a beloved child of the universe...

Farewell the faeries now, and leave a small offering to express your gratitude, an offering that reflects their care and protection of the natural world. You may wish to offer to them that you will be kind to animals, recycle more often, plant a tree, make a small donation to a conservation group doing work you admire... Whatever it is, let it be easy, small and sincere.

The faeries love you, and your faery godmother is with you, protecting you, loving you, guiding you at all times.

Farewell. Know you are loved by the fae, and loved by all creation. May you be blessed, at peace, and know the sweetness of love and light, all the days of your life...

The Faery Quizzes

"The universe is full of magical things,
Patiently waiting for our wit to grow sharper."
Eden Phillpotts, English poet and author

Quiz 1 : What's Your Faery Talent?

The faeries have come to represent so many different things to us – there are faeries with healing powers and deep wisdom, faeries who encourage us to protect and nurture the earth and its creatures, and faeries who inspire us to enjoy life more and appreciate every beautiful moment. Whether you believe they are real, are a personification of nature or a manifestation of your own magical qualities, you can explore these different personalities, adopt their good traits and attune yourself to your own faery energy.

1. What do you love most about faeries?
A) Their healing powers.
B) Their light-hearted joy.
C) Their connection to nature.
D) The way they inspire people.
E) Their wisdom and knowledge.

2. What do friends say is your best quality?
A) You have deep empathy and listen well, and help them to feel understood.
B) You make them happier and encourage them to enjoy life more.

C) You're committed and passionate, and inspire with your actions.

D) You're expressive, and your creativity moves them deeply.

E) You are wise and fair, give great advice and inspire them through how you live your life.

3. What character traits do you most admire?

A) Selflessness and caring.

B) A sense of humour and positivity.

C) Dedication and sacrifice.

D) Bravery and self-expression.

E) Kindness and wisdom.

4. What character traits do you most dislike?

A) Laziness and lack of discipline.

B) Seriousness and negativity.

C) Selfishness and consumerism.

D) Stubbornness and lack of communication skills.

E) Narrow-mindedness and self-doubt.

5. What inspires you?

A) Other people's growth.

B) Laughter and joy.

C) Being outside in nature.

D) Music, books and art.

E) Learning new things.

6. What did you want to be when you were a kid?

A) Doctor or nurse.

B) Performer or events manager.

C) Marine biologist or scientist.

D) Writer or artist.

E) Social worker or teacher.

7. What's your favourite charity?

A) The Cancer Council, Leukaemia Foundation.

B) Starlight Children's Foundation, Comic Relief.

C) Sea Shepherd, World Wide Fund for Nature.

D) Beyond Blue, Mental Health Foundation.

E) Red Cross, World Vision.

8. Which form of movement do you like best?
A) Yoga.
B) Dancing.
C) Rock climbing.
D) Boxing.
E) Walking.

9. What do you feel is your purpose in life?
A) To help people heal from illness.
B) To make people happy and spread joy.
C) To protect and preserve nature and the planet.
D) To express your own heart to help others connect with theirs.
E) To help people find peace and contentment.

10. Which of these weekend courses are you most likely to do, or have you already done?
A) Reiki, herbalism, angel therapy.
B) Acting, cooking, candle making.
C) Organic gardening, bushwalking.
D) Jewellery making or writing classes.
E) Counselling, self-development.

11. Who's your favourite faery?
A) Queen Mab, the faeries' midwife.
B) Tinker Bell from Pixie Hollow.
C) Christa from *Fern Gully*.
D) The Muses.
E) Lady Galadriel from *The Lord of the Rings*.

12. What's your favourite animal?
A) Dolphin.
B) Butterfly.
C) Panda.
D) Tiger.
E) Owl.

13. Which goddess do you most strongly connect with?
A) Brigid/Bride, goddess of healing.
B) Aphrodite, goddess of love.

C) Gaia, goddess of the earth.

D) Ceridwen, goddess of inspiration.

E) Athena, goddess of wisdom.

14. Which colours resonate most strongly with you?

A) Blues.

B) All the shades of the sunset.

C) Greens.

D) A rainbow of colours.

E) Purple, silver.

15. What kind of holiday most appeals to you?

A) Spending time at an ashram in India or with a healer such as John of God in Brasil.

B) A trip to a tropical island with your friends.

C) Camping, or working on organic farms in return for board.

D) A trip through the museums and art galleries of Europe.

E) A meditation or yoga retreat.

16. What do you most want to develop?

A) Strength and assertiveness.

B) Deep friendships and trust.

C) Strength and endurance.

D) Confidence and self-expression.

E) Spirituality and inner power.

17. Who do you most admire?

A) Fred Hollows, Doreen Virtue, neurosurgeon Wirginia Maixner.

B) The Dalai Lama, Thich Nhat Hanh, Ricky Gervais.

C) Paul Watson, Peter Garrett, Al Gore, Julia Butterfly Hill.

D) Paulo Coelho, Midnight Oil, Jessica Galbreth.

E) Bono, Shirley MacLaine, Cassandra Eason, Oprah Winfrey.

18. Which element – and elemental – do you most connect with?

A) Water.

B) Air.

C) Earth.

D) Fire.

E) Spirit.

Scoring

Mostly As – Healing Faery

You're a kind and caring person who resonates most strongly with the healing faeries. You identify as a healer, and feel that your purpose in life is to help facilitate other people's physical and emotional healing. You relate to the world through your ability to assist others, and spend a lot of your time and energy searching for the best way to be of service. You have a strong grasp of the mind-body-spirit connection, and understand that we can create our own reality through our thoughts and actions.

You try to maintain an environment of emotional calm around yourself, knowing that stress and worry can affect you physically. You want to help people live healthier, happier lives, avoiding ill health through prevention rather than cure, and you encourage them to pay attention to their physical health, as you know that eating well and exercising regularly are just as important to overall health as meditating and being spiritually aware. You have a passion for learning new healing methods, and feel truly alive when you're studying herbal medicine, crystal healing, nutrition, reiki techniques or any other subjects you feel will make you a more effective healer.

You understand that different healing modalities help different people, and you are open to trying new things and sharing your experiences to benefit others. You like to feel needed and useful, but make sure you don't continually put other people's needs before your own – you need to find a good balance, and allow other people to offer healing to you as well. Everyone should try to incorporate a little of the healing faery into their life, and share the things they learn and the skills they are blessed with. Thank you for your generosity of spirit and wonderful healing energy.

Mostly Bs – Fun Faery

You're the ultimate faery – light-hearted and filled with joy, and on a mission to help others appreciate the beauty and wonder of life. You relate to the world and express yourself through humour and a positive outlook, and have the ability to detach from issues you have no control over, which helps you solve them more quickly, and prevents angst accumulating in potentially heated situations. You have the gift of being able to calm a heavy atmosphere, and lift people's spirits, so they love being around you. You can be mischievous and a little cheeky at times, and you're always the life of the party, shining your own light on others and cheering them up (and on). You are genuinely happy when other people achieve their dreams – and you love celebrating and sharing the triumphs of your friends. You acknowledge your own success with humility, accept defeat with good grace, and appreciate everything you go through, good and bad, with a beautiful attitude of gratitude.

You perceive the world with pure, child-like eyes, and can always see the good in people, and in situations, which is a wonderful gift to have. It does not come lightly or easily though, and you are sometimes disappointed when others let you down – although you would rather think well of people, and occasionally experience disappointment, than live a life of mistrust, doubt and cynicism. People sometimes overlook the pain you're suffering because you don't complain, or even explain, when you are feeling down. Try to allow the people who are close to you to share your burdens sometimes, and see you in all your many moods.

We should all try to incorporate a bit of the fun faery into our lives, and develop the attitude of gratitude that helps you experience life in the way you do. Thank you for your joy and your sense of fun, and the light you spread to those around you.

Mostly Cs – Eco Faery

You're an environmental faery and eco warrior, whose mission in life is to help the planet and increase people's awareness of the issues that face us in an era of big business and consumerism. You relate to the world through your actions and passions, expressing who you are by what you do to help. You care about the earth and all its plants and creatures, and are passionate about animal welfare and climate change, protecting the forests, conserving resources, having clean air and creating a sustainable future.

You're likely to be found campaigning outside nuclear facilities or in a threatened forest, writing letters to politicians to express your concerns about local issues, or starting petitions to save the whales or get climate change on the agenda. You live your ideals too, recycling, composting, eating organic, avoiding foods and other products that involve cruelty to animals, and learning as much as you can about the issues that matter most to you.

In addition to doing your bit personally, you also try to educate people and corporations, raising awareness not just amongst your friends but also in the wider community. You're committed and idealistic, and probably a little sceptical of the political process and impatient with long-term goals. It is frustrating when so many people don't understand the urgency and importance of environmental concerns, but through your actions and your inspiring example you are slowly raising awareness and changing the way people see such issues.

We should all try to cultivate a little bit of eco faery energy in our lives, taking responsibility for, and action to save, this beautiful world we live in. Thank you for being so passionate and dedicated to the cause, and to the future of our planet.

Mostly Ds – Artistic Faery

You relate to other people and the world through expressing yourself – through music, art or the written word – which allows you to make sense of the world and the things you experience. You make the world more beautiful with your creations, be that through music, dance, painting, sculpture, writing, storytelling, film, jewellery making or other forms of expression.

Great art sparks the imagination, touches the heart and the mind, and teaches people things they don't know about themselves and the world. It is an expression of the inner self, reflecting back the conflicts, the drama and all of the good and the bad that the artist has experienced, which can help other people deal with their own issues by realising they are not alone.

Art can move people to tears, provide a form of catharsis, connect them to their emotions and give them a way to express and understand their fears, their sadness and their inner turmoil. It can also impart great joy and beauty, uplifting humanity and inspiring people to be more than they thought was possible.

Art reflects culture, society and history, either through capturing and recording it, or through the artist's reflection of their personal issues as a microcosm of the greater worldview. This gives it great importance, but art also has value as an action, allowing people, no matter how lacking in artistic merit they consider themselves, to express their inner heart and make sense of the world. Art therapy and literacy programs aim not to (necessarily) produce professional

artists, but to help people connect with their own emotions and heal through the process of expression and self-reflection.

We should all try to cultivate a little bit of artistic faery within us, for our own health and wellbeing, and we are grateful to you for offering us healing and inspiration through your expression.

Mostly Es – Wise Faery

You're a wise and gentle helping faery, and are determined to change the world for the better in any way you can. You feel that your purpose in life is to assist others to connect more deeply to their own intuition and knowingness, and you help people towards their own spiritual growth rather than doing things for them, showing them how to illuminate their own beautiful self and shine brightly. You relate to the world through a deep level of understanding and questioning, and you have always delighted in learning, and comprehended new concepts easily.

You have great wisdom and perspective, and you don't take things personally, which helps you give advice and assistance without a vested interest or motive. Your friends see you as a faery godmother of sorts, and come to you for practical and emotional help. You are selfless and caring, and always there for people when they need you. Just don't forget to take a little time out to enjoy your own life, to laugh and play and be child-like every now and then.

You have great inner strength, and are wise, emotional and sensitive. You've suffered your own pain, which has instilled great empathy in you, and made you want to alleviate the hurt of others. The suffering of friends, family members, strangers and the world as a whole affects you deeply. Inequality and prejudice of any kind causes you pain, and you embrace many different causes and charities in order to help as much as you can. We should all aim to access a little of the wise faery wisdom, and tap in to our own intuition, and we are grateful to you for showing us how.

A little of each – Balanced Faery

Congratulations! You incorporate a little of all the faery archetypes, and are living a balanced, giving, joyful and magical life.

Quiz 2 : What's Your Faery Bloodline?

Are you a dark Unseelie, bringing about balance in unexpected ways? A Shining One, part of the land, sea and sky? Or perhaps you are a Seelie courtier, with noble intent and good heart. You may be a friendly brownie, or a serious and graceful elven one. There are so many faeries, but to narrow down which type of fae blood may be thrumming through your bloodline, here's an easy, fun quiz that may have surprising insights to offer you. There won't always be your own personal favourite within a question and answer section, so choose the option you are most drawn to...

1. What is your ideal environment?
A) Mountainous and icy with distinct seasons.
B) Rolling hills, great forests and glens.
C) Bright green fields, stone cottages.
D) Rocky, wild coastlines.
E) A small, sweet garden filled with herbs and flowerbeds.

2. Which tree or plant are you most drawn to?
A) Pine.
B) Oak.
C) Rowan.
D) Wild weeds and flowers.
E) Hazel.

3. Imagine your most magical place. What is it most like?
A) A great hall of a castle atop a tall mountain.
B) A sacred well.
C) A grove of trees.
D) A Hollow Hill.
E) The fireside at home.

4. Physically you are:
A) Tall and slender.
B) Small, delicate, stronger than you look.
C) Curvy and sensual.
D) Thin, fast and always moving.
E) Plump, rounded and quite small.

5. Which of the following traits do you have?

A) Slightly pointed, tapered ears.

B) Tilted, bright eyes.

C) Creamy skin and reddish hair.

D) Wild hair, pointy teeth.

E) A small snub nose and rosy cheeks.

6. What do you prefer to wear?

A) Long gowns, beautiful silks and pretty hues.

B) Natural fibres in natural colours.

C) Linens and embroidered shirts and skirts.

D) Anything that makes you stand out.

E) Clothes which are pleasant and practical.

7. Which of your psychic senses is most developed?

A) Clairaudience (clear hearing).

B) Clairvoyance (clear seeing – the Sight).

C) Claircognisance (clear knowing – you just "know").

D) Clairsentience (clear feeling – you get tingles, chills and sensations of physical connection).

E) Clairgustance (clear taste – the ability to taste flavours psychically which relate to emotions and knowings).

8. When you are upset, how do you usually react?

A) You feel deeply sad, but you tend to stay quiet and private.

B) You know that if you do the right thing, it will all work out.

C) You try to see the funny side, drinking and making merry to distract yourself.

D) You become vengeful and angry – and sometimes your reactions scare you, or others.

E) You comfort eat, clean the house and tend to what needs to be done at home and work.

9. A friend is sad. What do you do for them?

A) Make or give them some jewellery.

B) Write them a poem, or give them a favourite book.

C) Sing them a song, or give them a CD.

D) Swear revenge on the person or thing that has hurt them.

E) Bake them a treat or take them to a cafe to cheer them up.

10. If you were able to change the world in one way, you would:
A) Heal pain and wounds.
B) Bring about peace and justice.
C) Give the gift of creativity to everyone.
D) Overthrow all rulers.
E) End hunger.

11. Which of these destinations are you most drawn to?
A) The fjords and mountains of Scandinavia and New Zealand.
B) The wells and ancient places of Cornwall, Wales and England.
C) The sacred sites of Ireland and Scotland.
D) New York, Los Angeles, London – cities with high energy.
E) A tour of historical country estates, manors and farmhouses.

Scoring

Mostly As – Elven

You're likely to have elven blood. You're dignified and quiet, with great physical beauty. You may be skilled at scrying and other forms of divination. Explore this link by reading Tolkien, casting runes, learning Anglo-Saxon magics and practising crafts like jewellery making. Elves are wonderful at healing, but they can be quite serious as they know what is truly going on in the world – like their mountaintop homes, they can see what is going on in every direction, throughout the ages. You may want to lighten up a little. Elves can become wonderful doctors, pilots, adventurers and travellers.

Mostly Bs – the Seelie Court

You are probably related to the Seelie Court. You always try to do the right thing, have noble intentions and are a person of great integrity. You love to learn, and do well as both a teacher and as a student. You like to know that you are working for the greater good, but be wary of thinking you are so strong that you can endure anything – you tend to take on too many tasks, and put up with too much. Learn to say no, and let go! Seelies make wonderful teachers and professors, magicians and wizards, writers and law makers, and provide the magical world with great examples of ethics and morals, and enjoy reading magical spellbooks, learning to speak other languages, and spellcasting for the good of all!

Mostly Cs – Shining One

You're most likely a beautiful Shining One. Cheerful, good-natured and a lover of trees and meadows, you are creative and love music, gatherings and conversation. Your uplifting nature brings laughter and delight, and can instantly clear away the cobwebs of doubt and misery. However, you need to learn how to finish what you start, and remember to give yourself quiet time alone, and take what needs to be taken seriously, seriously. Shining Ones are wonderful hosts, restaurant and pub owners, entertainers, artists, singers and storytellers. Their magical talents lie in chanting, singing, learning about herbs and trees, and working with animals.

Mostly Ds – Unseelie Court

You're one of the Unseelie, who are necessary agents of change and rebellion, the beings with the fresh thoughts and daring new attitudes and ideas that can see societies and people change swiftly. Unseelies sometimes do scare their faery brethren. Seeming reckless and almost too wild, and often unable to stop themselves from saying and doing destructive things, an out of balance Unseelie is a fearsome thing indeed. An Unseelie in darkness can be cruel and wicked, but an Unseelie in balance is a wise, brilliant being who brings the fresh winds of change! Unseelies make great rock stars, mad poets, scientists who wish to change the world and environmental activists. If they can channel their anger to do good, they are unstoppable! They may be drawn to dark magics though, and have to be talked out of binding, hexing and cursing at times.

Mostly Es – Brownie

You're a wee brownie, who loves their home, and homeliness. You are domestic, and love to help all those around you feel comfortable and well fed, warm and clean and happy. Brownies are unlikely to go on great adventures, but are very loyal and committed. Friends become family, and family is precious. Brownies love kitchen witchery and space clearing. They love to cook, and even find cleaning joyous and fulfilling. They are wonderful chefs, nurses, parents and designers, and have great pride in what they do. They are not subservient – so if you are a brownie, you need to be appreciated! Lots of faery godmothers have been through a faery incarnation as a brownie – so be proud, and know you are treasured!

Lucy Cavendish

"I greatly respect her work. Lucy is a modern-day Guenevere."

Deepak Chopra

Lucy Cavendish is a natural white witch who works with the terrestrial and celestial realms. She works magic every single day of her life, embracing it as a creed for personal and planetary fulfillment and happiness, and as a belief system that sees us as a part of nature, and thus gives us all the motivation to respect and revere and delight in our unique experience here on Planet Earth.

Lucy is the author of *The Oracle of Shadows and Light*, *The Lost Lands*, *The Wild Wisdom of the Faery Oracle*, *The Oracle of the Dragonfae*, *White Magic*, *Magical Spellcards* and *The Oracle Tarot*. She has created three magical CDs, *As Above So Below*, *Return to Avalon* and *The Seven Gifts of Faery*. Her work has been enjoyed by thousands of readers worldwide, and she is recommended by people as diverse as Fiona Horne, Louise L Hay and Deepak Chopra.

Lucy created *Witchcraft* in 1992, the first magazine of its kind in the world. She is a feature writer for *Spellcraft* and *Spheres* magazines, has a column in *Black Rose* and *Goddess*, contributes to *FAE* magazine, and appears regularly on mainstream and alternative radio and television, explaining the Craft and demonstrating the power of natural magics and intuition.

She is a classic book witch and adores reading and writing, listening to and playing music, connecting with the wild, and creating enchanted workshops. She is a founding member of the Goddess Association in Australia, as well as an active member of the international Order of Bards, Ovates & Druids.

Lucy lives in Sydney, Australia, with her pixie-like daughter and their menagerie of plant allies, animal companions, spirit beings and beloved faeries and elementals. Visit her website or join her on Facebook for updates on retreats, workshops, talks and refreshing insights into the daily life of a working white witch.

www.LucyCavendish.com

Serene Conneeley

Serene Conneeley is a Sydney writer with a passion for history, travel, ritual and the myth and magic of ancient places and cultures. She has written for magazines about travel, spirituality, health, news, social and environmental issues and entertainment, and contributed to international books on witchcraft, psychic development and personal transformation, as well as the best-selling history compilation *Dateline*.

She is a reconnective healing practitioner, and has studied magical and medicinal herbalism, angel therapy, reiki and many other alternative health modalities, as well as politics and journalism. She is the editor of the children's Love to Learn magazines *Little Friends* and *Playhouse Disney*, and has worked for publications as diverse as *Cosmopolitan*, *Dolly*, *Woman's Day*, *The Daily News* and *The West Australian* newspapers, *Hot Metal*, *Spheres*, *Spellcraft* and *Your Destiny*.

She loves yoga, hiking, reading, rainbows, drinking tea with her friends and celebrating the energy of the moon and the magic of the earth. Her heart blossomed as she climbed mountains, sat in stone circles, walked a pilgrimage, performed rituals with shamans in South America and priestesses in Avalon, wandered through ancient cathedrals and stood in the shadow of the pyramids, and she's also learned the magic of finding true happiness and peace at home.

Her first book, *Seven Sacred Sites: Magical Journeys That Will Change Your Life*, was published in 2008. Her second, *A Magical Journey: Your Diary of Inspiration, Adventure and Transformation*, followed in 2009. She's also created the CD *Sacred Journey: A Meditation to Connect You to the Magic of the Earth*, which includes seven meditations that take you on a deep inner journey, connecting you with the power of the elements – air, water, fire, earth, spirit – and balancing the masculine and feminine energies of your heart and soul to reawaken the divine spark within you.

www.SereneConneeley.com

"… she came into the Land of Faery,
Where nobody gets old and godly and grave,
Where nobody gets old and crafty and wise,
Where nobody gets old and bitter of tongue.
And she is still there, busied with a dance,
Deep in the dewy shadow of a wood,
Or where stars walk upon a mountaintop."
WB Yeats, *Irish poet*